AF669071

EDUCATION: Planning and Human Development

EDUCATION

Planning and Human Development

(In 8 Volumes)

Future Challenges of Learning

(Volume 8)

V.C. PANDEY

ISHA BOOKS
DELHI—110 033

EDUCATION: Planning and Human Development
(Education)

Rs. 7000 (Set in 8 Vols.)

© V.C. Pandey

ISBN: 81-8205-006-5 (Set)
ISBN: 81-8205-014-6 (Vol. 8)

All rights reserved. No part of this book may be reproduced in any manner without written permission.

Published in 2003 in India by
Isha Books, D-43, Prithviraj Road
Adarsh Nagar, Delhi-110 033

Lasertypesetting by: Varsha Graphics, Delhi
Printed at: Chawla Offset Press, Delhi

Preface

The twenty first century is witnessing rapid growth in the area of technology and human development. With the scientific and technological advancement taking place in leaps and bounds, change is inevitable in all walks of life. One of the great challenge faced by the new century is adapting education to the changing needs of the society. As the transmission of information and explosion of knowledge is very fast today, it is very urgent to take immediate steps to make education more useful and relevant.

In today's competitive world, varied sources of information are trying to educate the future generation on a wide spectrum of knowledge. In order to fulfil the requirements of the new millennium successfully all nations must determine the extent to which their educational systems are preparing the next generation for successful participation in the existing enterprise. For this it is essential to understand the requirements, possibilities and problems of a country, and prepare an alternative plan based on the challenges of the new millennium.

The structure and content of learning activities should be determined to equip all children, youth, and adults with the knowledge, skills, values and attitudes they need to survive, to improve their quality of life, to empower them to participate fully and responsibly in the life of their communities and nations, to initiate and to adapt to changing circumstances-and to continue learning according to their individual needs and interests. For the new era skill-based learning should be emphasised. Learning should be based on hardware and software. There will be global thinking in education. The teacher should be fully acquainted with the different teaching skills and they can use them successfully in the classrooms.

The International Commission on Education has put greater emphasis on the four pillars that it proposes and describes as the foundations of education: learning to know, learning to do; learning to be and learning to live together. The concept of learning throughout life is also emerging as one of the key aspect of new age learning. It goes beyond the traditional distinction between initial and continuing education. It has a key role in formulating and achieving a future vision.

The present book provides an insight on issues and challenges in the process of learning and their envisaged solutions. It will be of immense utility to educational planners, policy makers, researchers and educationists etc.

Editor

Contents

1

Basic Learning Needs

The basic learning needs comprise both essential learning tools such as literacy, oral expression, numeracy, and problem solving and the basic learning content such as knowledge, skills, values, and attitudes required by human beings to be able to survive, to develop their full capacities, to live and work in dignity, to participate fully in development, to improve the quality of their lives, to make in formed decisions, and to continue learning.

The scope of basic learning needs and how they should be met varies with individual countries and cultures, and inevitably, changes with the passage of time. The satisfaction of these needs empowers individuals in any society and confers upon them a responsibility to respect and build upon their collective cultural, linguistic and spiritual heritage, to promote the education of others, to further the cause of social justice, to achieve environmental protection, to be tolerant towards social, political and religious systems which differ from their own, ensuring that commonly accepted humanistic values and human rights are upheld, and to work for international peace and solidarity in an interdependent world.

Basic education facilitates the ability to meet other basic needs—adequate nutrition, shelter and clothing, and access to health services and clean water. All of these basic human needs are interdependent, but basic education promotes accomplishment of, and increases the individual benefits from, the satisfaction of other needs.

The possession of basic learning also is a prerequisite and a complement to other sources of social and economic development. It can help resolve the problems of economic decline, widening economic disparities, dislocation and disadvantage, environmental degradation, and excessive population growth. Another and no less fundamental aim of educational development is the transmission and enrichment of common cultural and moral values.

It is in these values that the individual and society find their identity and worth. Moreover, sound basic education is fundamental to the strengthening of higher levels of education and of scientific and technological literacy and capacity and thus to selfreliant development.

As the range and gravity of problems facing the world's nations have grown, so too has awareness of the need to emphasize human development on global and national agendas. From settings as diverse as the 1987 Asian Forum of Parliamentarians on Population and Development, the 1988 Cartagena meeting of Latin American Ministers of State, the 1988 North-South Roundtable in Amman, the ongoing work of the South Commission, and numerous United Nations meetings, a general understanding has emerged: Real development is human development, and long term economic growth and social wellbeing rest on the quality of life of every woman and man. Confidence in this view has grown as countries have accumulated experience in providing basic education.

Many countries have made remarkable societal improvements as a result of their sustained investment in basic learning opportunities. The experience of Europe and North America, and more recently of Japan, the Republic of Korea, and Singapore, strongly support the conclusion that basic education is a necessary part of an equitable and efficient foundation for national development. Despite the real financial constraints evident in the 1980s, some countries have had striking success in fostering a better quality of life for all.

Major global initiatives, such as those related to access to clean water and sanitation, primary health care, immunization, and child survival, have each saved millions of lives and enhanced the wellbeing of hundreds of millions of people. Since the 1970s, an estimated 1.1 billion people have benefited from improved water supply and sanitation facilities, and in four lowincome African countries the percentage of the population with access to clean water doubled from 1980 to 1985. Worldwide, over 60 percent of all children are now vaccinated against the six major diseases that kill young people, and the goal of universal immunization seems near. This is an astonishing improvement over 1974 when only 5 percent of the babies born in the developing world received these vaccinations.

One child survival technique alone, oral rehydration therapy, saves as many as a million infants' lives a year. These successes required major initiatives, concerted action, and the formation of development alliances. Equally indispensable was the use of new communication technologies to disseminate the knowledge and skills needed to deal with the problems of water, sanitation, and health. In sum, these examples are dramatic proof that where there is a willingness and a commitment, gains in human development can be attained, even within the financial and other constraints of the current global challenges.

Recently, the development literature has focused more on constraints than on opportunities. A review of the state of basic learning in the world will reveal, however, that these constraints are not the absolute barriers to progress that many have assumed; with strong public and private commitments, they can be overcome. Constraints and opportunities are part of a complex whole where demographic, cultural, sociopolitical, technical, economic, environmental, and strictly educational factors are interrelated in a circular pattern of causes and effects. Each nation must be viewed individually: its background characteristics, financial capacity, and past educational efforts combine to determine the ultimate impact of learning achievement on its population. Whatever the constraints, a societal willingness and effort can minimize the inhibiting effects of these constraints and allow each country to exploit the unprecedented global opportunity to meet its current challenges.

Since human development determines how well individuals and nations will meet the current global challenges, it is important to understand the present context and effects of basic learning in the world. National data sets on the state of basic learning have four significant limitations. First, data are more commonly available for the formal education system and are incomplete to nonexistent for the wide range of out-of school programmes for youth and adults. Second, the data predominantly include learning inputs, sometimes outputs, but rarely indicators of the learning process. Third, the data are highly aggregated and do not always reflect the internal diversity of nations, systems, or even institutions. And fourth, the data rarely reveal qualitative dimensions of the quantitative measures. Given these data limitations, it should be recognized that more is known about basic learning than can be validated with available data and techniques. Thus, when data or statistical results appear illogical or even counterintuitive, one should be prepared to re-examine the situation carefully before abandoning one's original conception of the learning relationships. The national data on basic education can be organize around five concepts:

— The economic and demographic background of the nation

— The specific financial characteristics that constrain or facilitate the nation's capacity to support social services

— The actual effort being made to support basic education activities

— The direct effects of these efforts as measured by access to educational services, continuing participation of students, and graduation

— The social impacts of basic education activities as measured by indicators of literacy, health, nutrition, fertility, and income equality.

There are no simple cause-and-effect relationships between the determinants and results of basic education; rather, the relationship is interactive. Education facilitates development and development further facilitates future education activities. Thus, the current indicators of the effects of basic education become part of the general background and financial determinants of a nation's future capacity to progress toward meeting the basic learning needs of all. Per capita GNP is a useful indicator of a nation's total measured economic production and thus of the economic resources potentially available to meet social needs. Therefore, when per capita GNP is compared with other national characteristics, other measures of financial capacity, and indicators of educational effort and its direct and social effects, the analysis of the state of basic education is structured in a logical and effective form.

With per capita GNP in 1987 (in U.S. dollars) as a standard, the nations are divided into three categories: the lowincome economies (less than $480 per capita GNP), the middleincome economies ($481 to $5,999), and the industrial market economies ($6,000 and above). The low and middleincome economies are categorized as developing economies and the middleincome category itself is divisible into lower-middle -income economies ($481 to $2,000) and upper-middle -income economies ($2,001 to $5,999). The "other economies" category represents those nations for which data are unavailable for most of the indicators used in the analysis.

A review of the background characteristics of the world's nations reveals a startling convergence of disadvantage. The lowest-income economies not only are poor but also suffer from a variety of other developmental disadvantages. Their populations are the least educated, are increasing in number at the most rapid rates, are the most dependent on subsistence agriculture, have the least access to clean drinking water and health services, and most often lack the communication benefits of radio and television. This convergence of disadvantage has resulted in only twelve of the thirtyseven lowest-income nations reporting positive growth rates during the 1980-87 period. However, the more positive growth forecasts for 1987-1995 reinforce the belief that the present period offers a special opportunity for dealing with the world's basic learning needs.

During the 1970s it became conventional to refer to the world's poorest nations as "developing" rather than underdeveloped. However, over the last decade, the term "developing" became a misnomer for the majority of the poorest nations. The economic gap between the advantaged and disadvantaged nations widened not simply because the poorer countries were growing at a slower rate but because some were not growing at all in per capita terms and other economies were actually contracting. The joint effects of economic stagnation and continued high population growth made the already severe situation of these nations even worse. The problem of nondevelopment has not been confined to the low-income economies. It also appeared among the lower- middle-income countries where only fifteen of the thirty-four nations report positive per capita GNP growth rates for 1980-87. Only seven of these countries have reduced their annual population growth rates to below 2 percent while eight have rates still above 3 percent; thus, the pressure in these countries to promote economic growth sufficient to offset population increases is intense.

Development problems are not just a phenomenon of the least developed economies, however. For the most prosperous nations, the major issue has been the continued m a rginalization of their disadvantaged populations. Aggregate prosperity does not automatically generate benefits for these groups. Thus, programmes specifically directed to the needs of these groups are required if gains in equity are to parallel aggregate growth. In the middle-income countries, a major issue is the potential for economic stagnation. As countries become less able to maintain real per capita growth, they may find it more difficult to maintain the gains in social development of the last thirty years. These countries need to renew growth, beyond that fueled by inflation and required to off set population increases, to maintain and improve the social condition of all, especially the most disadvantaged.

The major aggregate issue in the low-income economies is economic decline. Many of these nations already are losing the battle to keep up with inflation, and some cannot maintain positive growth rates even in the aggregate, let alone in per capita measures. In these societies, both marginal and central population groups suffer, although marginal groups to a greater degree. In such conditions, the tendency is for the privileged minority to sustain itself while increasing numbers of the population become economically disadvantaged and face reduced access to basic social services.

Change is occurring within the three categories of economies. Some of the more prosperous countries are threatened by economic stagnation; within the middle-income economies, stagnation is moving toward decline for some; and within the low-income economies, decline is accelerating for the most disadvantaged countries. The reversal of these trends will not solve all of the economic and social problems, but it will begin the process of reclaiming the positive effects of development. Marginalization, stagnation, and decline are simply degrees of failure in the ability of nations to produce economic growth and to share it equitably among their populations.

A nation's specific economic conditions will either facilitate or constrain its financial ability to support social investment. Among these specific conditions are the role of government in the economy, the relative status of the agriculture sector, the structure of international trade, the balance of international payments, the debt burden, and the receipt of development assistance. With the exception of the last condition, the low- and lower-middle- income economies again present a pattern of disadvantage. The expansion of public sector involvement is not inherently a constraint on development. In fact, average levels of reported government expenditure as a percentage of gross domestic product are higher in the industrial market economies than in the developing economies, and there does not appear to be a systematic relationship between government involvement in the economy and national growth. The least developed nations are expected to continue to depend on agriculture as a major source of aggregate employment and growth in the near future. They also will continue to depend on commodity exports and imports of manufactured goods.

Supply and demand conditions in these two categories of trade often leave the developing nations in a less favourable market position than the more developed nations. Without improvement in their terms of trade, developing countries will operate under an ongoing disadvantage in attempting to promote aggregate growth by increasing foreign trade. In part, the current account balances for 1987 reflect these different trade structures. All but three of the low-income economies reported a negative balance for 1987; only nine of thirty-four lower-middle-income economies had a positive balance, whereas five of sixteen upper-middle-income and ten of twenty-five industrial economies had positive balances. Because of the debt incurred by developing nations in the 1970s, their access to foreign financing became so limited that current account balances were reduced dramatically after 1982. This reduction forced the seventeen most highly indebted nations to increase their trade surplus from $2 billion in 1982 to an annual average of $32 billion during 1983-87. This surplus resulted from lower relative imports, reduced investment, and constrained per capita consumption. These adjustments were doubly damaging because reduced consumption lowered economic welfare immediately while reduced investment threatened the longterm potential for growth.

The debt burden problem is a general constraint on development in all three categories of developing nations. Twenty-four of thirty-four low-income economies reported debt service levels for 1987 above 10 percent of exports, and nine of these had ratios above 25 percent. For the lower-middle-income economies, only two of thirty reported debt service ratios of less than 10 percent, and thirteen exceeded 25 percent. For upper-middle-income nations, only two countries (Panama and Gabon) had a debt service ratio below 10 percent, and nine of the twelve reporting nations had ratios above 25 percent. For the poorest nations these debt burdens aggravate the existing patterns of stagnation and decline. For the middle-income nations the debt burden is slowing—in some cases reversing—the progress that once was being made in national development.

The longterm debt of developing countries has continued to increase since 1982; for the highly indebted countries, it rose from $390 billion in 1982 to $485 billion at the end of 1987. This increase in debt paralleled deterioration of creditworthiness through 1986, but since then conditions have been more stable and in some cases have improved. The compression of imports brought on by the debt burden reduces exports from the developed nations and further jeopardizes global economic growth. The debt service problem is linked to the potential for social investment spending, but only indirectly.

As a greater share of national resources must be used to service foreign debt, fewer funds are available for all investment and consumption activities. It does appear, however, that under heavy debt burdens, some governments tend to emphasize import substitution activities and the immediately productive sectors at the expense of social investments. Debt conditions also precipitate structural adjustments and reforms that often have an impact on expenditures within the social sectors. Despite the general economic and financial conditions described above, many nations have made impressive attempts to maintain their financial commitment to basic education. The pattern suggests that a willingness to support the meeting of basic learning needs is a necessary condition to offset the most harmful effects of financial restraints. Between 1980 and 1987, fourteen of the twenty-two low- income countries reporting expenditure data maintained or increased total education expenditure as a percentage of GNP. Fifteen of the twenty-four lower-middle-income countries and fourteen of the sixteen upper-middle-income countries did the same. A similar pattern exists for education as a percentage of total government expenditure.

Some countries, despite their economic difficulties, have made the commitment to reallocate government expenditures in favour of, rather than away from, education. An appropriate inference from this data is that although choices concerning educational expenditures are constrained, it is still within a country's own ability to choose education. A large number of countries have maintained or increased the share of primary education in the total education budget between 1980 and 1987. More than half of the low-income and lower-middle income nations reporting comparable data have managed to increase primary education's share in their education budgets. However, in two-thirds of these countries this increase was coupled with a decline in the per pupil expenditure during the same period, due to increasing enrollments. On the other hand, in the upper-middle-income economies, and notably in Latin America, primary education's share in some countries' education budgets has declined because of the relative expansion of secondary and tertiary education. Because total resources for education have increased in many of these nations, the relative decline of primary education's share does not automatically imply a decline in per pupil expenditures on primary education. Even with increasing primary school populations, five of the six countries in this category that experienced a decline in primary education's share, managed to increase their per pupil expenditure between 1980 and 1987.

As a further indication of education efforts, a large majority of countries continued to expand enrolment during the 1975-85 decade, and some even reduced teacher-pupil ratios. Because of governmental financial constraints and parental choice, many countries have an increased proportion of their primary school pupils in private schools. Even though many private schools receive some form of direct or indirect government subsidy, the expansion of private schools can allow governments to target a portion of their expenditures more directly on the needs of the disadvantaged; for example, through subsidy formulas based on community income. There always is the danger that the private system will evolve into an elite alternative with access determined by family income alone, or that public schools will be comparatively neglected. However, appropriate planning can avert these effects by assuring a recognition of the inevitable interdependency of the two sectors.

The development of private education has been more dramatic in the industrial economies than among the developing economies. Only seven of twenty-four low-income countries showed an increase in the proportion of pupils in private primary education, while twenty -three of forty-nine middle-income countries, and fourteen of twenty industrial market economies did so. One inference is that the more advantaged nations are benefitting from the mobilization of nongovernment resources for primary education, while in low-income countries, whose public budgets are already burdened in other ways, governments continue to assume the highest proportion of fiscal responsibility for educational services. Obviously, private resources in low-income nations also are constrained, but nongovernment alternatives can assist in financing even in the poorest nations. For example, Haiti has more than half its primary students in private schools, and there are initiatives to mobilize family and community resources for basic education throughout sub-Saharan Africa. Parallel efforts to provide out-o f-school basic education for children are harder to document in a comparable quantified manner. Despite difficult economic conditions, however, many nations have maintained and some have expanded their out-of-school programmes equivalent to formal primary education. These often provide instruction with the same content as that of primary schools and also often teach basic knowledge and skills to youth and adults. Better documentation of such programmes and their participants, costs, and results will be required for the future planning of basic education.

Ideally, a nation would want to know how educational efforts affect school processes, and the acquisition of knowledge, skills, attitudes and behaviour. In reality, data are available only to indicate access to schooling, continuing participation, graduation, and further learning attainment. The degree to which these indicators are adequate proxies for the hoped for effects of basic education activities will vary among nations, systems, and institutions. The gross and net enrolment ratios reveal once again the differences among nations and among the economic categories of nations in their priorities for and efforts in meeting basic learning needs.

Gross enrolment ratios include under- and over-age pupils in addition to those of the normal primary school age (usually six to eleven years old). Within the group of low-income economies, gross enrolment ratios for males range from 20 to 30 percent (Afghanistan, Mali, and Somalia) to over 100 percent (twelve countries). The gross enrolment ratios for females are consistently lower with only one exception (Lesotho with 125 percent for females versus 101 percent for males). Net enrolment ratios (restricted to the primary school age cohort) are less generally available but show a similar pattern: countries with comparable economic conditions show significantly different education results.

Among the low-income economies, reported net enrolment ratios for males range from 14 percent in

Somalia and 31 percent in Guinea to 87 percent in Togo, 89 percent in Madagascar, and 99 or 100 percent in Indonesia and Sri Lanka. Female net enrolment ratios reported for the same set of countries range from 8 percent in Somalia, 15 percent in Guinea, and 20 percent in Burkina Faso to 96 percent in Indonesia and 100 percent in Sri Lanka. Of course, these differences are not solely a product of policy choices and priorities, but they do support the contention that both societal willingness and effort must be considered in evaluating the constraining effect of a nation's financial capacity.

One of the most widely used indicators of educational development is the female enrolment rate. Since females commonly are the last to benefit from educational expansion and the first to suffer from reductions in learning opportunities, their participation rates are a more sensitive indicator of access than are total or male only rates. The general pattern of female participation is one of lower aggregate enrolment rates with a notably greater degree of equality at entry to primary schooling than at termination. This finding indicates that attempts to improve gender equity must focus both on access and on the continued participation of females. Not indicated in the available data is differential achievement.

Anecdotal reports suggest that, even where participation in learning programs is high, social and cultural factors which influence career expectations and role definitions can indirectly affect learning achievement. A wellknown example in the United States is the question of girl's achievement in science and math. Participation by students until the end of the primary school cycle may be, however, a necessary if not sufficient condition for achieving an acceptable level of basic learning. For 1 9 8 0-86, completion rates (the proportion of grade 1 enrollees who complete the primary cycle) reported by the low-income countries ranged from around 15 percent (Benin, Guinea-Bissau, and the Yemen Arab Republic) to 80 percent and above (Mauritania, Indonesia, Sri Lanka, and Zambia).

Since high completion rates can reflect policies that restrict initial access opportunities in favour of elites, this indicator needs to be viewed in the context of both access and achievement levels. Similarly, reported levels of secondary school access indicate the effect not only of primary schooling but also of other determinants, including the demand structure of the labour market and the availability of secondary school places. Educational patterns also differs among the middle-income and the industrial market economies. For example, one lower middle-income nation reports a gross enrolment ratio for males of less than 75 percent, while twenty-five countries report ratios of 95 percent or above. Among the higher income nations, the reported female net enrolment ratios range from 48 to 100 percent. A list of the desired effects of educational investments at the basic education level must include initial access, continued participation, equity for disadvantaged populations, and learning achievement. All of these are of some concern in all countries. As in the case of economic growth, however, the most disadvantaged nations face the most difficulty in achieving the desired effects. In summary, multiple indicators of educational processes and effects are required to assess the effectiveness and efficiency of a nation's attempts to meet basic learning needs.

Examination of a high-performing nation's willingness and effort may help identify aspects that can be transferred to other national contexts. The data on primary education efforts shed light on the incomplete coverage of the current systems; they also define more precisely the task of expanding basic education through primary schooling and equivalent systems, public information, and adult education and training programmes. The need for each nation to expand its outofschool efforts is strengthened by the realization that, for many nations, the goal of universal primary schooling will not be attained in the immediate future.

The desired social outcomes of expanded basic learning include higher levels of literacy, health, and nutrition, lower fertility, and greater income equality. Indicators of these effects can be used to appraise the social justification for past investments in basic learning. Although simple cause-and-effect relationships again are difficult to document, numerous studies have demonstrated that basic education has direct effects on these social measures by transferring information and skills and indirect effects by altering general economic conditions and individual and community preferences.

In reviewing the available data, it becomes obvious once again that, while a correlation does exist between background economic conditions and these measures of social progress, many countries succeed beyond their expected levels while others seem to be underperforming relative to their economic context and fiscal capacity. While literacy levels, with some exceptions such as the notable achievements of Tanzania, follow the pattern of primary schooling effects, the same is not true for the other societal measures. Under five mortality rates (U5MRs) have been notably reduced in such low-income nations as China, Kenya, Lesotho, Myanmar (Burma), Sri Lanka, Viet Nam, and Zambia. Poland, Jamaica, Costa Rica and Chile have outperformed the other lower-middle -income countries, and Greece and Portugal lead all higher-middle- income countries in this measure. In contrast, the United States is second in income, a leader in educational expenditure, and nineteenth in child mortality rates. Similar patterns of over and under-achievement exist among countries for the measures of life expectancy, caloric intake, fertility rate, and the shares of income possessed by the lowest 40 percent and highest 20 percent of the population.

Although economic development eventually will help achieve societal goals, some goals cannot wait for such progress. The data here show that, in fact, equivalent social development can be fostered at varying levels of economic development. Since social development · in the form of improved literacy, health, nutrition, population planning, and income equality - also promotes further economic development, this interaction provides clear grounds for an expanded vision and a renewed commitment to meeting the basic learning needs of all.

Because of the diverse nature of adult education activities, the available aggregate data fail to capture adequately the content, effects, and target populations of specific programmes. Even the coverage and detail of the aggregate data are not as complete as in the case of formal education. As economic development proceeds, the scope and content of basic learning needs change. The issue is not just that the level of enrolment in the developed nations is higher, but that adults in these countries typically have greater access to learning opportunities than adults in the developing nations. It is this combination of advantages that widens the knowledge gap between these two groups of countries.

When the advantages of adult education are compounded by other favourable circumstances in the economically developed nations, the challenge to developing nations to maintain, let alone increase, their relative position is made dramatically difficult. Information on female participation in adult education is not available for all countries. Among the thirty-four developing nations for which data are available, women represent half or more of the participants in only fourteen, though in five of these cases they represent twothirds or more of the participants. Because females have often been denied access to and participation in formal education, their share of the need for adult education is greater than their share in the population. Therefore even an equal gender ratio could be interpreted as less than equitable to women. In seven of the fourteen more developed countries reporting gender ratios, over 50 percent of the participants are women. But some of these countries have rates of female participation below one-third of all enrollees.

Adult education activities do not automatically serve their dual role of supplementing and extending the effects of formal education. The data here, as aggregate and dated as they are, suggest that basic learning opportunities for out-of-school youth and adults must be consciously designed to fit the needs that remain unmet by the primary education system and to meet the new learning needs created by the successful operation of primary education. Whether providing literacy, numeracy, knowledge to meet basic needs, or social and economic skills, the programmes to train youth and adults face rapidly evolving demands. The lack of adequate resources to meet those demands places an even greater burden on adult education programmes in most countries.

The state of adult education remains unclear because of data limitations and the internal complexity of the basic learning activities that occur. The available data do highlight a general pattern of increasing inequities among nations in participation and growing differences between genders in overall knowledge acquisition. More detailed data on the content and quality of programmes and on the characteristics of participants would not likely reverse this conclusion, and current observations of adult education in many developing and developed nations tend to reinforce it. Above all, there is a critical need to improve the data base on adult education to permit more detailed analysis and a more refined development of policy to meet the basic learning needs of adults.

Early child development can be considered a component of basic education because learning begins at birth. Moreover, a growing body of evidence demonstrates that health, nutrition, and psychosocial processes interact to affect survival and development in the early years of life. The outcomes of these interactions condition the readiness of the child for school and other learning opportunities, which in turn influences the child's chances of enrolment and success in basic education programmes. As with basic education for adults, the data on early child development is incomplete and does not lend itself readily to international comparisons. Early child development may include some or all of the following: nutrition supplementation, growth monitoring, caretaking, home instruction in preliteracy and numeracy skills, and parent education for the benefit of the child, which may also be considered under adult education.

According to 1980 data from the World Bank, enrolment in preschools, a subcategory of early child development, was quite low in most low-income economies, with a median of one percent of the age-group for countries reporting data. In middle-income developing economies, the picture is more mixed. Enrolment rates ranged from a low of one percent to a high of 57 percent, with 4.5 percent as the median for lower-middle income economies and 15 percent the median for upper-middle income.

In high income economies, median enrolment rates were 25.5 percent, with a range from less than one to 66 percent. However, most statistics focus on organized pre-school and child care programmes. Because of the difficulty in defining and identifying such educational programmes, the Unesco Office of Statistics points out that their estimates should be considered as the minimal figures for each country. What is clear from the data, however, is that in many countries, early childhood education has been the most rapidly expanding sector of education over the past decade.

From the growing body of studies and reports on specific early child development, two important impacts of early childhood development programmes on meeting basic learning needs have become evident. First, attention to the physical and psychosocial development of young children often enhances their ability to benefit from schooling, thereby increasing efficiency within the school system. Second, the positive effects on school performance of early child development programmes has been shown in many cases to be more significant for girls than boys, and for children from disadvantaged social groups than those from more affluent homes. Thus, early child development can have a substantial equity effect, by reducing disparities in subsequent educational attainment. So long as such programmes are only available to higher income groups, however, they may have the effect of further advantaging those groups, thus increasing inequities in learning achievement.

Since the 1948 Universal Declaration of Human Rights articulated the right of everyone to education, the nations of the world frequently have established specific targets to make the right a reality. The 1956 Lima meeting and the 1963 Santiago Conference of Ministers of Education focused on free and compulsory education in Latin America and the Caribbean; similar conferences in 1960 in Karachi and 1962 in Tokyo established the Asian model" with goals of primary school gross enrolment ratios of 70 percent by 1964 and 90 percent in 1980.

The Addis Ababa conference in 1961 affirmed the goal of universal primary education in Africa by 1980. Ironically, the primary enrolments attained in 1970 and 1980 exceeded those projected by these UNESCO regional meetings, and yet universal primary education still was not achieved in many countries. The phenomenal growth of aggregate enrolments during the 1960s and 1970s was offset by rapid population growth and a widening divergence among the achievements of individual countries and geographical regions. In the 1980s, Asia has consolidated its gains, and in the more developed countries emphasis has shifted from concerns with aggregate access to issues of achievement and equity for disadvantaged populations. In much of sub-Saharan Africa and in the least developed economies elsewhere, however, the 1980s have been a period of stagnation and, for some, a retreat from the goals of universal access. The low-income economies have seen growth in primary enrolments fall from an average annual rate of 5.6 percent in 1975-80 to 2.7 percent for 1980-87. During this same period population growth increased annually from

2.7 percent to 3.4 percent on average and was accompanied by negative real economic growth rates for certain Sub-Saharan countries. Most middle-income countries maintained enrolment growth in proportion to population growth, but many faced mounting concern about the effectiveness of education and the efficient utilization of funds. The lower-middle-income countries have not been able to maintain their 1 9 7 5-80 enrolment growth rates into the 1980s, while the higher-middle-income countries have benefited from a decline in population growth rates that more than offset the slowing growth in enrolments.

According to UNESCO estimates, in 1985 approximately 105 million schoolage children were not participating in formal education. Of these, 70.2 percent were in the least developed nations and 60 percent were girls. If current trends continue, by the year 2000 the number of out-of-school children will almost double to approximately 200 million. Despite significant progress in the aggregate expansion of primary education, a growing number of children are not in school, nor ready when they do enter, the number of illiterate adults is increasing, and the unmet needs for basic knowledge and skills continue to accumulate. These needs are expanding so fast that many formal primary education systems do not have the capacity to meet them. Without significant changes, many nations will have to forgo improvements in educational quality, and some will be forced to accept deterioration. High rates of dropout and repetition of grades will continue to characterize many basic education programmes - symptoms of the overwhelming needs and the current inadequacy of resource provision.

The challenge for the future remains the assurance of access to an acceptable quality of primary education, of literacy training, and of basic knowledge and essential life skills for all children, youth, and adults. However, universal access to primary education alone by the year 2000 would require raising enrolment by more than 7.5 percent a year for the low-income countries, 3.2 percent for the lower-middle-income countries, and 3.0 percent for the upper- middle-income countries. The current growth rates for the three categories are 2.8, 2.4, and 1.7 percent respectively. One fact is obvious, therefore: a linear expansion of current growth patterns will not be sufficient to meet the basic learning needs of all.

Government, families, communities and nongovernment organizations will all need to do more. For the economically advantaged economies, increased efficiency and the availability of new resources will better their chances of improving educational quality for all and extending basic learning opportunities more effectively to currently marginal populations. For a middle range of countries, substantial increases in efficiency and effort will allow them to concentrate more on reducing the inappropriate repetition of grades and the number of dropouts. These countries can work toward providing universal access to primary education, encouraging completion of the primary cycle and the achievement of an acceptable level of learning, and improving opportunities for youth and adults to attain literacy and the basic knowledge and skills their society requires.

Under projected patterns of economic growth, however, a third group of countries simply will not be able to meet basic learning needs for all with their own resources. Greater government fiscal support, the mobilization of family, community, and nongovernmental resources, and increased efficiency — even if all a re achieved — will not provide sufficient resources. External assistance, substantial and sustained, will be required to allow these countries to join those in the more advantaged categories in meeting the basic learning needs for all. The challenge for all countries is to devise a feasible way to meet the basic learning needs of their population. This requires more than a recommitment to basic education as it now exists. What is needed is an "expanded vision" that builds on the best of the present policies and practices but goes beyond existing resource levels, institutional structures, curricula, and conventional suppliers and incorporates whatever is needed to meet the basic learning needs of all.

The structure and content of learning activities should be determined to equip all children, youth, and adults with the knowledge, skills, values and attitudes they need to survive, to improve their quality of life, to empower them to participate fully and responsibly in the life of their communities and nations, to initiate and to adapt to changing circumstances-and to continue learning according to their individual needs and interests. "An expanded vision" commensurate with the extent of the basic learning needs of children, youth, and adults can be conceived in terms of the following components:

— Universalizing access and promoting equity;

— Focussing on learning;

— Broadening the means and scope of basic education;

— Enhancing the environment for learning;

— Strengthening partnerships.

Universalizing access and promoting equity: Basic education should be provided to all children, youth and adults To this end, basic education services of quality should be expanded, and consistent measures must be taken to reduce disparities. For basic education to be equitable, all children, youth, and adults must be given the opportunity to achieve and maintain an acceptable level of learning. The most urgent priority is to ensure access to, and improve the quality of, education for girls and women, and to remove every obstacle that hampers their active participation.

All gender stereotyping in education should be eliminated. An active commitment must be made to removing other educational disparities. Underserved groups should not suffer any discrimination in access to learning opportunities: the poor; street and working children; rural and remote populations; nomads and migrant workers; indigenous peoples; ethnic, racial, and linguistic minorities; refugees; those displaced by war; and people under occupation. The learning needs of the disabled demand special attention. Steps need to be taken to provide equal access to education to every category of disabled persons as an integral part of the education system. In nearly every society, specific social groups have historically lacked the social conditions necessary to meet basic learning needs. Adequate supply of basic education programmes such that all members of society have access to them is a necessary but not sufficient condition for meeting the basic learning needs of all.

Factors conditioning demand, such as the appropriateness of programmes to learners' needs, their design and delivery in accordance with learners' circumstances, and an environment that provides incentives and rewards for learning, all impinge on efforts to meet basic learning needs. Eliminating disparities in basic education will require that equity effects be taken into account in the design, implementation, management, and evaluation of all basic education programmes.

Focussing on learning: Whether or not expanded educational opportunities will translate into meaningful development for an individual or for society - depends ultimately on whether people actually learn as a result of those opportunities, i.e., whether they incorporate useful knowledge, reasoning ability, skills, and values. The focus of basic education must, therefore, be on actual learning acquisition and outcomes, rather than exclusively upon enrolment, continued participation in organized programmes and completion of certification requirements.

Active and participatory approaches are particularly valuable in assuring learning acquisition and maintenance, allowing learners to reach their fullest potential. Therefore, it is necessary to define acceptable levels of learning acquisition for educational programmes and to improve and apply systems of assessing learning achievement. This focus on learning acquisition should help prevent policies which encourage access for all but adequate learning only for the more advantaged. For school systems in many developing nations and in disadvantaged areas of some developed nations, the danger is that the sacrifices in quality that have occurred in recent years may not soon be removed or ameliorated. At the very least, continued educational expansion without attention to learning achievement will raise substantially the eventual cost of providing quality learning opportunities to the most disadvantaged populations. The other aspects of the expanded vision should help promote the expansion of basic education without the sacrifice of necessary learning achievement.

The focus on equitable achievement of learning outcomes includes, but is not restricted to, measurable cognitive gains. Demonstrable achievement in other areas, such as attitudes, values, and behaviour, can be part of each country's definition of acceptable learning acquisition for all. The nature of learning will vary by country, and within countries, by age groups and by level and purpose of instruction.

Basic learning opportunities may be designed to meet intrinsic individual needs, to facilitate meeting other basic human needs (e.g., health, nutrition), and/or to provide learning which is instrumental in achieving larger community or societal concerns. Whatever the purposes of learning, evidence of demonstrable effects can help justify the sacrifices made by individuals and society to support learning. Particular efforts will have to be made to maintain basic learning skills once they are acquired. Such postbasic education efforts should make more efficient use of existing media, such as the rural press, radio, television, etc. Isolated or marginal populations will need reading materials that are relevant, stimulating, group specific, and culturally acceptable. Similar efforts are needed to further develop their writing and numeracy skills.

Broadening the means and scope of basic education: The diversity, complexity, and changing nature of basic learning needs of children, youth and adults necessitates broadening and constantly redefining the scope of basic education to include four components. These components should constitute an integrated system complementary, mutually reinforcing, and of comparable standards, and they should contribute to creating and developing possibilities for lifelong learning. First, as learning begins at birth, this calls for early childhood care and initial education. These can be provided through arrangements involving families, communities, or institutional programmes, as appropriate.Second, the main delivery system for the basic education of children outside the family is primary schooling. Children who complete this level successfully should possess essential life skills and the capacity to benefit from further education. Achieving universal primary education will be the goal for many countries in the 1990s.

For a large number of developing countries, however, it is unlikely that enough primary schools can be built, equipped and staffed at an acceptable level of quality to provide a place for every child in the immediate future. Other vehicles for primary education, such as religious and community-based instruction, radio, television, and learning activities in clubs and libraries, also can meet the basic learning needs of children. Provided that the same acceptable standards of achievement are applied to all vehicles of primary education, it is possible to encourage such diversity in delivery without creating differential learning effects. The lack of adequate access to schools need not prevent any child from attaining a common educational foundation for life and for further learning.Third, the basic learning needs of youth and adults are diverse and should be met through a variety of delivery systems. Literacy programmes are indispensable because literacy is a necessary skill in itself and the foundation of other life skills. Literacy in the mothertongue strengthens cultural identity and heritage. Other needs can be served by: skills training, apprenticeships, and formal and non-formal education programmes in health, nutrition, population, agricultural techniques, the environment, science, technology, family life, including fertility awareness, and other societal issues. Finally, all available instruments and channels of information, communications, and social action could be used to help convey essential knowledge and inform and education people on social issues. In addition to the traditional means, libraries, television, radio and other media can be mobilized to realize their potential to meet basic education needs. All of these can serve to provide direct instruction to children and adults, as well as to train instructors and supervisors. The success of one technology over another is rarely generalizable, as local conditions inevitably shape the choice and effective utilization of technologies. In their most effective applications, such technologies have generally been adapted to supplement conventional delivery systems such as the classroom teacher, the literacy worker, and the agriculture, health, and family planning extension agent.

Communications media and other information dissemination systems are of particular importance. Media can have a planned and structured application in support of learning activities or, more commonly, can have an indirect impact through informal learning processes. In some industrialized countries, children may spend on average five hours or more per day exposed to modern mass media, especially television, an exposure which rivals their attendance in formal education.

In developing countries, where imported foreign products often constitute as much as eighty percent of overall media programming, it is the image of the world conveyed by such media that feeds children's imagination and largely conditions their perceptions of cultural identity. The mass media have become major agents of learning, even though this learning is usually unstructured, unintentional, and sometimes socially harmful. At the same time, communications media both mass media, and smaller, community-based formats can be important adjuncts and supports to education and development processes. They can be employed within formal education as a means of direct teaching or enrichment; they can provide alternative delivery systems in such contexts as distance education.

Linked with computerized systems, they can help improve both the volume and quality of information accessible to learners. In some nations, these new forms of information dissemination, when combined with incentives for information acquisition and utilization, constitute an effective channel for basic education. All available means and technologies for communications, information, and social mobilization must be utilized to disseminate basic learning and to educate the public about such concerns as health, nutrition, family life, sanitation, child care, population, environmental protection, agricultural techniques, and drug prevention.

Enhancing the environment for learning: Basic education should be planned in relation to the preconditions and concurrent requirements of learning. The preconditions of learning include the health, nutrition, and physical and intellectual stimulation to which the learner has been exposed prior to the learning activity. Some negative preconditions, such as disease and malnutrition, can exert powerful constraining effects on the capacity of the learner to benefit from a learning opportunity. Positive preconditions, such as supportive parents, siblings, and peers, can raise the entry-level capacity of the learner and enable learning activities to achieve more substantial and extensive results. More attention needs to be given to preventing disabilities among young children and to developing their faculties for learning. One must also consider the concurrent requirements for nutrition, health, and stimulation. If these concurrent requirements are not met, the achievement of basic learning objectives will be limited. Therefore, basic education initiatives should be designed to promote a supportive learning environment in the home and community.

The social, cultural and economic contexts play a role in defining basic learning needs, in motivating individuals to learn, and in determining the capacity of the society to initiate and reinforce learning programmes. Knowledge and skills that will enhance the learning environment of children should be integrated into community learning programmes for adults. The education of children and their parents or other caretakers is mutually supportive and this interaction should be used to create, for all, a learning environment of vibrancy and warmth.

Strengthening partnerships: National, regional, and local educational authorities have a unique obligation to provide basic education for all, but they cannot be expected to supply every human, financial or organizational requirement for this task. New and revitalized partnerships at all levels will be necessary: partnerships among all subsectors and forms of education; partnerships between education and other government departments, including planning, finance, labour, agriculture, communications, health, social welfare, etc.; partnerships between government and nongovernmental organizations, the private sector, local communities, religious groups, and families.

Recognition of the vital role of families, teachers and other educational personnel is particularly important. In this context, the terms and conditions of service of teachers and their status, which constitute a determining factor in the implementation of education for all, must be urgently improved in all countries in line with the joint ILO/ UNESCO Recommendation Concerning the Status of Teachers. Genuine partnerships, which contribute to the planning, implementing, managing and evaluating of basic education programmes, are at the heart of the expanded vision and renewed commitment called for in the World Declaration on Education for All.

Policies and Programmes

Basic education can help meet the intrinsic needs of learners, assist them to meet other basic human needs, and promote social and economic development. However, these latter two effects cannot be achieved in isolation of other public efforts. The knowledge and skills concerning health and nutrition, for example, are effective only when the concomitant resources and means are provided. Without a primary health delivery system, access to water, or availability of necessary foods, knowledge and skill alone will be insufficient. Similarly, it is not adequate to orient education to prepare people for employment. Government and private enterprise must institute the appropriate rules, incentives, and support that will encourage wider demand for educated labour and more efficient utilization of it. More broadly, the effects of basic education are determined by the interaction of the full complex of government and private sectorssuch diverse activities as agricultural pricing, political participation, entrepreneurial regulation, cultural practices, and infrastructure development all help determine the usefulness of the education individuals receive. The planning and management of education must consider the full range of learning opportunities needed and relate them to the full range of other government and private activities necessary to make the learning opportunities effective.

Supportive policies in the social, cultural, and economic spheres are required in order to realize the full provision and utilization of basic education for individual and societal improvement. Attaining basic education for all depends on political will and commitment manifested in appropriate fiscal measures, educational policy reforms and institutional strengthening. Suitable economic, trade, labour, employment and health policies will provide incentives for learners and enhance their contributions to societal development. Similarly, public policy should ensure a strong intellectual and scientific environment for basic education. This implies improving higher education, developing scientific research, and utilizing them to enrich the content and methods of basic education, particularly through the application of contemporary technological and scientific knowledge.

To respond to the unmet learning needs, new resources will have to be sought from three sources:

(1) a broader governmental base of support;

(2) an increased financial effort from expanded participation by nongovernment agencies, communities, families, and individuals; and

(3) assistance from external funding agencies.

This entails identifying and drawing on the support of government, the private sector, nongovernmental organizations, local communities, and families. In most countries, all of these play some part in financing basic education from government's formal taxation and expenditure activities to the family's sacrifice of labour so that the child can attend schools or the adult can acquire new skills.

A broader base of government support can be achieved by mobilizing the resources of all government agencies that deal with some aspect of human development. Agencies responsible for agriculture, health, labour, defense, commerce, industry, and other development activities can be encouraged to make specific allocations within their own budgets to support basic education activities. Whether by developing new sources of revenue or reallocating funds from other sectors or within the education sector, government will need to take the lead in expanding new basic learning opportunities. Government resources alone will not be sufficient, however, to meet effectively the basic learning needs of all groups.

Greater participation by nongovernmental organizations, communities, families, and individuals is needed. Examples of these forms of participation include support provided by local community organizations, employers, labour unions, cooperatives, voluntary organizations, and religious bodies. Often, existing programmes or services can be reoriented or enlarged to include an educational component or to support ongoing education and training activities. In some cases, facilities and materials can be produced by volunteers or donated. This diversification of participation also can encourage the broad commitment needed to ensure that society gives a real priority to meeting the basic learning needs of all, and thereby investing in its future.

In many cases, no matter how well a country mobilizes and allocates its resources, it still will not be able to meet the basic learning needs of the entire population. Because of their disadvantageous conditions, the least economically developed countries will not immediately have the capacity to supply the necessary quantity and diversity of learning opportunities. Only external assistance, of a significant amount and sustained over time, can meet the resource needs for basic learning in these countries. The longterm return on this investment, and the goal of external assistance, will be the eventual development of each country's selfsufficiency in providing basic education.

Meeting basic learning needs constitutes a common and universal human responsibility, requiring international solidarity and cooperation. All nations have valuable knowledge and experience to share in this field and much to gain in doing so. International consultation and cooperative action regarding basic education through the many existing structures and institutional arrangements need to be intensified. The prospects for meeting basic learning needs around the world are determined in part by the dynamics of international relations and trade. A stable and peaceful international environment will facilitate socioeconomic development and hence the prospects for expanding basic learning opportunities. All nations must continue to work together to resolve armed conflicts and to end military occupations. The world community has a particular responsibility to settle displaced populations or to facilitate their return to their countries of origin and ensure that their basic learning needs are met.

With the current relaxation of tensions and the decreasing number of armed conflicts, there are now real possibilities to reduce the tremendous waste of military spending and to shift those resources into socially useful areas, including basic education. The world community and individual governments need to plan this conversion of resources for peaceful uses with courage and vision, and in a thoughtful and careful manner.

To achieve education for all, substantial and longterm increases in resources for basic education will be needed. While most of these resources must necessarily come from within each country, the world community will need to act through multilateral and bilateral agencies to alleviate the constraints and deficiencies that prevent some countries from meeting the basic learning needs of their populations. The least economically developed and lowincome countries have special needs which will require priority attention in international cooperative efforts during the 1990s. Measures to reduce or eliminate current imbalances in trade relations and to reduce debt burdens will enable many lowincome countries to rebuild their own economies and release and retain the human and financial resources needed for development and for providing basic education to their populations. In this connection, structural adjustment policies should protect appropriate funding levels for education.

To meet the basic learning needs of its population, each country must first diagnose its own societal resources and requirements in order to define the basic level of learning suited to its context. This diagnosis requires analyzing national background characteristics, financial constraints, current educational effort and effects, and present conditions of societal development. On this basis, a country can establish appropriate targets and derive suitable strategies for implementing policies and programmes to meet basic learning needs for all. The decisions implicit in this process will be difficult and may lead to adjustments in the education sector to incorporate the expanded vision of basic education. This could entail adjustments to the management structure, incentive measures, the content of basic education, and the methods of providing and monitoring basic learning activities.

As countries develop their own policies and programmes for the expanded vision of basic education, they must be especially concerned with four policy issues: relevance, quality, equity, and efficiency. The concept of relevance implies that the results of basic education must be evaluated in terms of how well the learner is prepared for immediate life survival, effective participation in society, and further learning. In some nations, further learning will include formal schooling beyond the primary level; in others, a variety of less formal activities will offer more advanced education, skill training, and opportunities to acquire and use specific information. The mix between these two forms of postbasic learning depends on the public and private supply of learning opportunities and on the demand for them as determined, in part, by their relevance and effectiveness.

The quality of learning activities has traditionally been defined in terms of the inputs to a programme, institution, or system. Preferably, measures of output should be used as substitutes for or, at least, complements to the input measures. Measures of the learning process the actual interaction of the learner with the learning resources and environment are least commonly used to indicate learning quality because of the methodological problems of measuring process effects. Therefore, the definition and analysis of learning quality has relied excessively on input and output measures without a clear understanding of how the available inputs are transformed into the desired outputs.

The analysis of the International Association for the Evaluation of Educational Achievement's Second Mathematics Study presents one example of how this understanding might be improved by the simultaneous consideration of inputs, processes, and outputs. Participation in basic education has increased impressively over the last thirty years but with varying degrees of equity in pupil's access to and continuation in programmes, as well as in learning achievement.

Most commonly, individuals suffer from learning inequities because of their poverty, gender, location, religious, linguistic, or ethnic identification, and physical or mental disability. In certain societies all of these characteristics operate to reduce learning opportunities, and in most societies they have some interaction that compounds the problem of inequity.

In all nations, the children of the disadvantaged are the least likely to be ready for, or to enroll in, and the most likely to drop out of, learning programmes. If the available learning opportunities for children, youth and adults (beginning in the preschool years) fail to provide the participants with necessary knowledge and skills, individual decisions not to attend or continue may appear logical, but in the longterm these individual decisions impose high costs on society. The effectiveness of a learning activity refers to how well its goal is accomplished; efficiency refers to how well the goal is accomplished relative to the resources spent.

By incorporating both costs and effects, measures of efficiency are the best indicators of how well individual programmes or learning activities are performing with the funds available to them. When the issues of relevance and equity are incorporated in the definition of educational goals, efficiency becomes a more meaningful concept and includes the common indicators of quality. Efficiency is not identical with reducing costs. Although cost containment may result from an efficiency analysis, an appraisal of a learning activity may well conclude that greater expenditure is needed. Whether or not expenditures can be increased depends on fiscal capacity and priorities, not efficiency.

Any learning activity depends significantly upon the characteristics of the learners. Research has documented that the most critical determinants of the learning capacity of children entering primary school are nutrition, health, and the early social environment. The appropriate policy response to these relationships is twofold. First, health, nutrition, and social development programmes must look beyond their immediate benefits to their longterm positive effects on learning. Second, basic education and training alternatives can offer wider and more equitable access to preschool opportunities, and to nutrition and health services, such as school feeding programmes. In their content, basic education programmes can include the lifeskills necessary to improve the environment for meeting the basic learning needs of the next generation. The first response is preventive; it combats the cognitive and behavioural disadvantages that originate from malnutrition, disease, inadequate caregiving or an unstimulating social environment. This response recognizes that basic learning begins at birth and not at entry to formal learning activities. Early intervention programmes among poor children in countries as diverse as Brazil, Colombia, Haiti, India, Thailand, and the United States demonstrate the longterm advantages to children and society that such programmes offer. These programmes experimented with a variety of alternative strategies including:

(a) attending directly to the child through childcare centres;

(b) educating parents and other caregivers to enrich their understanding and practice of caregiving; and

(c) fostering community development activities designed to enhance the environment of the young child.

Benefits to children participating in such programmes include subsequent higher levels of academic achievement and higher success rates in primary school than children who have not received similar early enrichment. Moreover, these benefits are especially strong for girls and disadvantaged children, who have a higher risk of physiological underdevelopment and who have limited access to and lower achievement in schools, when such early intervention programmes do not exist. The second response is not only preventative but also compensatory and reinforcing. The provision of early childhood learning opportunities and of health and nutrition services can offset some of the damage to infants from inadequate preconditions for learning. In addition, health and nutrition services offered concurrently with basic learning programmes reinforce the ability of individuals to benefit from the basic learning provided.

The World Food Programme allocates approximately 17 percent of its $600 million of development food assistance to education. The benefits of this assistance include increased access to education, improved quality of learning, and more effective use of learning after leaving education. Early intervention is essential to prevent and overcome disablement. Any interruption of normal development in an impaired child is often far more serious than the direct consequences of the impairment. Thus the validity of intervention must be measured by the degree to which it enhances normal child development and supports the family in achieving this objective.

Not all of the determinants of the favorable conditions for effective learning are within the influence of education policy or even general public policy. Nevertheless, these conditions must be considered in the design of policies and programmes to meet the basic learning needs of children, youth, and adults. For most countries, a discussion of basic learning needs of children will focus on the primary school age group, normally those six to eleven years old. Enrolments may include pupils one to two years younger and up to three years older. The main vehicles for delivering primary education are the school and the out-of-school programmes that provide equivalent instruction.

Primary schooling is the most formal method of providing basic learning. Normally an institutionalized, graded, and hierarchical system, in most nations it is characterized by the highest levels of participation, standardized curricula, and significant government involvement in the initiation, financing, regulation, and/or provision of schools. Primary schools are often the most visible and widely disseminated social institution in a country. Therefore, primary schooling is central to the expanded vision of basic education. First, because it is the major vehicle for meeting basic learning needs, highquality primary schooling for all children is a vital concern. Second, the shortfalls in access to primary schooling in any country define the immediate and intermediate demand for alternative, equivalent programmes.Third, the accomplishments of primary education determine the demand for literacy activities and knowledge and skill programmes for youth and adults. Fourth, appropriate learning achievement in primary schools and equivalent programmes will help establish a sound basis for further learning and prepare future instructors and teachers. Research findings demonstrate that primary education can improve labour productivity and entrepreneurial skills, help develop appropriate values, attitudes, and behaviour, and have positive intergenerational effects on families and communities.

These results justify the importance attached to the relevance of primary education. In most countries, primary schools have a dual function. First, their chief objective is to impart essential cognitive skills and knowledge: almost everywhere, the curriculum gives priority to reading, writing, and basic mathematics. In most nations, the curriculum also attempts to provide the basics of the scientific method and to promote moral and civic education. In the more successful cases, the curriculum also promotes the attitudes and essential life skills necessary for individuals to function effectively in their society. Second, in addition to imparting a common core of knowledge and skills, primary schools prepare students for further learning. The extent to which primary schools emphasize preparation for further academic education should depend on the availability of opportunities to continue formal education, most notably in secondary schools, and on the benefits to be gained from further learning.

Primary schooling also is the foundation for future vocational education, much on-the-job training, and for immediate employment in some occupations. All primary schools have multiple cognitive and non-cognitive objectives. Over the last two decades, the schools of the world often have been given a variety of new goals without sufficient funds to fulfill these new expectations. In both developed and developing nations the result often has been not only poor achievement in these new areas but also erosion in the achievement of the core of the primary school curriculum. A primary school should be allowed to give the highest priority to its explicit responsibility for imparting cognitive skills and essential knowledge and attitudes to all its pupils. National authorities should add other responsibilities only when the school is provided with the resources necessary to carry out these new tasks effectively. A primary school that graduates pupils who do not have basic literacy, numeracy, and problem solving skills has failed as a school regardless of how effective it may have been in meeting other cultural, social, or political needs. In contrast, the primary school that succeeds in imparting its core curriculum is laying the best foundation for meeting these other critical needs as well. Properly designed curricula and instructional materials can promote a greater synergism between cognitive and other objectives of the primary school.

In many developing countries, primary school graduates are the local leaders in acquiring and disseminating the information needed to achieve the cultural, social, and political goals of the nation. In localities where few people have achieved literacy, primary school graduates act as community leaders and teachers. The ultimate validation of the primary school's emphasis on literacy, numeracy, and problemsolving skills will depend on the school's ability to produce graduates who use these newly acquired skills to benefit their community and nation, not just themselves. To measure relevance it is first necessary to specify the desired effects of primary schooling and to define the relative value of those effects.

Because many of these effects are qualitative and some occur long after the students leave school, relevance is usually measured in terms of more easily quantifiable school outputs, which are assumed to be proxies for the more qualitative and less immediate effects. Standardized tests and attitudinal and behavioural appraisals commonly are used to help assess relevance. However, standardized testing can be a means of either increasing relevance or distorting instruction away from relevance.

Tests are administered at the end of the primary cycle for two reasons: to assess the level of measurable learning achievement and to select individuals for further learning, usually in formal secondary schools. Although there should be substantial congruence between the two purposes, it is possible for the design of the test to be biased. If it overemphasizes the selection function, it may not adequately assess the important knowledge and skills relevant for those students who will leave formal schooling at this level.

When properly designed and used, standardized examinations to measure learning achievement can help promote accountability within primary schools. In addition, test results can be used to identify weaknesses in the learning process and thus to promote more effective school processes in the future. Both as an indication of learning achievement and of unmet learning needs, measurement of learning outcomes is a valuable part of education management.

Countries will need to design or improve examinations in order to take advantage of the useful functions they can perform; for those learning outcomes not amenable to measurement by examinations, other accountability measures can be developed. Much has been said about how to increase the relevance of primary education, including schooling. A danger is that relevance to the local and immediate environment can take precedence over the more general and longterm conditions for which basic education should prepare the individual. Primary education can prepare people to be better farmers or craftsmen without precluding other possibilities for them. In addition, primary education can contribute to nation building, development of civic responsibility, and values formation.

The relevance of learning will change as individuals change their location and as the characteristics of communities change over time. If vocationalization and localization of the curriculum are carried too far, the learners will not have the skills necessary to adapt to the changes that are inevitable in all nations. The curriculum should make appropriate use of local materials, local examples, local languages, and local personnel to create a relevant and efficient learning experience; however, the core content of the learning experience should focus on literacy, oral expression, numeracy, and problemsolving general skills and essential learning tools that are applicable across locations and over time. Ultimately, of course, each society will have to decide for itself the appropriate balance between local, immediate relevance and general, longterm relevance. In making this decision, educational authorities should keep in mind that primary schools and their equivalents cannot do everything, nor can they do more than their resources allow. Primary education is only one part of a larger basic learning process, and concurrent and subsequent opportunities for learning can help address the need for more specific forms of relevance.

School or educational quality has a variety of meanings, depending on what measures are selected. The characteristics of pupils in a school are one indicator of school quality. The policies that most affect this factor are those concerning early childhood development. The key implication for primary schools is that premature placement of pupils in different learning "tracks" on the basis of perceived differences in their competence may be both inefficient and inequitable. It is inefficient because cognitive development proceeds at a different pace for different children, and it is inequitable because economically disadvantaged children are more likely to be perceived as lacking ability.

The mix of pupil characteristics within a school or classroom often is a product of the preconditions for schooling. Where nutrition, health, and opportunities for physical and mental stimulation are poor, pupils may lack many of the characteristics most conducive to learning. Elsewhere, the mix of characteristics will be a result of the social, economic, or demographic patterns of the society. Improved equity in early childhood experiences will greatly advance equity in learning achievement within schools and will improve the chances to complete the primary cycle. Programmes that give all children the necessary health and nutritional support while in school, as well as access to positive learning experiences and encouragement within the community, also can do much to resolve problems of both efficiency and equity in school learning. Among input measures, those most commonly used to indicate the quality of primary education are teacher characteristics, availability of educational materials, availability of equipment and facilities, administrative and supervisory activities, and summary measures such as expenditure per pupil. The teacher characteristics are used because the teacher is the primary source of instruction in most societies and has been recognized as such by most curricula and forms of classroom organization.

For many countries, the focus on learning achievement implies increasing teacher capacity and performance through preservice and inservice training and improved school and classroom management. Teacher effectiveness usually is indicated by such characteristics as formal academic study, teacher training, subject mastery, verbal ability, attitudes toward teaching, and availability. The first two relate to the formal preparation of the teacher and are assumed to be positively related to subject mastery and pedagogical skills. Most national authorities determine whether teachers are "qualified" on the basis of their having attained some combination of formal academic study and teacher training. For primary school teachers the requirements for subject mastery are relatively low in many countries, not because of choice, but because of the supply of teachers.

Nearly all nations have standards for primary school teachers that are less rigorous than those for teachers at other levels. However, given the critical cognitive period covered by primary schooling, the fact that it has the most equitable access, and the indicated social returns to investment in primary education, it is ironic, if not indefensible, that greater emphasis is not placed on the quality of instructional personnel at this level.Several studies have shown the verbal ability of the teacher to be a significant predictor of student learning; this is a logical finding given the importance of verbal instruction in all classrooms, especially where instructional materials are scarce. The teacher's attitude about the instructional process will be affected by both intrinsic and extrinsic factors.

Although in the developed nations teacher remuneration has begun to improve in real terms, many developing nations have declining levels of real wages for teachers. When low wages are combined with poor working conditions, the intrinsic incentives to remain an effective teacher can be overwhelming. Teacher absenteeism is a critical concern in many nations. The issue of pupil/teacher ratios is less clear. Although research indicates that very small classes can have learning advantages, the differences in learning achievement among larger classes are harder to identify.

By 1985 developing nations had reduced average class sizes to a range of twentyfive to thirtynine students per teacher, but it is unclear that this was a costeffective policy for raising quality compared with policies emphasizing the availability of learning materials or innovate instructional technologies. And it is not obvious that reduced ratios have increased the actual amount of time pupils interact with the teacher. The major benefit of reducing class size apparently has been in improving teachers' working conditions; such policies thus may have increased teachers' motivation and kept them on the job longer, but the costeffectiveness of achieving these results cannot be evaluated from available information.

The number of teachers is so large and their salaries represent such a high percentage of the educational budget that improving teacher quality in the short run is a difficult alternative in all but the wealthier nations. The linkage between teachers' salaries and general civil service regulations or standards is often underappreciated in attempts to improve school performance by increasing the prerequisite training of teachers. Increasing teachers' salaries is difficult in most countries without incurring general wage increases throughout the civil service, or at least among its professional staff. Non-monetary incentives to recruit and retain teachers constitute a form of benefits which can be granted to teachers without the obligation of extending them to other civil service employees. The availability of educational materials is one of the most powerful and consistent determinants of learning achievement; inequality in access to such materials is a major source of rural/urban and regional inequalities in achievement. Where teacher quality is poor, the value of instructional materials is even more important. Properly designed materials can help train unqualified teachers while providing instruction to students.

The critical concerns are the appropriateness of materials to the curriculum, their cost, and their dissemination. Language and cultural issues restrict the direct transfer of learning materials among and even within countries, but in the short run the adoption and adaptation of existing materials may be of value where local materials have not yet been developed. The issue of cost involves weighing the initial expense of producing or acquiring materials against their useful life expectancy. Lowcost materials may not be a bargain if they are not durable enough for extensive use in the classroom.

Finally, dissemination must be a part of any consideration of the availability of materials as an indicator of school quality.

Unless the instructional materials reach the classrooms they cannot be effective, and unless they reach all classrooms they cannot promote equitable learning opportunities. The value of buildings or equipment as an indicator of quality is not as clearly supported by research as that of instructional materials. There is not a consistent positive relationship between the availability of facilities or equipment and learning results. However, there does appear to be a clear threshold of general availability and quality of facilities necessary for learning to take place. Equity may also be affected: provision of separate lavatory and toilet facilities for girls have been documented as an important determinant of female attendance. Also, overcrowding in primary schools, especially in the early grades, is a major source of poor achievement and attrition. In addition, some research indicates a correlation between special facilities, such as science laboratories, and achievement in specific domains of learning, but the correlations are consistently small and of questionable significance for policies toward primary schooling.

Although the availability of equipment is normally not a major indicator of quality in primary schooling, it becomes an important consideration when special technologies are used for instruction. Radios, film projectors, and tape recorders are now being supplemented in some nations by televisions, videocassette recorders, and computers. As with instructional materials, providing instructional equipment to some pupils but not all can be a source of learning inequality. The results of research in North America on the effectiveness of schools, and observations of schools throughout the world, emphasize that school and system administrators are potentially critical in influencing instructional activities, in motivating teachers, and thus in determining school effectiveness. Greater decentralization that places more authority in the hands of teachers, the principal, the community, and local education officials can make an individual school more relevant and efficient through increasing its accountability.

In decentralized systems, district and regional administrators usually continue to be the logistical link with national authorities but serve primarily as facilitators rather than implementors. Similarly, school principals and inspectors must be free to interact with teachers and students in ways that encourage learning rather than merely enforce policies.

The principal or head teacher appears to have the greatest impact on school quality by establishing clear goals for individuals and creating a school climate conducive to learning achievement. Summary measures of inputs, such as per pupil expenditure, dramatize a problem that exists for all analyses of inputs as indicators of quality. They represent the availability, but not the use, of a resource. Per pupil expenditure indicates only how much was spent, not the quality or effectiveness of the learning experience. Such measures may indicate whether enough resources are available but not whether they are being used well. All input measures, suffer from this shortcoming which limits their relevance for policy. For countries that do not yet have even the minimal supply of inputs, however, these summary measures will be appropriate indicators of educational efforts, even if they are questionable proxies for quality.

Improving quality by changing the instructional process is an ambitious endeavour. Many systems have very little information on how pupils and teachers use their time. As a minimum foundation for reform, it is necessary to know how much time teachers spend on their work and how they allocate their time among activities (preparation, instruction, review, evaluation, and remediation) and among various contacts with pupils (full class, subgroups, and individuals). Similarly, information is needed on the time pupils spend in contact with the teacher, other pupils, and instructional materials and equipment, including time devoted to homework. Analyses should refine these measures so as to estimate the time pupils actually devote to specific tasks or learning activities. An accumulation of evidence indicates that learning achievement is proportional to the time spent in learning activities. Teacher and pupil absenteeism, holidays, and the needs of agricultural and other employment cycles are all sources of divergence between the official school year and the effective learning time in school.

In many developing nations pupil learning time is less than half of the 800-1000 hours a year that is common in developed nations. Thus, less time is available for access to fewer resources, so the learning disadvantage of pupils in the developing nations is compounded. Differences in teacher-pupil interactions and pupil use of materials and equipment can create inequities even within a single class or school. A critical question is how teachers allocate their time in relation to disadvantaged learners — do such pupils receive more, less, or the same investment of teacher time and effort? The answer will tell a great deal about the efficiency and equity with which school resources are utilized.

A special equity concern is the tendency, in some schools, for females to receive less attention from the teacher and to experience lower expectations in terms of their school performance. Although measures of educational outputs and outcomes are a popular means of assessing school quality, they often are not considered a means for i mproving quality. In the case of school examinations, however, the psycho metric properties that allow them to assess learning performance also determine both the correctness of the appraisal and the propriety of allocating resources on the basis of examination results. Another measure of educational outputs is graduation from primary school, but if this is to guarantee possession of a necessary level of basic knowledge and skills, then the standards for graduation must be understandable and acceptable to the teachers who will have to apply them. If pupils are promoted automatically, graduation can become merely an indicator of age and perseverance, rather than evidence of learning.

Graduation from primary school must provide the pupil with more than a certificate for employment and further education; it must also provide the prerequisite knowledge and skills for the graduate's continued learning and successful participation in the community and society. To summarize, a systematic effort to improve school quality requires specification and measurement of the desired school outputs and identification of how the multiple inputs of the system interact within the learning process to produce the desired school outputs. The current understanding of these relationships suggests the following priorities for primary schooling reform:

(1) improving the availability and use of instructional materials;

(2) enhancing teacher effectiveness by emphasizing subject mastery, communication skills, and teacher motivation;

(3) improving managerial skills, community and institutional structures, and individual and organizational incentives; and

(4) increasing the time actually spent on learning. When these priorities are linked with improved preconditions for learning that enhance pupils' initial capacities, and with community environments that reinforce learning, true gains can be made in school quality and learning acquisition for all.

Inequities most commonly relate to poverty, gender, location, religious, linguistic, or ethnic identification, and physical or mental disability. Poverty creates inequity in learning in multiple ways. It is correlated with a low educational achievement of parents, poor nutrition and health care, inadequate intellectual stimulation for young children, a paucity of local nonschool learning opportunities, a reduced motivation for and benefit from schooling, and difficulty in absorbing learning expenses whether they be explicit fees or implicit opportunity costs. In country after country, studies have revealed that poverty affects both the ability of the family to support schooling and its willingness to bear the costs. Society's responsibility is to see that the children of these families, as well as poor orphans, receive an education appropriate to their needs and accurate information about the probable benefits of primary schooling. Other social investment programmes, including those that provide credit and generate employment, can complement the efforts to provide schooling by increasing the probable benefits to the poor who become educated.

With the exception of Latin America, female rates of enrolment in primary schooling continue to lag behind those of males: the rates for six- to eleven-year-olds in Africa are 69 percent for males and 56.5 percent for females; in Asia the respective rates are 77.4 and 59.3 percent. The gap has actually widened since 1970 in Afghanistan, Nepal, and Pakistan, and in many other nations female enrolments remain very sensitive to economic or social disturbance.Female pupils also often suffer from the negative attitudes of teachers who underestimate girls' competence and from unsupportive family and community perceptions of the Appropriate" levels of education for women. Assignment policies that concentrate women teachers in urban and economically advantaged areas prevent many female pupils in other areas from having relevant role models and the teachers best able to appreciate the specific learning needs of girls.

In cultures where parents are reluctant to send girls to coeducational programmes, they may be educated in segregated schools or alternative systems such as those that instruct via radio or television. These alternative programmes are not available in all nations, however, and where available are mostly in urban settings. The debate over gender segregated schools versus coeducation is complex and influenced by social and cultural history and traditions. Even where special social provisions are made to educate females, family demand for a girl's household labour and a cultural emphasis on the early marriage of women can impede attempts to equalize opportunities. For those females who gain access to and complete primary education, gender biases in instructional techniques, learning materials, and test designs further reduce the probability that their measured achievement will equal that of males. The results of the national comparisons undertaken by the International Association for the Evaluation of Educational Achievement indicated that boys did better at the primary school level; the difference was even greater at higher levels of schooling. An immediate goal of primary education must be to minimize the gender differences in achievement as much as possible. Because of the special role of women in the intergenerational transfer of knowledge, attitudes, and behaviour, raising their learning achievement to equal that of males will enhance the efficiency of overall learning in society. Closing the historical gap between female and male learning achievement requires concerted, compensatory efforts, not simply an expansion of access for females. Locational equity is a concern because of both rural/urban and regional differences in the quality of primary schooling in many countries. Because the presence of a school is the minimum condition for participation, the unequal distribution of schooling in a nation causes unequal access. According to one estimate, only half the rural children in most countries have the opportunity to complete four years or more of schooling.

The barriers to learning attainment in rural areas include the limited quantity and poor quality of schools, poor reinforcement from the nonschool environment, irrelevance of the curriculum, high opportunity costs for children whose labour is needed at home, and long distances between the home and the school. Another disadvantage is that the language of instruction used in schools often differs from that used in the home. These disadvantages translate into differences in learning achievement, with pupils in urban schools scoring consistently higher except when the increased age or more frequent repetition of pupils in a rural or other disadvantaged area has an equalizing effect on measured achievement. Few data exist on issues of ethnic and religious disadvantage. In some countries, a minority group is disadvantaged not so much because of its ethnic or religious identity as because it is poor and/or rural. The situation of castes in South Asia and indigenous populations in parts of Latin America and Southeast Asia, however, suggests that differences can emerge even when other determinants are the same. Special basic learning programmes may be necessary for these populations. Ethnic and religious discrimination can operate either through formal practices favouring a privileged group or more informal biases in employment networks. Whether or not the discrimination is explicit, the negative effects soon will be: discrimination reduces the incentives for the disadvantaged children to participate in and benefit from the primary schooling system.

Again, the immediate sacrifice of equity promotes a longerterm loss of societal efficiency. Another major category of inequity is that of disabled children and adults. This group is a heterogeneous one with impairments ranging from mild or moderate to severe or profound; the more severely disabled are fewest in number. The needs of many disabled people can be met within existing services, as long as they are augmented by appropriate arrangements to support the special requirements of the child and the family. There is a need to demystify educational provision for disabled persons; the main barriers continue to be misinformation about their capacities. This misinformation leads to a gross underestimation of their potential to benefit from education of all kinds. Even though many developing countries face shortages of financial and human resources, education for all means that all groups, including the disabled, are entitled to a fair share of resources. Whatever the current conditions, assisting disabled individuals to reach their learning potential should be a part of the strategies for meeting the basic learning needs of all.

Developing countries considering action in the education of disabled children, youth and adults should have confidence in their own initiatives and should not feel that their efforts must follow those patterns established by the industrialized countries. A special equity issue is that of refugee populations. These groups, suffering already from the dislocation and deprivation inherent in their refugee status, often face inequities because of other conditions. Refugees are usually poor; a majority are females; they often are located where selfsufficiency in agriculture or other employment is least probable; and their religious and ethnic origins may differ from those of the host population. To meet the learning needs of these multiply disadvantaged individuals may require special programmes, alternative means of providing learning services, and new forms of financing. Refugees need an equitable share in basic learning opportunities and in their benefits.

To reduce inequity, whatever its source, requires an aggressive commitment on the part of government and society. Helping to incorporate presently disadvantaged populations into the larger society should be one of the explicit goals of primary schooling. No conflict need exist between equity and efficiency if goal attainment is defined explicitly in terms of the dimensions of equity. Achievement of equity goals requires specific interventions and acceptance of the reality that in the short run compensatory resources and measures may be necessary for certain groups to offset their disadvantages in the preconditions for, access to, completion of, and patterns in achievement in primary education. Of all the problems of equity in primary education, the participation and successful achievement of girls deserves the highest priority.

Removing the many barriers to primary education for girls will require a multifaceted approach. Countries need to address restrictive attitudes and beliefs about gender roles and capacities; adapt the education system, if necessary, through inhome instruction or separate schools for girls; provide day care for younger siblings and find other ways to reduce the family's need for girls' domestic labour; and improve learning achievement so that the benefits of primary education will off set the sacrifices imposed on the girl pupil and her family.

The special conditions of poor families may require assistance with the costs of school fees, uniforms, and transportation. Equity in rural areas may require flexible scheduling of the school year to minimize conflict with the agricultural planting and harvesting cycle. Sensitivity to special religious and cultural values, and the preservation and development of a people's cultural identity, may be necessary in dealing with ethnic and religious minorities. Disabled pupils and their families may require special help and alternative systems of instruction.

A different type of equity issue concerns out-of-school equivalents for primary schooling. If these "different but equal" pro grammes are to fulfill pupil expectations, standards of learning achievement must be the same as for the formal primary school system, and the credentials received must have the same value for both employment and access to further learning. Secondclass or deadend programmes cannot satisfy the need for equal learning opportunities and achievement; they simply substitute a new inequity for an old one. Once equity is established as part of the efficiency goal, it is necessary to measure the attainment of equity and to reward it. Teachers and principals must be convinced that the nation has a true commitment to the equitable treatment of previously disadvantaged populations. Equity in meeting basic learning needs may come at a cost, but in the long run it will be a lower cost to society than the continuation of inequity.

Efforts to improve efficiency in primary schools emphasize reducing costs without significantly altering the desired effects, or enhancing effectiveness without increasing costs. For example, programmes to produce lowcost, durable facilities expect to reduce expenditures on maintenance. The introduction of split shifts to increase the utilization of facilities is an appropriate way to enhance efficiency in locations with sufficient pupils to justify extra shifts. Similarly, literacy and other basic skill programmes can make use of primary school teachers, facilities, and appropriate materials when school is not in session and thus reduce the proportion of the cost of these resources that must be charged to primary schooling.

While controversy exists about the practicality and effectiveness of all such proposals, alternatives to the current structure of primary education deserve consideration. In many countries, and particularly in developed nations, there is an emerging Crisis" in teaching due, among other factors, to the perceived irrelevance of curricula and to the difficulty in recruiting good candidates to the profession. The task of the teacher has become increasingly complex and demanding; to fulfill this task, teachers must see themselves as educators and can no longer be satisfied with merely delivering a given body of knowledge.

The teacher is a key contributor to improving the quality of education. Other institutions play coordinate roles: the family, the media, cultural institutions and others. Therefore, there is a need for nations to develop more coherent policies and plans to further improve teacher education and training and to continue to seek ways and means to maximize the use of existing resources. There also is the need to strengthen efforts to promote an integrated approach to preservice and inservice training programmes and to harmonize the training of teachers in the formal and non-formal systems. In addition, teachers have unique roles to play in research activities, instructional experimentation and in the development of evaluation mechanisms. The provision of teacher resource centres and learning materials is seriously deficient, and often lacking altogether, in almost all of the poorest countries. This seriously inhibits the motivation of teachers to continue their education. Also it often appears that not enough is done in the school environment itself to facilitate exchange of experiences among teachers, and to organize effectively the staff development of .the teaching corps.

The effectiveness of these activities in meeting the objectives for pupils' learning can be assessed only if these objectives are explicitly stated in the school curriculum. The systematic evaluation of learning gives feedback that allows assessment of the e efficiency of teachers and instructional materials. A special form of educational inefficiency is that described as "wastage" — this normally refers to the effect of pupils repeating a grade or dropping out of school. Since both actions increase the number of years of schooling provided relative to the number of graduates produced, such wastage is seen as synonymous with inefficiency. Ideally, with adequate preconditions for learning and schools of appropriate quality, neither attrition nor repetition should occur. In many nations, however, repetition and attrition result because enrolments have increased so much that schools are unable to benefit all pupils. Similarly, wastage can occur if schools do not have the time or resources to remedy learning disadvantages or to allow the slower learner's development to catch up with that of the other pupils. If repetition resulted in increased achievement, it could be considered a pedagogically useful mechanism. However, the evidence shows that the achievement gains from repetition are minor, rarely costeffective, and often promote lower selfesteem and an increased propensity to dropout. Prevention of repetition through improved instruction and in class remediation is often less expensive than accepting it as an unavoidable part of the education process. The control and governance of primary schools raise questions of efficiency throughout the world. Because the central educational bureaucracies are geographically and administratively distant from individual schools and must base plans on a variety of aggregate measures, decisionmakers may not be informed about the specific resources and needs of local communities.

Central government authorities have a natural responsibility to initiate programmes, monitor school performance, and ensure the equitable provision of schooling among economically diverse settings. Many nations have recognized, however, that efficient management of schools requires involvement of the local community and increased authority for the school principal.With decentralization, the school remains accountable for its use of public funds and must continue to meet curricular standards and conform to general educational regulations. But the school can be given greater discretion on how to generate and utilize the resources for its learning activities. Research has found that individuals and communities are more willing to finance primary schooling when they participate in the decision making concerning it. Thus, decentralization and local support can increase efficiency and mobilize new resources for schooling. Many countries are examining new ways for private education and nongovernmental agencies to complement the existing primary school system. Regardless of the final set of partnerships or alliances developed, all nations will need to shift their priority concern away from the interests of the providers of schooling to those of the users: the pupils, the families, the community, and the nation. The interests of the providers cannot be ignored, but for the sake of efficiency, they must be considered only in the context of how to promote improved benefits for the users of the education system.

In the poorest nations, enhancing efficiency will help prevent the most dire consequences of domestic fiscal constraints and external debt burdens. In the more economically prosperous nations, efficiency measures can make the difference between an education system that degenerates into inadequacy and one that significantly promotes societal and individual development. Ultimately, efficiency reforms will be judged by what happens in a nation's classrooms and by the individual pupil's success or frustration in learning. The goal is for primary schooling to provide cognitive and non-cognitive learning opportunities both efficiently and equitably, and to become a true human development activity that provides skills for individual success in life and resources for national development.

The basic learning needs of youth and adults are considered separately from those of children; not only is the target population older, but also the learning needs and the methods of meeting them differ. However, there may be a significant overlap in the essential learning tools. Literacy, oral expression, numeracy, and problemsolving will, in many countries, represent an important part of the curriculum for meeting the basic learning needs of certain youth and adults, as well as children. This is particularly true for those who did not attend primary schooling, who failed to complete the cycle, or who completed primary school but did not attain the necessary level of learning achievement.

Because of the complexity, diversity, and frequent incomparability of the forms of basic education for youth and adults, increasing the ability of planners and providers to diagnose, test, and evaluate learning activities is essential. The development of a diagnostic capacity in each country is necessary and should include not just identifying specific needs and means of meeting them, but also the interaction between the youth and adult programmes and earlier and subsequent learning activities of participants. Pilot testing of programmes and evaluation of their effectiveness must include consideration of instructors, curriculum, materials, equipment and facilities, management, and costs and financing. It is important to establish a clear distinction between essential learning tools and basic learning content for youth and adults.

The essential tools include literacy, oral expression, numeracy, and problemsolving, but may also encompass such other tools as computer operation, library use, and the ability to interpret messages relayed by radio, television, and emerging information systems. The tools defined as Essential" depend on each country's present context and expectations for development. The basic content will be even more varied and contextspecific; it will cover the full range of knowledge and skills necessary for an effective life in one's community and larger society.

Literacy is a life skill and the primary learning tool for personal and community development and selfsufficiency in a rapidly changing and increasingly interdependent world. Over the last thirty years the definition of literacy and the design of literacy programmes have undergone dramatic change. Literacy is now seen as the foundation for life skills ranging from basic oral and written communication to the ability to solve complex scientific and social problems.

With this broadened definition of literacy, nations may need to change the way they think about and promote literacy. The idea of illiteracy as a disease that can simply be eradicated is outdated. Nor can illiteracy be used as a convenient label that implicitly blames 'victims' for their own victimization. The new definition makes it clear that literacy is the primary enabling force for all further education. It is a uniquely effective tool for learning, for accessing and processing information, for creating new knowledge, and for participating in one's own culture and the emerging world culture.

Basic learning content is appropriately viewed as an array of knowledge and skills organized to meet the basic needs of learners, both as individuals and as actors in the contexts of the family, the work place, and the community. For example, basic knowledge and skills could address the need of the individual for selfesteem, knowledge of one's language and cultural heritage, and understanding of gender roles and social relationships. In the family and household sphere, there is the need to plan and manage a household and to raise healthy children, and, therefore, to know about health, nutrition, and infant stimulation and care.

Learning needs relating to community life include knowledge about civic rights, a clean environment, and community organization and advocacy. Learning for the work place focusses on the skills required to earn a living and to adapt to changing economic and technological conditions. Beyond training specifically for the home, the work place, or the community, basic knowledge and skills programmes need to enable people to develop the appropriate values, attitudes, and skills for critical thinking, creativity, and community problemsolving. In practice, literacy activities often are incorporated into larger training initiatives that provide knowledge or skills for youth and adults. The line between literacy and other basic knowledge and skills, therefore, is not always distinct both are often broadly defined and provided to the learner in similar ways. In this sense, literacy is both a means to other knowledge and skills, and a knowledge/skill in itself. Certain basic knowledge and skills can be provided before literacy is achieved. Where resources are sufficient, basic knowledge can be disseminated simultaneously with the teaching of literacy or other basic skills. Where literacy already exists, it will facilitate the transmission of this basic knowledge. But national authorities should recognize that literacy is not a precondition for the spread of some forms of basic knowledge and skills, however much it would be facilitated by literacy. It can be argued that the literacy and basic education potential of the new communication technologies (and educational innovations) has never been fully realized.

Many reasons have been put forward to explain this relative failure: inadequacy of investment, the inability to transform utilization habits to match a new teaching and learning environment, and an unwillingness to accept and apply the practical applications of change. Such concepts as the 'information society' and the 'global village', even if they are largely metaphorical, highlight the social and economic transformations that are taking place as a result of massive and instantaneous information transfer, the increasing acceptance of information as possessing an economic, social and cultural value, and the consequent importance of information handling as a significant aspect of economic activity. Commentaries on social and economic disparities between societies now treat information availability and use as significant determinants of these disparities. In some contexts these activities can be interpreted as representing a major educational channel, supplementing primary education and programmes for youth and adults to meet the basic learning needs of all.

At the very least, therefore, future understanding of literacy is likely to include media literacy as a functional skill important on several counts. In the first place, given the volume and variety of information now available from a wide variety of media sources, an ability to discriminate between media messages, and to evaluate both their objectivity and utility, is becoming a basic individual need. Secondly, the ability to operate and process information and communication technology may eventually rival traditional literacy and numeracy skills in determining the individual's ability to be effective in society. These arguments have a number of implications, both for an expanded vision and for constructing appropriate policies and programmes. In relation to the informal learning that comes from the media, there is a need to know more about the degree, q uality, and relevance of that learning, the processes through which it takes place, and the ways in which it can be channelled productively. This is not only a research question, but also implies a need to involve the information producers in the overall educational process, by acknowledging their impact and importance. There is a parallel need to build some elements of media literacy into basic education programmes, encouraging an understanding of how the media work and how they can be used and evaluated. Such understanding comes most easily from practical contact: learning through doing. This practical contact also helps build up the functional skills in handling information and communication technology, upon which vocational effectiveness is becoming more dependent. It extends well beyond technical competence, embracing the development of a full range of communication abilities in the individual.

At another level of education and development programming, a new and innovative programme of research is necessary if planned applications of communication are to become more effective. If educational technology has in the past been an ineffective, or only partially effective, instrument of change, a better knowledge of the reasons for this is needed. The definition of literacy and the need for basic knowledge and skills evolve along with social, economic, and cultural change. As a result, all individuals continue to face new learning challenges throughout their lives. In the end, literacy whether oral, written, computer, or scientific is evolving to meet many diverse and changing needs. No fixed set of information or competencies defines basic knowledge and skills for all countries. Thus, the question for each country is how best to define and provide the literacy and basic knowledge and skills appropriate to each individual and community and how to devise mechanisms that improve the scope, relevance, and quality of the essential learning tools and content.

The content and relevance of basic education for youth and adults depends on the fit between policies and programmes and the context and needs in which the learning activities take place. Since that context is always changing, the learning process must be continuous and learning activities designed to take account of the changing context. In the final analysis, the dissemination of literacy and basic knowledge and skills takes place within the more complex activities of technological and political development. Although some may assert that the larger goals of development can be achieved without meeting the basic learning needs of youth and adults, the existing evidence suggests that teaching literacy and basic knowledge and skills is among the most costeffective means of promoting a synergistic development effort.

In many settings, in both developed and developing nations, training programmes conducted by employers may have to continue emphasizing essential knowledge and skills literacy, numeracy, and problemsolving tools that, in principle, should have been learned at school. Thus employers become trainers and educators as well.Preemployment training in specific vocational skills increasingly is recognized as i n sufficient for successful employment. As more and more skills are specific to a single occupation or employer, the relevance of preemployment programmes will cease to be defined in terms of an exact fit between training and an occupation. Instead, there will be more concern with assuring the future trainability of workers, or equipping them with the basic knowledge and skills that define capacity and adaptability, rather than to fulfill the requirements of narrow job descriptions. In the informal sector, on-the-job training, apprenticeship, and training with production are already common and compete with the vocational training offered in many schools and institutes. Even where generic pre-employment skill training is necessary, it no longer will be sufficient preparation for employment. No matter how well prepared the initial entrants are, occupations evolve, often during a single working life, and technological change keeps requiring new and expanded knowledge and skills.

Many of the research findings concerning the quality of primary education also apply to basic learning programmes for youth and adults. Examples are the critical importance of the instructor's qualifications and the great potential for learning materials to contribute to learning effectiveness. There are, however, some distinctive aspects to providing learning for youth and adults. For example, motivation is even more critical in a noncompulsory programme—motivation to join, to continue, and to succeed. The motivation of youth and adult learners will depend on the actual relevance of the learning opportunity and the effectiveness with which this relevance is communicated to the potential learners. The variation of age and experience among adult learners is a second characteristic that must be taken into account in the design and scheduling of learning opportunities. Programmes should not underestimate either the sophistication of youth and adult learners or their ability to make practical choices about joining or persisting in learning activities. Variety and flexibility are necessary if programmes are to match the mix of learning capacities and needs of this population.

Learning inputs for these programmes will focus on the instructor and on learning materials. Learners who are already literate, however, may be able to use instructional materials in the absence of a teacher or to extend on their own the learning provided by a teacher. Equipment is likely to be a more important input here than in primary education, especially for mechanical and related skills training. The media and public information systems can be expected to play even more significant roles in promoting behavioural change for this population than was the case in primary education.

Evaluations of programmes that use a variety of pedagogical techniques suggest that the most effective curricula and materials are learner-centred, participatory, and relevant to local needs and aspirations. The programmes that achieve the most tend to present their content in conformance with accepted learning theory, in an entertaining and interesting fashion, and in accordance with the competencies of instructors and the resources available for training. Materials and methods for teaching literacy and basic knowledge and skills work best when they appeal to all the stakeholders —learners, instructors, families, communities, implementing agencies, and governments.

Teachers/Instructors will remain central to many youth and adult basic learning activities. The subject mastery, verbal ability, and attitudes that make successful schoolteachers also will be positive factors in these settings. Effective teachers/instructors of literacy and basic knowledge and skills share the characteristics of high-quality curriculum and materials: they are appropriate to the learners and their environment. Those recruited from other socioeconomic and cultural contexts to work with preliterates normally are burdened with preconceptions that have to be "unlearned" and often are never overcome. Also, when primary education teachers are used in programmes for youth and adults, they may need special training to sensitize them to the different needs of older learners and how to meet those needs.

A reciprocal benefit can occur in that working in the learner centred orientation of programmes for youth and adults may help these teachers be more responsive to pupil needs when they return to primary school classrooms. It is important to recognize the need for recurrent training of teachers/instructors to enable them to deal with different learners, evolving learning needs, and content levels that also change rapidly over time. One should not underestimate the significance of appropriate wages, benefits, rank, and recognition for nonschool-based educators. In fact, the myth that literacy efforts can succeed with volunteer and part-time, underpaid instructors alone has become a major excuse for government underfunding and a dominant liability of many programmes. The proper management of youth and adult learning activities is an especially important consideration for programme quality. Management issues apply over the entire administration of learning: from the design and implementation of local programmes to the national establishment of standards. Because of the diversity of this second channel of basic education, the monitoring and evaluation functions of management are paramount.

The lack of analytical research and comparable experiences emphasizes the need for more documentation on basic education activities for these age groups. The instructional process for young and adult learners is a topic of considerable controversy. The question of the appropriate psychological and pedagogical models to apply to this population has not been resolved. Some agreement exists, however, on the critical role of learner time utilization. On the one hand, although the time spent on any given learning task may vary among learners, each learner can be seen to improve dramatically as the timeontask increases. On the other hand, the timing of learning activities is essential as the high opportunity costs of youth and adult learners impose often severe demands for the efficient use of learner time.

Instructional methods used in programmes for youth and adults abound —functional, Freirian, intergenerational, whole language, psycholinguistic, and others — but no single approach or method of instruction has been shown to work in all situations without adaptation to the local culture, context, language, and learning needs. Although existing models can offer a point of departure and comparison, the key to achieving successful learning is to use a method that is adapted to the situation. It should be accompanied by systematic monitoring and evaluation to profit from experience and thus deter the waste of scarce educational resources. Measures of the outcome and output of basic learning activities for youth and adults will be extremely varied. Standard measures of learning may be appropriate for some literacy activities and for skill training programmes that are comparable in content. However, many learning opportunities will not be comparable because they differ in context, content, and participants. Follow-up to these basic learning activities has been shown to be essential. In the long term, programme quality is revealed by how frequently and appropriately learners are able to use their new knowledge and skills. Thus, monitoring of outputs and outcomes will have to consider the postlearning supports provided to the learner.

The quality of basic learning programmes for youth and adults is an even more complex issue than in the case of primary education. Usually, adult education does not have the benefit of a large supervisory system or a long tradition to direct the focus on quality. Although the management and supervisory system of primary education does not always perform effectively, the first channel of basic learning does have the advantage of an organizational foundation on which to build. In youth and adult programmes, planning and management activities must incorporate quality considerations by developing better data bases, appropriate diagnostic and analytical skills, and management capacity. The inequities in programmes for youth and adults originate from two sources:

(1) the residual inequities created because an acceptable quality of primary education is not universally available, and

(2) inequities within the supply of learning opportunities for youth and adults.

The second source is especially critical since youth and adult learning opportunities can either compensate for earlier inequities or reinforce and exacerbate them. Inequities can worsen, even though such programmes attempt to equalize learning opportunities for those who have gained less benefit from primary education than others. Inequities in youth and adult programmes are related to the same characteristics of individuals as in the case of primary education: poverty, gender, location, religious or ethnic identification, and physical or mental disability.

A special characteristic to be considered, however, is age. Given the accumulation of learning needs in the population over time, it may not be realistic to expect every nation to meet immediately even the basic knowledge requirements of all of its adults. Some societies have made implicit choices about the age groups that will be given priority; these decisions have direct implications for equity among age cohorts. One quantitative indicator of inequity in learning is the literacy rate. Clearly, the greatest number of illiterates is in Asia, particularly China and India, while the highest rates of illiteracy are in Africa, especially the Sahelian nations. Consistently, women are disproportionately represented in these numbers.

A majority of the world's illiterates, female and male, live in rural areas or urban slums, impoverished and marginal members of their societies. Both the proportion of a population that is illiterate and the large absolute number of illiterates must be considered in targeting literacy e fforts; illiteracy has serious consequences for national economic wellbeing because of both the relative and absolute burden it imposes. In 1990 there will be an estimated 882 million adults (fifteen years and over) who are illiterate, 27.7 percent of the world's adult population. Nearly 98 percent of the world's illiterates will live in developing countries. Asia will remain the heart of the problem with about 659 million illiterates; Africa will have about 165 million, and Latin America and the Caribbean region 42 million.

North America and Europe will have only about 17 million illiterates, but the position of these individuals is particularly disadvantageous in relation to the basic learning needs of their societies. There is no statistic comparable to the literacy rate that indicates how many people lack basic knowledge and skills. It may be inferred, however, that given changing demographics, increased instructional provision, and the variable standards by which literacy is measured throughout the world, the problem of aggregate illiteracy may, indeed, be actually shrinking, whereas the number of semiliterates and those lacking basic knowledge and skills is increasing.

The increasing number of individuals with unmet basic learning needs, alongside scarce resources and an inadequate capacity to implement programmes, suggests that some decisions must be made concerning who will benefit first from renewed efforts to disseminate literacy and basic knowledge and skills. Strong arguments exist for giving women highest priority. This precedence is justified by their history of being educationally underserved, by their economic contributions to agriculture and industry, and by their influential role as mothers and often heads of single-parent households. One proverb notes, When you educate a mother, you teach a nation." Their strong inter-generational effects as caregivers, their immediate effects on child health and family planning, their crucial role in food production and trade in many agrarian societies, and the rapidly changing nature of their societal roles place women in a pivotal position to enhance the wellbeing of their families and communities.

Meeting equity goals for women and other underserved groups does not depend solely on provision of services. In the past, adult education programmes, particularly skill training activities, implicitly have endorsed traditional male conceptions of female roles and vocations. This limits female contributions by closing access to training in nontraditional occupational roles for women. In many instances men have monopolized training opportunities, although women actually predominate in the occupations for which training is provided. Agriculture extension and small scale enterprise development provide two examples of such gender bias in adult knowledge and skills development. Not only are women often unable to get the training they need, they frequently cannot obtain the credit, land titles, and other assets required to complement the training and improve their overall resource base and productivity. Fortunately, many training programmes are now emerging specifically for girls and women, in which the content is explicitly linked to modern sector occupations. Programmes to meet the basic learning needs of youth and adults, if they are also to succeed in meeting their equity objectives, must take into account the barriers to participation in learning and to the productive use of learning. Learning inequities exist within a context of social inequities. To redress inequities will require initiatives to:

— Expand the number and size of programmes to provide more learning opportunities

— Establish priorities for the participation of presently underserved or disadvantaged persons and groups

— Take special measures to ensure that these priorities are fulfilled.

Efficiency issues have not been addressed adequately in many analyses of youth and adult programmes, in part because of the small size, noncomparability, and volunteer nature of many of these activities. Also, since such programmes do not normally represent a significant share of public expenditure, they usually have not been monitored and held accountable to the same extent as larger, formal education programmes. In the past, many countries have seen literacy programmes, particularly national literacy campaigns, as having political goals and have used them to consolidate national identity or demonstrate government concern. Others, in contrast, have viewed literacy and basic knowledge and skill training for youth and adults as part of a comprehensive educational system to prepare people for employment and civic responsibility. The former approach tends to focus on a certain time frame and specific targets for the participants, while the latter endeavours to develop institutions and skilled personnel capable of designing and implementing enduring literacy and basic skills programmes. Both approaches have merit; neither is ideal.

The process of meeting basic learning needs can encompass both approaches. Intensive national campaigns can provide literacy and basic knowledge and skills education to large numbers of people within a short time. The institution-building approach develops institutional capacities and competent staff that in the longer term can assess and meet the multiple basic learning needs that are emerging. Even when conventional educational institutions can provide basic literacy to all, there will be a continuing need for basic knowledge and skills training. A nation's effort is, and must inevitably be, pluralistic to reflect the diversity and changing nature of needs and the alternative means of meeting these needs in every society. Experience in the provision of basic learning for youth and adults suggests that the design of an efficient programme will:

— Identify priority populations and learning needs

— Mobilize demand by potential participants

— Promote effective local decisionmaking and management

— Broaden participation by diverse institutions

— Utilize public information systems

— Coordinate basic learning with other societal activities

— Provide support after basic learning.

All of these seven elements are linked, and programme design should incorporate decisions about each.

Identify priority populations and learning needs: There is a need to identify priority populations and learning needs because the demand for basic learning is far greater than its supply. Some populations may be assigned priority status because basic learning will increase their productivity in economic and social development. Others might be emphasized so as to redress current inequities. In either case, there is a need to protect the investment of the scarce resources made available.

Mobilize demand by potential participants: One way to do this is to target the motivated, a second is to motivate those targeted. This mobilization of demand will promote the efficient use of resources as well as the effective use of learning.

Promote effective local decisionmaking and management : The third efficiency need is to promote effective local decisionmaking. This should be done by allowing decisions to be made by the individual or agency that is best informed in each case. For example, certain decisions on delivery, content, and participant needs might best be made at the local level, whereas the national authority should establish standards for performance and coordinate efforts to promote economies of scale. Examples of such economies may exist in the areas of personnel training, curriculum design, materials production and delivery, and resource needs assessment and monitoring. In fact, governments can play several facilitating roles in meeting the basic learning needs of youth and adults: initiator, motivator, financier, and standard setter. Governments also can create a policy environment that is supportive of learning opportunities. This environment might include tax incentives to private sector firms and nongovernmental organizations to provide literacy programmes.

The efficiency of literacy and basic knowledge and skills programmes could be enhanced by labour and wage laws that reduce opportunity costs and increase benefits to workers who participate in such programmes. Incentive structures could be developed for motivating institutions, communities, and individuals to participate in and promote basic learning efforts. A government could take the lead in those efforts that target the most disadvantaged populations. Given the arguments for basing literacy efforts in the community and the work place, governments need not, and probably should not, be the primary coordinators and implementors of all basic learning programmes. These two tasks do not reflect the unique comparative advantages of governmental authority.

When communities are consulted and allowed to determine their own priorities and contribute to the design and financing of learning and development projects, they begin to see themselves as the managers of change. They develop a trust in their own information, insights, and leadership capabilities that makes them better able to understand, integrate, and sustain development messages and technologies. Therefore, decisions concerning the efficient use of resources should be made at the local level whenever possible.

Ultimately, it is the community that best knows its own needs and the environment or culture in which learning will take place. Decentralization is an administrative means to encourage responsive basic learning programmes throughout a nation. A government service agency could serve as the technical, financial, and managerial intermediary in a national network of basic education agencies and activities. It may offer technical competence in areas such as participatory training techniques and the design of instructional materials; project planning, monitoring, and evaluation; and organizational development.

By training the direct providers of basic learning whether in various government ministries, private enterprises, or community and other nongovernmental social agencies an intermediary agency can have a significant multiplier effect. It could also promote the horizontal exchange of information among the providers. However, decentralization, to be concomitant with increased efficiency, must be preceded by or concomitant with the development of local capacities to acquire, process and use information in a form adapted to local needs.

Broaden participation by diverse institutions: Public and nongovernmental organizations, the private sector, communities, families, and other agencies all have a potential role in basic learning for youth and adults. The larger the number of agencies involved and the greater their diversity, the better the chances of increasing the aggregate resources available and enhancing the flexibility of programmes to meet participants' special requirements and there fore of improving efficiency. The decentralization of decision making can create an environment conducive to broader participation. Comparative advantage should be the organizing principle for decisionmaking responsibility. Nongovernmental organizations, for example, have proven to be innovative and adaptable. They often have strong local networks and are closer to the learners than many government agencies; thus, they find it easier to recruit and motivate participants. Governments, however, have greater resources at their disposal and often can realize economies of scale, for example, in printing literacy materials or providing village libraries and newspapers. Communities often possess a vast array of untapped resources, such as instructional and managerial ability and useful indigenous knowledge. Local private entrepreneurs typically are most attuned to the special appeal of a magazine, comic, or poster which could be adapted to produce entertaining and interesting basic learning materials.

Utilize public information systems: This systems can deliver both information and instruction directly to the individual. More generally, it reinforces earlier basic learning activities. By allowing the learners to use their new knowledge and skills, the information system becomes an integral part of the basic learning process. Its diversity can add to the comprehensiveness and efficiency of basic learning activities, and it has the potential to update information and knowledge continuously. Even educators and communication experts often fail to regard the information system as a major component of the nation's total education system. It is essential that nations expand their understanding of what constitutes the full range of educational institutions and delivery systems if they are to realize the goal of providing educational opportunities for all youth and adults.

Coordinate basic learning with other societal activities: Lifelong learning is becoming a fact of life in modern economies, and a global trend toward multiple learning solutions is involving organizations in roles they never performed before. Training institutions are becoming producers, while production enterprises are becoming trainers. A broad range and mix of workrelated training opportunities is provided by private industries, professional associations, and other nongovernmental organizations to meet the changing learning needs of youth and adults. In addition, basic learning programmes are being offered by a host of indigenous institutions, such as a Buddhist wat in Thailand, a pesantran in Indonesia or Morocco, a local library in North America, and a maison de la culture in France. A crucial challenge to such programmes is to provide marginal populations with modern sector skills.

Countries should reexamine the allocation of the resources already devoted to basic learning so as to assure their effective use for each given population or situation. In Lesotho, Venezuela, and other settings, "service centres" supply the skills of literacy professionals and nonschoolbased educators to tackle fundamental basic learning problems in an integrated development context. The professionals serve as agents in sectoral programmes such as agriculture, health, cooperatives, and forestry, using their unique skills to develop learning materials and participatory training. Within such programmes, government may have an effective role as information broker, source of technical assistance, financial creditor, and standard setter.

With a variety of policies, technical assistance, and financial incentives, a government can become less an implementor of largescale, bureaucratic basic education and more a facilitator and evaluator of many smallscale, locally controlled basic education services. The financial as well as programmatic benefits are that scarce governmental resources are spent not on meeting programme costs or administrative demands, but on supporting grassroots efforts with the knowledge and skillbuilding that is needed.

Provide support after basic learning: For investments in basic learning to be efficient over the long term, learners must continue to have opportunities to use their new knowledge and skills and to build on them. Although there are many similarities between the provision of education and health services, a critical difference is that there is no one preventive action, no Cognitive inoculation" in the shape of schooling, but rather a series of lifelong Knowledge and skill boosters" that reinforce the early lessons and provide new ones throughout adulthood. As consumers and producers, youth and adults whether illiterate rural mothers struggling with their children's health, urban street vendors in search of licenses, or senior citizens seeking to make a meaningful social contribution must have the information, social support, and practical services that only continuous education can provide. This analysis of policies and programmes necessarily has concerned itself with the common or modal patterns of basic education that exist in the world. As noted initially, each country has the responsibility to identify and select those conclusions or inferences that can assist them in the formulation of their own policies, programmes, and research agendas. One generalizable finding does exist, however: all nations will need to seek courageous and creative means to meet their basic learning needs.

The present state of basic education is inadequate to meet the basic learning needs of all children, youth and adults. If current trends and conventional approaches to education and training continue, the situation of learning in the world will certainly worsen, and will aggravate the global problems, rather than help to address them. An expanded vision of basic education is urgently required, one that encompasses five components: universalizing access to basic education activities and promoting equity of treatment; focussing on actual learning; broadening the means and scope of basic education to cover a wide range of delivery systems and population groups; enhancing the environment for learning in the home and community; and strengthening partnerships at all levels among the various authorities, organizations, groups and families involved in basic education.

Available data indicate that countries with similar socioeconomic conditions may have very different levels of educational attainment, due to differences in policies and priorities affecting education. This fact should encourage each country to set courageous targets for meeting the basic learning needs of its people and to develop a feasible plan of action to reach those targets in a reasonable time.

Success or failure in meeting the basic learning needs of all people will depend ultimately on the actions taken within individual countries. Regional and international cooperation and financial assistance can facilitate improvement, but national governments and their domestic partners will be the key forces for change. Given the diversity of situations, capacities and social goals among countries, it is possible here to indicate, in general terms only, certain key areas that merit priority attention in most developing and industrialized countries. A major national effort to meet the basic learning needs of all requires a comprehensive, multisectoral plan of action. Given the multisectoral nature and scope of basic education, the plan of action will probably differ from past or present education plans, which are generally limited to activities under the ministry responsible for formal education. Of course, the plan of action to provide basic education for all will need to take into account, or even incorporate, elements concerning primary and other forms of basic education contained in any existing education plan. Similarly, it will need to conform to the relevant objectives of other sectoral plans and the country's overall development plan and strategy.

In general terms, the action plan should specify:

— the basic learning needs to be met, including cognitive skills, values, attitudes, as well as subject knowledge;

— studies for the evaluation of existing systems;

— the languages to be used in education; means to promote the demand for, and

— broadscale participation in, basic education;

— modalities to mobilize family and local community support;

— targets and specific objectives;

— the required capital and recurrent resources, duly costed, as well as possible measures for cost effectiveness;

— indicators and procedures to be used to monitor progress in reaching the targets; priorities for using resources and for developing services and programmes over time; the priority groups that require special measures;

— the kinds of expertise required to implement the plan;

— institutional and administrative arrangements needed;

— modalities for ensuring information sharing among formal and other basic education programmes; and

— an implementation strategy and timetable.

A plan should clarify priorities for the phased development of services and programmes and for the use of public and private resources. In this connection, it should provide for mobilizing and allocating new resources within and among the several sectors concerned to meet basic learning needs in a comprehensive manner. A national plan of action should set clear objectives and measurable targets in a realistic timeframe. The definition of targets is a demanding task, but is important in mobilizing commitments and resources, and is crucial in monitoring progress. The more meaningful targets for basic education include a definition of the acceptable level of learning to be achieved; more common but less meaningful targets specify the enrolment levels or ratios to be attained. Specialists in several disciplines, from pedagogy to economics, can help define meaningful and measurable targets.

Widespread public discussion of proposed targets can help build understanding and acceptance of the targets and the plan of action. Even though targets must be established specifically for and by each country, five general principles should inform the process of establishing intermediate targets: The ultimate goal for each country is to meet the basic learning needs of all children, youth, and adults. All plans of actions, strategies for special groups, and assignment of priorities must be part of a phased, longterm systemic approach to universalize the achievement of basic learning at an acceptable level. The focus on learning acquisition is central to the meeting of all basic learning needs. Access, continued participation, and graduation should therefore be defined only in terms of access to, continued participation in, and graduation from activities that produce an acceptable level of learning achievement.

No regional or global standards can be imposed on countries, and regional plans of action cannot set the rate at which individual countries will progress from the current status of basic education to the attainment of the ultimate target. Such aggregate and external specification of the process would represent an abrogation of national autonomy and will not help in the planning or monitoring of basic learning activities. However, regional plans of action to mobilize and coordinate collective resources and support activities may be useful. Each country should monitor its own progress and trace improvements from the present situation through the intermediate targets to the ultimate goal. The intermediate targets should be established and readjusted in accordance with each country's own evolving needs, resources, and priorities. All intermediate targets should specify the proportion or number of individuals who will attain an agreed level of necessary learning achievement.

Although learning achievement will continue to vary among individuals, specification of the acceptable level of learning achievement for all can help reduce the dramatic inequities in actual achievement reported in many countries today. The intermediate targets should not be simple projections of current trends and resources but should reflect the expanded vision and its components. The intermediate targets should be realistic and courageous, because basic learning needs can be met more effectively in the future within the expanded vision.

Countries may wish to set their own targets for the 1990s in terms of the following dimensions proposed in the Framework for Action to Meet Basic Learning Needs:

1. Expansion of early childhood care and developmental activities, including family and community interventions especially for poor, disadvantaged and disabled children;
2. Universal access to, and completion of, primary education by the year 2000;
3. Improvement in learning achievement such that an agreed percentage of an appropriate age cohort attains or surpasses a defined level of necessary learning achievement ;
4. Reduction of the adult illiteracy rate to, say, onehalf its 1990 level by the year 2000, with sufficient emphasis on female literacy to significantly reduce

the current disparity between male and female illiteracy rates;

5. Expansion of provisions of basic education and training in other essential skills required by youth and adults, with programme effectiveness assessed in terms of behavioural changes and impacts on health, employment and productivity;

6. Increased acquisition by individuals and families of the knowledge, skills and values required for better living and sound and sustainable development, made available through all education channels including the mass media, other forms of modern and traditional communication, and social action, with effectiveness assessed in terms of behavioural change.

Insofar as possible, targets established in respect to these dimensions should define acceptable levels of performance and the proportions of participants who are expected to reach these levels in specific basic education programmes. Targets should be consistent with the expanded vision of basic education which focusses on universalization of access and on learning acquisition as joint and inseparable concerns. In all cases, performance targets should specify equity by gender.

The first dimension concerns the general provision of early childhood care and developmental activities, but emphasizes its particular importance for children who are disabled or disadvantaged in other ways. Targets might specify the number or proportion of such children who will be reached by this form of basic education activity. While universal primary education is usually defined in relation to the age-group 6 to 11 or 12, this dimension actually concerns the provision of basic education opportunities for children and adults, both in and out of school, at least at the level of primary education. In many countries today, "basic education" in accordance with the expanded vision extends into secondary education as well.

Targets concerning the second dimension should not be limited to formal schooling, and they may need to be formulated to cover access to, and completion of, basic learning activities corresponding to a post-primary level of education.

The third dimension implies some form of assessment to determine whether the defined level of learning achievement has in fact been attained. This might be based on a sample of fourteen-year-olds, by which age all children should have completed primary school or its equivalent. If an unacceptably low percentage of individuals are able to demonstrate the basic knowledge and skills they should have acquired, alternative learning strategies could be introduced to increase the proportion of successful learners.

The fourth dimension suggests that a country with an estimated illiteracy rate of 30 percent in 1990 would strive to reduce the aggregate rate to no more than 15 percent by the year 2000. If females in that country represent a larger proportion of adult illiterates than they do of the adult population, then literacy programmes should promote female participation so that, by the year 2000, the proportions of male and female literates are equal. Because of the special contributions of literate women to development activities in most contexts, some countries may plan an even greater emphasis on reducing female illiteracy. Each country should establish priorities for other population groups as appropriate.

The fifth dimension covers a diverse and growing range of learning activities provided as basic education for youth and adults. No generic quantitative targets are possible for these varied activities but specific targets for the largest or most significant activities would be justified for the reasons noted above — mobilization of support, focussing on effort, and monitoring of progress. An example of such a target would be the proportion of participants who should complete a skill training class with the appropriate set of demonstrable abilities. Other targets, for instance, might specify changes to be attained in the proportion of learners who smoke cigarettes, or who practice family planning, or who become self-employed.

The sixth dimension also concerns a wide range of activities available to the general population. Some activities, such as radio and television broadcasts, may not currently be considered "educational" in the strict sense, but they may nevertheless stimulate public awareness and provide information that can lead to beneficial changes in behavior. Targets relating to this dimension might resemble those defined for the fifth dimension, but would need to be formulated in respect to behavioural change in the general or adult population, since everyone is presumed to be a potential learner. To be fully effective, a multisectoral plan of action must be supported by the overall policy environment; therefore, the policies governing the sectors concerned may have to be adjusted. The purpose of such adjustment is to ensure that the relevant aspects of all concerned sectors interact so that they are mutually supportive, more effective, and in line with the country's overall development goals. Action to meet basic learning needs should be seen as a vital part of the country's total development efforts.

Because basic learning needs are intersectoral in nature, various agencies and institutions, in addition to the official education authorities, are actually involved in meeting those and related needs. Probably few, if any, governments have managed to create a policy environment that takes this complexity fully into account. Sectoral policies should interact to promote cooperation among all the concerned agencies and institutions so that they can work together to attain interrelated policy goals, such as better health, rural development, employment generation, and basic education. Legislative and administrative measures may be needed to create consultative mechanisms and to introduce incentives for parents, communities, employers, the media, and other partners to allocate more resources to basic education activities. Official and voluntary channels can be used to build public awareness of, and commitment to, the goal of education for all. Public participation at all levels in developing education policy generally has positive results.

Visible and continuing support for basic education by the political and administrative authorities is essential in creating and sustaining a policy environment conducive to meeting basic learning needs for all. The relevance o f basic education to actual learning needs is a precondition of educational quality, equity and efficiency. The key issue concerning relevance is to achieve a suitable equilibrium in the content and methods of basic education between the immediate needs and environment of the learners, and the longterm and more general needs of society. A specific strategy should be designed to improve the quality and relevance of basic education services and programmes, focussing on at least three crucial aspects: instructional and supervisory personnel, learning materials, and time spent on actual learning.

In respect to instructional and supervisory personnel, the strategy should provide for improvements to preservice training programmes and for incentives and opportunities to upgrade knowledge and skills through inservice training; it should also include measures to upgrade status and career prospects. Where instructional materials are scarce, the strategy should include measures to supply suitable textbooks and other learning materials in adequate quantities through out the country. Increasing the use of the information media in educating the public should also be prominently featured. The strategy should provide ways to reduce absenteeism by teachers and pupils, and to enable pupils to spend more time in actual learning. In certain countries, the strategy should include measures to maintain and, where necessary, rehabilitate existing educational facilities and equipment, and to provide for phased expansion and upgrading of the physical plant to meet future requirements, drawing on community participation and responsibility wherever feasible.

Expanding access to basic education is an effective way to improve equity, provided that the quality of education offered is satisfactory. Ensuring that girls, women and other disadvantaged groups stay involved in basic education activities, until they have attained at least a satisfactory level of learning, should be encouraged through special measures, designed in consultation with representatives of these groups wherever possible. In addition, improvements to educational quality and relevance should be implemented to support greater equity. Measures to keep learners in basic education programmes also help improve efficiency, by using available resources to obtain the intended results at the lowest per unit cost. Both the educator and the administrator should try to ensure that the maximum possible number of learners complete educational programmes in the allotted time; that they achieve at least the stipulated level of learning; and that all available resources are used fully and efficiently.

The action areas outlined above presuppose a range of analytical and managerial capabilities, from policy analysis and planning, through administration and financial management of programmes and institutions, to design and implementation of educational development projects. To a greater or lesser degree, all these management functions require reliable, upto date data and other information. However, there is a serious lack of sound information on basic learning needs and on how and to what extent these needs are being met. This lack is particularly evident in developing countries, but many industrialized nations also lack reliable statistics on certain education and training activities outside the purview of the government authorities. Because present levels of resources allocated to meet basic learning needs in developing countries are substantially inadequate, decisive action by all domestic and external partners is needed to increase the total volume of available human, material and financial resources and to use them in more costeffective ways. Once the current allocation and use of financial and other resources for education and training in different sectors has been analyzed there are essentially, four options for obtaining additional support for basic education:

(i) improving efficiency in the use of available resources;

(ii) prioritizing expenditures;

(iii) reallocating resources within government budgets; and

(iv) finding new sources of funding within and outside government budgets.

Each country will need to seek the appropriate mix of these options to assure adequate financing to meet the basic learning needs of its population. Some specific efficiencies can be achieved, for example, by utilizing educational buildings and equipment more intensively, improving the use of learners' time, and providing appropriate instructional materials for learners and instructors. Such measures may actually reduce per unit costs, or they may lead to better learning achievement for the investment made. Developing ways to assess learning achievement is important for this reason, among others. Reducing the rate of attrition (dropout) and repetition of pupils can be an effective strategy to increase the efficiency of a programme or entire system, as well as to improve equity.

However, the social investment in education is efficient and equitable only if the learning achievement of all pupils is at an acceptable level. Initially, it may cost more to provide quality education to the potential dropout or repeater, but it should be borne in mind that dropouts and repeaters require expenditures that do not result in graduation or in appropriate learning achievement. It is obviously more efficient to use funds to finance learning instead of wastage. Furthermore, if improvements in the quality of education lower the rates of attrition and repetition, the savings from the reduced wastage can be used to open new places in schools for children currently denied access. For society, an investment in the preconditions for learning and compensatory measures for pupils at risk in the early years of schooling can prove less expensive in the long run than financing their failure in school and their subsequent dependency or delinquency, and receiving a reduced return because of their lower earning capacity. For the individual and the family, the stigma of failure and the consequences of not having one's basic learning needs met are very high costs to bear. Certain investments, such as improving the quality and availability of instructional materials, may pay for themselves through their positive effects on participation and achievement. In certain situations, programmed instructional materials and electronic educational technologies can enhance learning and efficiency, especially in offsetting the negative effects of multigrade classrooms, large classes, and inadequately trained teachers.

By increasing the effective utilization of available resources, efficiency gains in basic education activities also have a secondary effect. Those who supply resources for these activities are more willing to continue or increase the supply if they believe the resources will be used efficiently. Thus, efficiency in the use of current resources is a strong argument when seeking additional resources. Prioritizing public expenditures is necessary because every country, in the short run, faces a greater demand for basic learning opportunities than it can meet.

The priorities established should promote programmes that reach certain groups without explicitly excluding any potential participant. Efficiency and equity considerations suggest that primary education should have the first claim on public resources. However, to be equitable and to meet the basic learning needs of all, priorities should be established within a longterm, phased and comprehensive approach to ensure that everyone will eventually have the opportunity to benefit from basic education. Prioritization can complement strategies to promote greater efficiency. All countries need to prioritize public expenditure and enhance efficiency, but this need will receive particular attention in countries where resource utilization is a more critical concern than the level of financial effort. These nations already may provide extensive opportunities for basic learning, but the benefits and beneficiaries may still be limited by existing inefficiencies.

Reallocating resources means shifting funds within the education budget, as well as from other government budgets, to support basic education. Because such a large part of the benefits of basic education accrue to society and not just to the individual, there is a strong argument for allocating a greater relative share of public resources to basic education than is now the case in many countries. This does not necessarily imply taking funds away from the other levels and types of education. Rather, reallocation can occur over time by directing a larger proportion of new resources to support basic education. In this way an appropriate equilibrium between the several levels and types of education can be reached without sudden or drastic changes.

The reallocation of resources from one sector to another may be more difficult to effect because of competing claims for scarce government funds and because of misperceptions of the value of basic education in relation to other social and economic activities. However, planners and decisionmakers can more easily encourage other sectors to make basic education activities an explicit part of their own programmes and of major development projects. The ministries in charge of labour, agriculture, industrial development, health and other aspects of human development generally organize some basic education activities already. In the short term, it is probably easier to obtain additional funds for these forms of basic education through reallocations within the budgets of other sectors than reallocations from these budgets to the education budget. However, such additional funding for basic education in other sectors is likely to be targeted on programmes for youth and adults, rather than children. In the long term, any substantial increase in funding for primary education may require increasing the education budget's relative share of government funds by reallocating resources, at least new resources, to it from other sectors.

Finding new resources for basic education can involve developing new sources of government revenue, encouraging private employers to help fund and provide basic learning opportunities, and facilitating the efforts of individuals, families, communities, and various kinds of nongovernmental organizations to support or to organize basic education activities. Government can increase the effect of its own investment in basic education by targeting funds to stimulate and support greater community and private financial participation. Such Leveraging" can be achieved, for example, through incentives to local communities to build and maintain schools and teachers' homes, guarantees of public bond issues, local control of school funds, and compensatory formulas that grant additional government funding to schools to help them remediate or compensate for the educational disadvantages of their pupil population.

Assistance must be substantial enough to allow the disadvantaged nation to achieve the level of educational quality and access essential to the expanded vision of basic education for all. Assistance must be sustained until the nation has achieved a level of social and economic development that will allow it to meet the basic learning needs of its population with its own resources.

An often neglected but vital resource that needs to be mobilized is the individual learner. The demand for, and participation in, learning opportunities cannot simply be assumed, but must be actively encouraged. Potential learners need to see that the benefits of basic education activities exceed the costs the participants must bear, such as earnings foregone and reduced time available for community and household activities and for leisure.

Women and girls especially may be deterred from taking full advantage of basic education opportunities because of reasons specific to individual cultures. Such barriers to participation may be overcome through the use of incentives and by programmes adapted to the local context and seen by the learners, their families and communities to be "productive activities". Also, learners tend to benefit more from education when they are partners in the instructional process, rather than treated simply as "inputs" or "beneficiaries". Attention to the issues of demand and participation will help assure that the learners' personal capacities are mobilized for education. Family resources, including time and mutual support, are vital for the success of basic education activities. Families can be offered incentives and assistance to ensure that their resources are invested to enable all family members to benefit as fully and equitably as possible from basic education opportunities.

Basic learning needs must be met through action within countries, but there are many forms of cooperation between countries with similar conditions and concerns that could and do assist them in this endeavour. By exchanging information and experience, pooling expertise, sharing facilities, and undertaking joint activities, several countries, working together, are able to increase their resource base and achieve economies of scale to the benefit of them all. Such arrangements are often set up among neighbouring countries, among all countries in a major geocultural region, or among countries sharing a common language or having cultural or commercial relations. Regional and international organizations often play an important role in facilitating such cooperation between countries. Some regions already have relevant development plans, such as the Jakarta Plan of Action on Human Resources, adopted by the Economic and Social Commission for Asia and the Pacific (ESCAP) in 1988, within which cooperation can be further strengthened. Various regional mechanisms, both intergovern-mental and nongovernmental, promote cooperation in education and training, health, agricultural development, research and information, communications, and in other fields relevant to meeting basic learning needs. Within the limitations of their respective mandates, resources and constituencies, such mechanisms can be utilized to exchange information, experience and expertise among institutions, organizations and government services involved in basic education.

The industrialized countries should also consider establishing appropriate mechanisms for co-operating on basic education, including functional illiteracy. In addition to the technical and policy consultations organized in connection with these programmes, other mechanisms could be utilized for consultations on policy issues concerning basic education, as needs arise: the regional conferences of ministers of education organized by UNESCO and by several regional organizations, and certain trans-regional conferences organized by the Commonwealth Secretariat, CONFEMEN (standing conference of ministers of education of francophone countries), and the Organization of Economic Co-operation and Development (OECD), the Islamic Educational, Scientific and Cultural Organization (ISESCO), as well as consultations among funding agencies convened by the newly created Task Force of Donors to African Education. In addition, numerous conferences and meetings organized by nongovernmental bodies provide opportunities for professionals to share information and views on technical and policy issues. The conveners of these conferences and meetings should consider ways to extend participation, where appropriate, to include representatives of other sectors engaged in meeting basic learning needs.

There are numerous opportunities, still largely unexploited, for further regional co-operation in developing national capacities to more effectively meet basic learning needs for all. Joint regional projects in education and related fields have already demonstrated their usefulness to the participating countries and institutions - i.e., when the projects had enough sustained support and political commitment. Training of key personnel is often more costeffective when countries share the facilities for in-service programmes or courses at a specialized institution that serves an entire region. Among those who could benefit from such training are planners, managers, teacher-educators, researchers, evaluators, curriculum specialists, and those who write educational radio and television programmes.

Certain categories of personnel, such as teacher-educators, can multiply the effect of their own training experience by training others when they return to their own countries. The earlier regional training institutions for school architects and educational planners and administrators pioneered this kind of collaboration, with generally favourable results. However, when the financial burden of institutions shifted to the host country, their regional character diminished or ceased. Currently, the dominant formula is ad hoc inservice training for selected personnel from groups of countries; but multi-year programmes with regular external funding are providing such training in English, French and Portuguese for several countries in Africa.

The growing need for various specialists, both in and outside the field of education, to design and implement basic learning opportunities of all kinds raises the possibility of reviving regional institutions to train certain personnel. The magnet programmes used for agricultural training in some regions are one model that could be adapted for this purpose. In these programmes, technical training institutions in the cooperating countries agree to a division of labour based on their respective comparative advantages. The development of information and research capacities is particularly well suited to collaboration among countries. Developing countries have a great need for data and research in education and related fields, particularly applied research useful for policy and pedagogy. Such research requires appropriate data collection mechanisms and a "critical mass" of scholars for mutual intellectual stimulation and criticism. However, the research communities in many countries are too small to provide the necessary depth of experience and breadth of disciplinary perspectives and lack good data collection facilities.

Through inter-country joint research projects and networks of institutions, the critical mass of researchers is more likely to be achieved and the quality of research thereby enhanced. The greater challenge of joint research offers incentives that help keep professionals from migrating to permanent positions in the industrial countries. Also, certain data collection activities and research subjects can be dealt with more effectively across national borders. The five regional networks for educational innovation, which operate under the auspices of UNESCO, provide established structures for exchanging information and cooperating in research related to meeting basic learning needs:

— Asian Programme of Educational Innovation for Development (APEID);

— Network of Educational Innovation for Development in Africa (NEIDA);

— Programme of Co-operation in Research and Development of Educational Innovation in South and South-East Europe (CODIESEE);

— Caribbean Network of Educational Innovation for Development (CARNEID);

— Educational Innovation Programme for Development in the Arab States (EI-PDAS).

These five networks link some 500 institutions and projects in 104 countries. According to a recent evaluation, they have had a significant multiplier effect in many of the participating countries. Other useful mechanisms for co-operational include UNESCO's International Institute of Educational Planning (IIEP) and its net-works of trainees and research, the International Bureau for Education's (IBE) information network, the

Unesco Institute for Education (UIE), the research and review advisory groups (RRAGs) associated with the International Development Research Centre (IDRC), the Commonwealth of Learning, the Asian Cultural Center for UNESCO, the participatory research network established by the International Council for Adult Education (ICAE), and the International Association for the Evaluation of Educational Achievement (IEA), which links major national research institutions in some 35 countries.

The production of educational materials presents two major problems for many less advantaged countries: developing appropriate content and manufacturing attractive materials in large quantities. Inter-country ventures have been attempted, with mixed success, but the potential economies of scale have not yet been systematically explored. Even countries using different languages should be able to collaborate in producing teaching materials, such as pictures, rulers, science equipment, films, and certain textbooks. Particular attention could be given to collaboration in developing and producing 'learning packages' or modules for basic education and skills training of children, youth, and adults. The packages could provide or reinforce basic literacy and numeracy instruction while dealing with topics related to basic learning needs common to many countries, such as sanitation, provision of safe water, care of infants, or food storage. A careful review of existing materials would probably reveal a wealth of good texts and illustrations which, with proper editing and audio-visual supports, could be drawn upon to develop useful prototypes. Individual countries could then adapt and translate the most appropriate packages for use in their own basic learning programmes.

Distance education is another area in which significant economies of scale could be realized, particularly among countries with the same language. For example, participating countries could share the expertise and development costs of radio or television programmes, and broadcast costs as well. Sateliites have been used successfully to transmit educational programmes, including some for rural areas, but the cost apparently discourages individual developing countries. However, as the number of communication satellites grows and the corresponding land -based technologies become simpler and more affordable, countries can explore the possibility of joint education projects that use satellite transmission.

2

Education and Human Development

Today, the sheer quantity of information available in the world—much of it relevant to survival and basic well-being — is exponentially greater than that available only a few years ago, and the rate of its growth is accelerating. This includes information about obtaining more life-enhancing knowledge—or learning how to learn. A synergistic effect occurs when important information is coupled with another modern advance — our new capacity to communicate. The financial, technological, and human resources available on a world scale to meet basic learning needs today are unprecedented.

When these factors are combined with the reaffirmation of political commitment to meeting basic learning needs, the next decade and the new century can be seen to provide an opportunity for human development sufficient to help meet the real and serious challenges the world faces. During the four decades since the 1948 Universal Declaration of Human Rights affirmed the right of everyone to education, substantial and sincere efforts have been made by the countries of the world to implement this right. Concurrent with International Literacy Year (1990) and in line with the objectives of the World Decade for Cultural Development (1988-97) and of the Fourth United Nations Development Decade (1991-2000), there is a need to reinforce and extend basic education to bring into being forms of sustainable national development that reconcile cultural and technological change within social and economic development.

Over the past decade, per capita gross domestic product (GDP) has fallen from 10 to 25 percent in much of sub-Saharan Africa and Latin America. South Asian countries on the whole have maintained more steady macro-economic growth, but substantial parts of their populations still live in absolute poverty, with food and nutrition problems among the most serious in the world. Although the incidence of unemployment is worse in developing nations, unemployment rates in the industrial market economies of Western Europe rose to over 10 percent in the 1980s.

These economies are now home to over 13 million of the world's estimated 100 million formally unemployed. Also, substantial disagreement exists over the sustainability of current growth levels among the developed economies, particularly in view of their interdependence with the weakened economies of developing countries and environmental degradation. The 1980s have seen economic disparities widen both within and among nations. Rising debt burdens, falling prices for commodities, and policies restricting the free flow of trade have created a net outflow of as much as US$60 billion per year in capital and other resources from developing countries to wealthier nations.

Industrial countries, in turn, face shrinking markets for exports, with negative effects on their own labour markets and on prospects for fiscal revenue. With the unprecedented expansion of knowledge during the past decade, inequitable access to formal education and other learning opportunities has engendered even greater economic disparities among people within a single nation. The wealthy become more educated; the uneducated grow poorer.

Armed conflicts and civil disorder continue to command public attention and resources in many countries. More than 14 million people, uprooted from their homelands, lived as refugees in foreign countries in 1987, and some 13 million of them reside in the most impoverished countries of Africa, the Middle East, and South Asia. War, human rights abuses, and natural disasters have created an even greater number of internal refugees who are displaced within their own countries and have little recourse to international protection or assistance. Increased urbanization and unemployment, with the concomitant problems of crime and illegal drug use, have created intolerable living conditions for millions more people the world over. In addition, historical conditions of ethnic and linguistic minorities and the poor have created disadvantaged groups within many societies.

Exploitation of the natural environment and pressures on the land from the growth and relocation of populations have accelerated the rate of environmental degradation alarmingly. Improper waste disposal, unregulated use of toxic chemicals, and industrial accidents imperil the biological integrity of land, air, and water. Deforestation from commercial logging and the cumulative effects of many subsistence activities have caused environmental destruction from landslides, flooding, desertification, and reduced production of oxygen. The environment knows no national or regional boundaries: a natural resource depleted in one place is lost to the world. Pollution tends to spread both geographically and over time, and the costs of environmental repair, where repair is possible, far exceed the costs of prevention.

Population growth continues to exacerbate economic, social, and environmental problems, particularly in the poorest parts of the world. In 1987, the world population exceeded the 5 billion mark, an increase of 1 billion in less than fifteen years. Ninety percent of this growth took place in Asia, Africa, and Latin America, and most of it was in the countries least able to care for or utilize the additional population effectively. The harsh reality of absolute poverty, with its guarantee of high infant mortality and a precarious livelihood for the sick and the aged, encourages high rates of reproduction that further entrench a lifestyle of poverty among the growing numbers of the poor. Demographic trends in industrial countries follow a different aggregate pattern, but even there the more disadvantaged groups are growing at a higher rate than the population as a whole.

Education for Human Dvelopment: Lessons from History

For much of human history, education has been viewed as a means to other ends, rather than as an end in itself. Nation-building, national security, political imperatives, economic growth, and the socialisation of children have all been advanced as justifications for the provision of education, sometimes to the frustration of reformers. In short, education was 'rediscovered 'as a development theme in the 1970s; but this owed less to the view that education was intrinsically important than to a recognition that it was essential for economic growth, which was seen as the real measure of development. In the terminology adopted and popularised by the World Bank, education was a form of 'human capital 'capable of generating high returns for economic growth.It was not until the early 1990s that the idea of education being an end in itself became part of mainstream thinking about development. Women's education in particular is among the most powerful determinants of trends in public health and child mortality. Income-poverty reduction is a function of two factors: the rate of growth and the distribution of income.

Education generates important benefits in both areas. It is positively associated with the rising productivity and innovation upon which economic growth depends. Equally importantly, improved access to education can help the poor to participate in markets on more equitable terms, improving the distribution of income in the process. Globalisation, and the associated emergence of increasingly knowledge-based systems of production, is strengthening the links between education and poverty reduction, both nationally and internationally.

The human-development gains generated through education are the product of acquired skills and attitudes. At another level, they reflect a less tangible but more powerful set of advantages conferred through education. These relate to empowerment, or the capacity of poor people to influence institutions, processes, and policies that affect their lives. Educated women and their children enjoy better health than their uneducated counterparts, partly because they have better access to information; but also because they are more confident and assertive in demanding services. What is true for individuals is also true for society. Education does not provide a guarantee of formal democracy, let alone of genuinely participatory democracy. But popular education is a necessary condition for democracy to take root. That is why the struggle for education has always been a central theme in the struggle for democracy. One way of capturing the human-development benefits associated with education is to consider how progress towards the 2015 target of universal primary education might influence progress in other areas.

At a time when development thinking was dominated by economic indicators of welfare, Sen shifted the debate to define poverty in terms of 'capabilities '–a term denoting the potential of poor people to do the things that contribute to their welfare. He wrote that low income was one aspect of poverty, but deprivation was about something more than material wealth: it was also about the absence of what Sen called 'fundamental freedoms ',which included the attributes associated with good health and education, and the ability to influence institutions affecting one's life.Education is for Sen as important as income, because it is needed to realise human potential in a broader sense. The new approach did not deny the broader benefits of education; but it powerfully reasserted the view, first elaborated by Aristotle, that education did not have to be justified in terms of its instrumental value. In Sen's words: 'Something that is of intrinsic importance can, in addition, be instrumentally momentous without compromising its intrinsic value.' The intrinsic importance of education –and the importance of Sens's work –is today reflected in its inclusion in the international development targets agreed by governments. These were adopted at a series of UN meetings in the 1990s, and later by the Development Assistance Committee of the Organisation for Economic Cooperation and Development (OECD). These targets marry income-based indicators of human development with wider capability indicators. They include the following goals:

- *Income-poverty reduction*: The proportion of people living in extreme poverty, defined as less than $1 per day, should be reduced by at least half by 2015.
- *Child health* : By 2015, the death rate for infants and children under the age of five should be reduced by two-thirds of the 1990 level in all countries.
- *Maternal health* : Maternal mortality rates should fall by three-quarters of their 1990 level by 2015.
- *Education* : There should be universal primary education by 2015, with the disparity between girls and boys in primary and secondary schools eliminated by 2005.

International development targets (IDTs) figure prominently in the dialogue between aid donors and developing countries. The IDTs are regularly reaffirmed at high-level summits, endorsed by governments, and included in the policy statements of donors and international financial institutions. Unfortunately, reaffirmation has not been accompanied by progress on anything like the scale required. While there are large variations in performance within and between regions, the IDTs will be missed by a wide margin if current trends continue.

The 2015 target of reducing child-mortality rates (CMRs, or deaths below the age of five years) by two-thirds provides a yardstick against which to measure wider developments in public health. Mortality rates among children are a highly sensitive indicator of health and nutritional status, and of access to basic services.Improved access to education, especially for girls, has the potential to accelerate progress towards the targets set for reducing the rates of child deaths and maternal mortality. Evidence presented in this chapter suggests that education may be the single most powerful force for achieving the 2015 goals. As in the case of health, the international development targets for income-poverty reduction are ambitious –and progress has been equally disappointing. The 2015 goals now look increasingly unattainable. In stark contrast to the hyperbole that accompanied UN summit commitments on poverty, the achievements of the 1990s were limited.

The decade began with 1.2 billion people living on less than $1 a day –and it ended with a similar number in the same position. While the incidence of poverty declined, so that the percentage of people living in poverty fell from 29 per cent to 24 per cent, this was insufficient to counteract the effects of population growth. There were marked regional variations in income-poverty performance during the 1990s. These can be briefly summarised as follows:

— *Sub-Saharan Africa*: As with other development indicators, there is a widening gap between sub-Saharan Africa and other developing regions. The incidence of poverty did not change during the 1990s, leaving almost half of the population – 291 million people – living on less than $1 a day. Both the incidence of poverty and the poverty gap, or the average distance of the poor from the poverty line, are wider in Africa than in any other region.

— *South Asia* :Economic growth rates for South Asia have been stronger than for Africa, but the decline in the incidence of poverty has been insufficient to offset an increase in the number of poor people, by around 27 million.

— *East Asia* :East Asia continued its rapid progress in poverty reduction during the first half of the 1990s, with 174 million people being lifted above the poverty line, and the incidence of poverty falling from 27 per cent to 15 per cent. However, the financial crisis in 1997 represented a huge setback, with the incidence of poverty rising by almost 50 per cent in Indonesia alone. Economic recovery from the crisis has been stronger in some countries (such as Korea) than others (like Indonesia), raising questions about the capacity of the region to remain on track to meet the 2015 targets.

— *Latin America*: Like South Asia, the Latin American region achieved relatively strong growth in the 1990s, but poverty incidence has remained constant, with another five million people being added to the ranks of the poor.

— *Middle East*: Income-poverty incidence, using the $1 a day indicator, is lower in the Middle East than for any other region, and it continued to decline in the 1990s. However, the absolute number of poor people fell only slightly, to 5.5 million.

Future trends in income poverty will be determined by the overall rate of economic growth and the extent to which poor people participate in growth. For any given level of average income, the extent of poverty will depend on how income is distributed. The larger the share of any increment to growth captured by the poor, the stronger the linkage between economic growth and poverty reduction. Conversely, the greater the initial level of inequality, the lower the rate at which income poverty will fall at any given growth rate. Crudely stated, more unequal societies are less efficient at converting growth into poverty reduction. This has important implications for poverty reduction. Distributional factors have had an important bearing on income-poverty reduction trends. One survey, based on changes in household-income data from 44 countries, found that similar rates of growth had produced rates of poverty reduction that varied by a factor of five, depending on patterns of income distribution. Some regions have been far more successful than others at converting economic growth into poverty reduction. For instance, each percentage point of economic growth in East Asia reduced the incidence of poverty at around three times the rate achieved in Latin America. The abysmal rate of poverty reduction achieved by Latin America during this period, and the rise in the absolute number of poor people, owes as much to distributional factors as to slow growth.

In situations where initial income inequalities are high,and where the poor fail to capture a bigger share of any increment in growth than the non-poor, wealth creation is unlikely to translate into rapid poverty eduction. Extreme income inequality not only weakens the link between growth and poverty reduction, but also undermines economic growth. It was once assumed that any attempt at redistribution would act as a brake on growth by creating disincentives to investment. More recently, a large body of evidence has emerged to suggest that high levels of inequality are bad for growth, as well as for poverty reduction. There are various explanations. Large land-holdings tend to produce less efficiently than small and medium-sized holdings. Meanwhile, poverty and inadequate access to productive assets and marketing infrastructure create obvious barriers to risk-taking, while incomes restrict both the size of local markets and domestic savings and investment. Whatever the underlying causes, economic efficiency and equity are inextricably linked. This suggests that improved income distribution has the potential to produce a double benefit for poverty reduction, in the form of more dynamic and more widely dispersed economic growth.

There is a counter view to the argument that redistributive growth is the most effective mechanism for poverty reduction. Researchers in the World Bank have claimed that economic growth is the primary motor for poverty reduction, and that distributional issues are, at best, of secondary importance. Their claim rests on empirical data purporting to show that, on average ,growth benefits the poor and rich alike on a one-to-one basis, because the benefits of growth are distributed in accordance with the existing pattern of income distribution. The argument has had an important influence on the debate on growth and poverty reduction, shifting the emphasis away from policies for achieving redistribution and towards a more narrowly 'growth-oriented 'perspective. Few people would deny either that economic growth is a necessary condition for poverty reduction, or that the poor generally benefit from growth. But averages obscure large variations. Some countries are far more efficient than others at converting growth into poverty reduction. The real policy goal in any poverty-reduction strategy, especially in any highly unequal society, should be that of increasing the share of income captured by the poor, since this will increase the rate of poverty reduction. Even if it is true that rich and poor benefit from growth in proportion to their existing share of national income, in highly unequal societies this means that growth will simply reproduce inequality. Failure to change distribution patterns, with the poor capturing a bigger share of growth than their existing shared national income, will slow the rate of poverty reduction, rather than simply reproducing inequality.

There are three broader problems with the World Bank's perspective. First, it is based on data up to the early 1990s, and has therefore failed to capture the increasingly unequal income-distribution patterns associated with more recent growth periods. Second, it ignores some of the lessons of recent history. In Latin America, the number of people living in poverty increased by more than 50 million during the 1980s. Research by the Inter-American Development Bank attributed over half of this increase to changes in income distribution favouring the wealthy against the poor. Third, whatever the broad relationship between growth and distribution, it is increasingly clear that, with existing patterns of income distribution, the 2015 targets will not be met through growth alone.

Benefits in health sector

The potential benefits of education for poverty reduction would flow partly from more rapid economic growth; and partly from improved income distribution, both at a national level and at a global level. Accelerated progress towards the 2015 goals for reducing child-mortality rates will require action across a wide range of policy areas.

Improved provision of public services is one such area. But developments in health will be shaped by progress in other areas, including income-poverty reduction and education. A 'virtuous circle 'operates here, because better health is one of the requirements for raising the incomes and educational status of the poor. Education influences health outcomes through a variety of channels. Increased access to information, changing attitudes, and increased confidence are among the most important. In terms of improving prospects for reaching the targets set for reducing child deaths, improved access to good-quality education is among the most important requirements.

Nowhere are the human-development costs associated with mass exclusion from education more apparent than in relation to women's education. While the educational status of men makes an important difference to child health, it is a far less important variable than the education of women. Mothers typically assume responsibility for the welfare of children, including their nutritional status and their contacts with health-service providers. Education can empower women to make more informed choices, to demand better services, and to influence family decisions in a direction conducive to child welfare. The correlation between parental education and child mortality has been extensively documented. In almost all countries, child-death rates are inversely related to the level of maternal education. The more educated the mother, the healthier she and her child are likely to be. Comparative research focused on 33 countries during the 1980s found that each additional year of maternal education reduced childhood mortality by about 8 per cent. For mothers completing five years of primary education, the risk of childhood mortality decreased by around 45/1000 births. In countries where one child in every four dies before reaching the age of five, as in much of sub-Saharan Africa, the mass exclusion of girls from basic education has clear implications: it is costing millions of lives. Mortality rates for the children of Ghanaian mothers with some education are twice as high as for children born to mothers with no education. The benefits of women's education for child health are especially marked in countries with deeply entrenched patterns of gender inequity. In most countries, there are slightly more females in the total population than males. However, there are marked deviations from this pattern.

National income distribution determines the rate at which particular countries translate growth into poverty reduction, but international income distribution also influences the scope for poverty reduction, since it determines the average income levels in different countries. The size of that average income, and how wealth is distributed among different groups, will determine the incidence of poverty at the national level. Other things being equal, the bigger the share of global wealth captured by the poorest countries, the higher their average incomes and –subject to domestic income-distribution factors –the lower the incidence of poverty.

Global distribution trends are as disturbing from a poverty-reduction perspective as national income trends. International income inequality has been increasing at a rate that is probably without precedent, widening the gap between the average incomes of the rich and the poor in the process. The ratio of the average GNP per capita of the richest countries with one-fifth of the world's population and countries accounting for the poorest fifth has increased from 30:1 in 1960 to 60:1 in 1990, and around 74:1 today. Extreme as national income inequalities may be, even in Latin America, the world's most unequal region, they are less extreme than international inequalities. One way of measuring inequality is through the Gini coefficient, measuring the extent of departure from a situation of complete income equality. Income is shared among rich and poor countries even more unequally than it is shared among rich and poor Brazilians. Global income-distribution trends reflect the way in which global wealth, and any increment to it, is shared between rich and poor countries. At present, high-income countries accounting for about 20 per cent of the world's population account for 80 per cent of global GDP. Sub-Saharan Africa, with 10 per cent of world population, accounts for 0.6 per cent. Because economic growth has stagnated in many developing countries, the wealth gap is widening. The average annual growth in income per capita was negative in 50 countries during 1990 –1998, only one of them an OECD country.

Changes in global income distribution are needed if the poorest countries are to achieve the 2015 targets. Capturing a larger share of global GDP will require a dramatically improved growth performance on the part of these countries, but it will also mean that they have to capture a larger share of world trade. Education can empower women in their interactions with service providers. It makes it more likely that they will have read information about health problems, and that they will be more confident in explaining these problems and demanding treatment. In the Ibadan region of Nigeria, detailed research at health facilities found that literate women bring in sick children for treatment at an earlier stage, and that they are more likely to demand –and get –a specific diagnosis.

There is an unfortunate tendency in some quarters to view education as little more than a tool for achieving lower birth rates. Education does have this effect. In South Asia, the fertility rate for women with seven or more years of education is 35 per cent lower than for women with no education. But changes in fertility reflect a more important change in the ability of women to exercise greater control over their lives. The ability to make use of information, openness to new ideas that challenge conventional assumptions about gender, and improved understanding of nutrition all play a role. So does increased confidence in dealing with service-providers. Educated mothers are not only better able to gain information about health matters and nutrition: they are also far more likely to make use of preventative health-care services and to demand timely treatment.

The timeliness of referrals, uptake of immunisation, and use of antenatal services and clinics are all positively associated with education. Each of these factors reduces the risks associated with many potentially life-threatening illnesses. For example, swift responses to acute respiratory infections and early treatment of diarrhoea through the use of simple rehydration therapies could save many lives. Evidence from Zambia, educated women are more likely both to identify the need for treatment at an earlier stage and to demand treatment.Women with a secondary education are some 30 per cent more likely to take their children to a clinic for treatment than women with no education. This is consistent with evidence from a large number of countries. In rural south India, the participants in an adult education programme demonstrated a far better understanding of common illnesses and their causes, as well as of potentially life-saving remedies, than did nonparticipants. They were also far more likely to use modern health services. Primary education is similarly correlated with service uptake. In Mozambique, a government survey in 1998 found that mothers who had completed grades 1 –5 were almost twice as likely to vaccinate their children as illiterate mothers. The same mothers were 22 per cent more likely to possess a health card, indicating a higher level of contact with health clinics. Research in India found that mothers with four years of education were twice as likely to register for antenatal care as mothers with no education, and three times as likely to immunise their children. Both antenatal care and immunisation were significant determinants of mortality.

The HIV/AIDS epidemic represents a global threat which will slow down, or even reverse, improvements in health indicators in many countries. Apart from its direct impact on health, the epidemic is impoverishing families and overwhelming already under-financed health services.The most recent of the international development targets, adopted in 1990, envisages a 25 per cent reduction in HIV infection among 15 –24 year olds by 2005. Education has a vital role to play in meeting this target. Drawing on responses to household surveys from 32 countries, recent research has shown that knowledge and awareness of HIV/AIDS-related problems is strongly linked to education, especially among women and girls. For instance, the proportion of women who do not know that HIV infection can be transmitted to children is three times higher for uneducated women than for educated women, while the proportion believing that there is no way of avoiding HIV/AIDS is four times higher.In Zambia, infection rates among educated women started to decline in the mid-1990s, while the infection rate among women without any formal education has remained constant. There is similar evidence from Uganda,where infection rates among women with a secondary education have fallen, relative to those for illiterate women. Disaggregating child-mortality data for Kenya to take into account the education of mothers also illustrates the potential for reducing vulnerability. While the national CMR began to increase at the end of the 1980s, it continued to decline for the children of mothers who had attained post-primary education. It would be wrong to overstate the potential role of education in combating the HIV/AIDS epidemic. Yet it is clear that improved access to education could make a difference. Attendance at school provides children with an opportunity to gain access to relevant information and to transform this information into behavioural changes. At the same time, education can empower women to exercise greater control. Given that teenage girls in Africa are five times more likely to be infected by HIV than boys, girls 'education is an obvious priority.

Education and women empowerment

Womens's education does not merely create one-off benefits for child health. Apart from being an important objective in its own right, it helps to overcome wider gender-determined inequalities and to create virtuous circles of human development and poverty reduction. The critical role of female literacy and education in furthering human development emerges forcefully from comparisons between different countries, and between different regions of the same country. Differences in education have played an important role in the social development of Indias's States, as contrasts between

Kerala and northern States such as Uttar Pradesh and Bihar clearly demonstrate. One of the distinguishing features of Kerala's development was the early promotion of female literacy. This provided a basis for advances in public health and other areas. Unlike Kerala, female literacy rates and enrolment rates for girls in other States are much lower than for boys.

Better education creates opportunities for employment and income generation, which in turn create incentives for later marriage. Improved access to information and increased self-confidence raise the demand for contraception, and enable women to express that demand. Whatever the precise mechanisms at play, maternal education is one of the keys to achieving the 2015 targets for reducing maternal mortality rates.

Important as education is to improved public health, it is not the sole factor. Income-poverty is the primary driver of child malnutrition –and education does not override the structural disadvantages associated with poverty. Moreover, it is difficult in practice to separate the influence of education from that of income in explaining household behaviour. Better-educated households are less likely to be poor, and the poorest households are more likely to suffer educational disadvantage.

The benefits of education are conditioned by local social, economic, and cultural conditions. In some cases, the benefits may be weaker among the extreme poor than among less disadvantaged social groups. But even within low-income groups, maternal education is positively associated with better nutrition, partially compensating for other aspects of deprivation. Given that some 160 million children worldwide suffer from malnutrition, which is the main cause of premature death, this underlines the scale of the potential benefits of achieving universal education.

The multiple benefits of female education are cumulative, in that they become mutually reinforcing over time, with the advantages transmitted across generations. It is not just that educated children are likely to be more productive and healthier, with attendant benefits for poverty reduction. They are also more likely to educate their own children. Here too the benefits of maternal education are particularly strong, with educated mothers far more likely than uneducated mothers to send their daughters to school. In Tanzania, the daughters of mothers who have had a primary education are 11 per cent more likely to enrol in primary school than are the daughters of uneducated mothers. To the extent that education enhances the ability of women to control their fertility, lower population growth will also generate advantages for education. Slower growth in the school-age population will reduce pressure on the education system, and enable the government to increase spending per pupil and provide a better-quality education. It follows that investing in girls ' education today is one of the most effective strategies for progressing towards universal primary education in the future.

Education and poverty eardication

Recognising the potential of education as a catalyst for development does not mean that education policy can be treated in isolation. Schools are not islands that are somehow separated from the wider social and economic environment; nor are they immune from the effects of poverty, malnutrition, and ill health. Educational deprivation contributes to poverty, helping to transmit it across generations. But poverty also limits the ability of poor households to take advantage of educational opportunities. In the absence of integrated strategies for addressing these problems, many of the potential benefits of education will be lost. Despite the enormous shortfalls that remain, governments have significantly increased access to primary education. Four out of every five children of primary-school age now attend school, a greater proportion than ever before. However, the widening coverage of education systems has exposed the problem of poverty-related illness. Millions of children are attending school in a state of poor health or poor nutrition –or both. In the early 1990s, the World Bank estimated that children in the age range 5 –14 accounted for 11 per cent of the total global burden of disease, with infectious and parasitic diseases the largest contributor. More than 95 per cent of this disease burden was concentrated in developing countries. Poor health before and during school years can have devastating consequences in terms of impaired cognitive development, under-performance, and withdrawal from school.

Education systems can provide a useful mechanism for addressing health problems. Early-childhood development programmes can help to counteract the educational disadvantages associated with poverty. These programmes provide primary-care interventions, including prenatal care, immunisation, oral rehydration therapies, control of respiratory infections, and vitamin supplementation. Apart from the immediate health benefits, they can contribute to improvements in educational attainment later in life. Schools can provide a focal point for community health efforts. For instance, the

Partnership for Child Development, an international collaboration between UN agencies, non-government organisations, drugs companies, and academic institutions, has pioneered low-cost systems for delivering de-worming drugs to children through schools. Pilot programmes in Ghana and Tanzania have trained teachers to administer simple tests for identifying infection and administering low-cost treatments. The need for intervention by medical personnel in determining individual dosage for treatment has also been reduced.

Well-designed in-school nutrition programmes can help to alleviate the nutritional problems of school-age children. In the Indian State of Gujarat, more than three million children receive free school meals, with vitamin A and iron supplements. Studies in Benin, Burkina Faso, and Togo have all found that school meals have the effect of raising childrens's test scores.In Peru, a school-breakfast programme, which included an iron-fortified ration, was shown to increase dietary intakes of energy by 25 per cent and iron by 46 per cent. Other positive outcomes reported include reduced vulnerability to seasonal hunger, improved immunity to infectious disease through reduced micronutrient deficiency, and increased motivation for parents to send their children to school and have them attend regularly .Programmes can be targeted to reduce inequalities between boys and girls.In Pakistan, an intervention supported by the World Food Programme provided two tins of oil to families whose girls attended school for a minimum of 20 days a month. Attendance in the schools participating in the programmes increased from 76 per cent to 93 per cent.In some countries it accounts for up to half of school days missed for medical reasons. Diarrhoea, which claims the lives of 3.3 million children annually, has highly adverse consequences for school attendance and performance. Parents and teachers reported that children –especially young girls –were frequently withdrawn from school to tend sick relatives, missing valuable learning time a result. The cost of treating health problems was another important factor. In extreme cases, unaffordability resulted in poor households simply being excluded from health provision. More commonly, it leads to delayed treatment, with attendant implications for child health. This strongly suggests that the policy of introducing free primary education should have been linked to initiatives aimed at reducing –or eliminating –the costs of basic health care.

As in health-related studies, causal connections are difficult to establish. Income levels typically reflect educational attainment, but poverty –and its associated problems of illness and poor nutrition –is a powerful barrier to educational attainment. The precise patterns of association between income poverty and deprivation vary from country to country. What does not vary is the disproportionate representation of the under-educated in the ranks of the poor.For households, as for national economies, educational deprivation is a passport to low income, vulnerability, and poverty. In Vietnam, two out of three households headed by somebody with no education live below the poverty line.

Education is critical to the achievement of the 2015 target of reducing the incidence of extreme poverty by half. At a household level, educational status is one of the strongest influences on income and poverty. The lower the level of educational attainment, the greater the vulnerability to income-poverty. What is true for households is true also for national economies, with average income levels reflecting levels of access to education.

The rate of poverty reduction is dictated by the rate of economic growth and the share of national wealth captured by the poor. Improvements in both areas depend critically on advances in education. For households living on the margins of subsistence, these are significant gains. To a Ugandan coffee farmer, they can mean the difference between being able to afford urgently needed medicines, new tools, seeds, and food and having to manage without them. The benefits of education are equally pronounced in labour markets. One of the reasons why education offers an escape route from poverty is that it creates opportunities to earn higher incomes, whether in the form of wages, or through trading activity. Education cannot compensate for disadvantages associated with working in low-wage environments in which the poor are often discriminated against, but it can increase relative earning power.

In Latin America, workers who have completed primary school will earn on average 50 per cent more in their first job than workers who have not attended school. In Brazil and Mexico, they earn twice as much. The gap widens to 120 per cent for a worker with twelve years of education. There is a positive correlation between income and education even in the informal sector, where school qualifications are of limited relevance. Evidence from Honduras, Guatemala, and El Salvador indicates that each additional year of education is linked to a 5 –10 per cent increase in informal-sector earnings.

Gender is one of the key determinants of the distribution of benefits from education. Where women face unequal access to productive resources and services, the scope for realising the potential gains of education is restricted. The same is true where women earn less than men for doing similar work, as they do in most countries; or where men capture a disproportionately large share of higher-paid jobs. From a poverty-reduction perspective, what matters more than estimated rates of return are the real effects of education in terms of increasing the value of the main assets of the poor: namely, their output and their labour. The benefits of education are especially strong in agriculture. Evidence from many countries shows a positive association between productivity and the number of years spent in school. Higher productivity in turn leads to increased output and income flows, reducing the vulnerability of poor households.

Cross-country research based on data covering 13 developing countries suggests that, after taking into account differences in land, labour, and capital, each year of additional education raises farm output by 2 per cent. Here too the potential benefits of education are cumulative, because growth in the incomes of the rural poor generates demand for small-scale enterprises and manufacturing. In Indonesia, the multiplier effect of rural growth on manufacturing during the 1970s was large, with each percentage-point increase in farming matched by a 1.5 per cent increase in non-agricultural output. The precise causal links between education and productivity are difficult to establish, but an enhanced capacity to innovate appears to be one of the most important. More educated households are more likely to adopt new technologies, and to generate higher returns from those technologies. One study in India found that four years of basic education increased economic returns to innovation by about one-third – considerably more than the returns to spending on agricultural extension. Such studies clearly indicate the economic potential inherent in education, but realisation of that potential depends on access to productive assets and marketing infrastructure. In the Indian case, returns were highest in areas where the availability of infrastructure and producers 'access to marketing facilities were most developed,underlining the fact that public investment in education can increase the efficiency of public investment in economic infrastructure.

The distribution of educational opportunity has an important bearing on the distribution of income. Illiteracy and the absence of skills provided through education prevent poor people from participating in markets on equitable terms, and from responding to the opportunities created by economic reform. In countries where rapid growth is increasing the demand for, and returns to, skilled labour relative to unskilled labour, income inequalities will widen, slowing the rate of poverty reduction. Creating growth on the foundations of highly unequal education systems results in benefits biased in favour of the wealthy. Empirical research has found that the effect of educational inequality in producing income inequalities rises until the average time in school reaches 6.3 years, after which it declines. In much of sub-Saharan Africa, the average time in school is three –four years, and it is less than six years in Latin America. The time-honoured comparison between East Asia and Latin America illustrates the consequences of educational inequality. In Korea, the proportion of workers with high-school and post-secondary qualifications increased rapidly after the early 1970s, while the proportion of workers with elementary-school qualifications or less fell to only 8 per cent of the total.

The wage premium for skilled labour consequently fell. Over the two decades up to the mid-1980s, the average income of those who had completed higher education declined from 97 per cent above the average wage to 66 per cent above it. By 1986, the income gap between workers with high-school qualifications and those with only primary-school qualifications had fallen by one-third. In Brazil, by contrast, the wage premium earned by workers with higher education, already much larger than in Korea, remained unchanged. The earnings of those with the benefit of higher education had reached 156 per cent

Education may be a necessary condition for achieving more rapid economic growth, but it is not a sufficient condition. It cannot be assumed that increasing educational attainment automatically generates higher growth. Improved access to good-quality education has the effect of increasing the supply of skilled labour. But the growth generated as a result will be determined by the ability of the economy to absorb that abour at rising levels of productivity. It is perfectly possible to combine outstanding progress in education with an abysmal economic performance, as witnessed by the experience of countries such as Cuba, Zimbabwe, and Russia. Where weak macro-economic management is restricting employment opportunities or depressing productivity, increase in the supply of skilled labour may not be matched by increased demand for that labour. This in turn will have the effect of limiting productivity and wage gains, leading to skilled labour replacing unskilled labour and declining wages for the latter.

During the 1990s, the country invested a higher proportion of its national income in education than almost any other country, achieving near-universal primary education in the space of a few years after Independence. Secondary-school enrolment also rose sharply. However, slow economic growth meant that by the end of the decade only 30,000 formal-sector jobs were being created for every 200,000 school-leavers. Weak macro-economic policies geared towards capital-intensive, rather than labour-intensive, growth undermined the benefits of investment in education.

The unequal distribution of opportunities for education has had a profound and growing impact on the trend towards increasing income inequality. The underlying reasons for this trend are disputed: some accounts stress the role of technological change, others the impact of cheap imports, and still others failures in manufacturing policy. What is not in dispute is the fact that differences in education and skill levels are increasingly linked to income inequalities. Income disparity has widened fastest between people who graduated from college and those who graduated from high school, or dropped out before graduation. Average wages for those who graduated only from high school have fallen by 15 per cent over the past two decades.

Education and globalisation

Differences in education provide an important part of the explanation for existing inequalities in the distribution of wealth between countries and within countries. However, important as education is today, it will play an even more important role in determining future patterns of income distribution. This is because knowledge, and the ability to process it, is increasingly shaping the production of wealth, and the distribution of wealth between countries and between households. As education grows in importance, income distribution within countries will increasingly reflect the distribution of educational opportunity. At an international level, the distribution of global wealth will follow similar patterns.The existing income gap between 'education-rich 'and 'education-poor 'countries has the potential to turn into a chasm, with devastating implications for global poverty-reduction prospects. As Nelson Mandela has written: 'Eliminating the distinction between information rich and information poor countries is critical to eliminating other inequalities between North and South.' Technology transfer has a role to play in the elimination of this division; but without rapid progress towards universal primary education, the foundations needed to close the 'digital divide 'between rich and poor nations will not be in place.

International economic life is being transformed by a revolution that began approximately two decades ago. Globalisation, or the surge in flows of trade and finance, is part of that revolution –but only a minor part. The more fundamental shift has been in the way that wealth is produced. Two hundred and fifty years ago, the first Industrial Revolution was driven by steam power, physical labour, and money. Comparative advantage was defined by endowments of these resources. The textile mills of Lancashire were able to produce cloth because they had access to water-power and capital. Technological innovation was important, but the technologies that drove the Industrial Revolution wer-erelatively simple. This began to change during the second industrial revolution at the end of the nineteenth century, when industries were transformed by innovations in organic chemistry and electromagnetism.

Today, new technologies are further weakening the relationship between physical resources and wealth production. In future, economic wealth and prosperity will be derived largely from an intangible resource widely referred to as 'knowledge capital '. The transformation from a world dominated by physical factors of production to one dominated by knowledge implies a shift in the locus of economic power as profound as that which took place after the first Industrial Revolution. It is a shift which has important implications for the role of education. As production processes and trade become more knowledge-intensive, patterns of wealth distribution will increasingly reflect the distribution of educational opportunity, both within countries and between countries.

Failure to close the education divide now separating rich and poor will undermine efforts to achieve the more equitable patterns of economic growth essential for the reduction of poverty. Countries that fail to develop education systems capable of responding to the challenge will fall further behind, with attendant costs to their citizens. In the nineteenth century, Britain failed to manage the transition from the first to the second industrial revolution partly because of the chronic neglect of basic education –a salutary lesson for governments at the start of the twenty-first century.

Information technologies are at the heart of the new processes driving wealth creation. Productivity and competitiveness are, to an increasing extent, determined by knowledge generation and information processing. New information and communications technologies, based on microelectronics and telecommunications, provide the infrastructure for the new economy. The background to the development of this infrastructure is complex, but the key point is that telecommunications and information technology are converging, since both depend on the digital transmission of 'bits ',or data written in the binary language understood by computers. The resulting technological advances have been dramatic. The capacity of computers, communications networks, and information storage and retrieval systems has grown faster than any technology in history. Over the past decade, the processing power of computers using the same-sized microchip has increased one hundredfold, while the speed with which they operate has multiplied a thousandfold. At the same time, the cost of digital transmission and computer equipment has fallen dramatically, and the range and sophistication of services provided (from faxes to virtual private networks) is constantly increasing. One service in particular –the Internet –has transformed the flow and accessibility of information.

The World Wide Web has created some 60 million documents since 1992. The Internet is one of the fastest-growing sites of international commercial activity. According to some accounts, the increased volume of trade and investment activity in international economic relations is what is driving globalisation. This is at best a partial truth. While economic transactions between countries are intensifying, this aspect of globalisation is not new. The changes are more quantitative than qualitative. What is new is the technological infrastructure underpinning globalisation. The convergence of computers and telecommunications has created a global community in which time-zones are more important than geographical borders. Information technology has removed time and distance from the competitive equation. It has also produced a new source of wealth: knowledge applied to create value. For firms and national economies alike, wealth generation is now largely based on the application of ideas and information to production and marketing. This change is reflected in efforts in the World Trade Organisation and elsewhere by transnational companies to increase the returns to knowledge through patents. Since knowledge is the key input in the production of profit, there is a powerful corporate self-interest in maximising returns through patents that raise the cost of knowledge transfer.

Some aspects of the Information Revolution are immediately visible, especially to populations living in rich countries. Others are less visible, but no less important in the way that they are reshaping social and economic life. The rise of service industries, the development of global financial markets, the increasing mobility of capital, the globalisation of production under the auspices of transnational companies, and the expansion of an English-language, USA-dominated, homogenised 'world culture 'and 'world media 'are all manifestation of the Information Revolution. Changes in economic life have been equally dramatic. The average weight of one dollars's worth of US exports has halved since 1970. The intimate relationship between education and national prosperity is not a recent discovery. At the start of the twentieth century, the British Prime Minister, Arthur Balfour, lamented the fact that his country was 'behind all continental rivals in education'. He was not understating the problem. By 1870, when Britain was embarking on the timid reforms that would ultimately lead to the principle of State financing for compulsory universal primary education, one child in every 1000 attended secondary school – one-quarter of the ratio achieved in France. But it was not until the turn of the century that British policy makers finally acknowledged that the country's under-financed, poor-quality and class-ridden education system had helped to erode the competitiveness of the national economy.

Some historians have challenged the view that education, or a generalised lack of it, contributed to Britain's industrial decline. They point out that the enormous expansion of national wealth produced in the century after the Industrial Revolution was achieved without a huge investment in education. During the second half of the nineteenth century, the pattern of innovation changed, with the marriage of science and technology opening a new era. The major technological advances required knowledge of scientific subjects such as organic chemistry and electromagnetism, and their application required increasingly skilled workforces.

In the United States, the textile magnates of New England laid the foundations of a mass public education system in the 1840s. Their motives were not even remotely altruistic. They wanted better-educated workers to raise productivity and scientists to innovate, all in the interests of enlarging profit margins and overtaking Britain. The increasing reliance on formal mass education for the diffusion of scientific knowledge had momentous consequences, both in opening up new branches of knowledge and in linking education systems to economic activity. Yet in the midst of this explosion of educational activity, British governments agonised over the merits of using taxes to pay for education, and over the political threats of educating the working classes. By 1850, when countries such as the Netherlands, Switzerland, France, and Germany had achieved virtually universal primary education, Britain had fewer than half of its children in school, and was spending far less per pupil.

The main purpose of mass public education was to provide working-class children with the rudiments of instruction as cheaply as possible, and with a premium on values stressing obedience. State support was linked to pupils passing tests in basic literacy and numeracy and to 'payment by results' – a system which encouraged rote-learning and was condemned by a contemporary Chief Inspector of schools as 'an ingenious instrument for arresting the mental growth of the child'. Like any process of historical change, globalisation is changing the distribution of economic wealth and power. It is creating winners and losers, both at an international level and within countries. The winners are those with the skills and assets that they need to participate in the new knowledge-based global economy; the losers are those without. For poor people in poor countries, there are major opportunities; the creation of jobs linked to software industries in India is one example. But the threats are immense. Globalisation and new technologies are rapidly increasing the returns to education at a time when there are massive inequalities in educational opportunity. For the millions of poor households denied the chance of even the most rudimentary education, and for countries where average education levels are low, globalisation points clearly in the direction of rapid marginalisation. As wealth becomes more concentrated in rich countries and among higher-income households, the prospects for reaching the 2015 target of halving income poverty will recede.

Part of the problem can be traced to 'the digital divide' or inequality in access to new technologies. The changes in communications and information technology underpinning the new economic order have been concentrated overwhelmingly in North America, Europe, and the Pacific Rim, regions with high per capita incomes and almost universal access to telephones. More than 90 per cent of telecommunications traffic takes place between countries in these regions. Almost all people in these countries depend on telephones, to a greater or lesser degree, in their daily lives. But more than half of the world's population, living in poor countries, has never used a telephone. Almost one-third of the world's population lives in countries that, taken together, have fewer than 19 million telephone lines between them – fewer than in Italy.

Whereas developed countries have 37 telephone lines for every 100 people, developing countries have only 2.3 lines, and there are more telephone lines in Tokyo than in the whole of sub-Saharan Africa. Access to information technology is equally distorted. Most high-income industrialised countries have more than 315 computers for every 1000 people. Some 70 per cent of the average value in US cars can now be traced to this source, according to one estimate –and more North Americans are now employed in making computers than in the car industry. For the industrialised countries as a whole, the World Bank estimates that more than half of GDP is accounted for by the production and distribution of intangible knowledge.

The growing importance of information to the generation of wealth is most clearly apparent in the US economy. By one calculation, the value of the USA's stock of intangible investment overtook the value of the stock of physical capital in the 1980s. In terms of market capitalisation, Microsoft long ago overtook companies such as Ford and General Motors, which have traditionally dominated the industrial landscape. Capital-intensive, knowledge-based industries are the new growth centres in the US economy. At the beginning of 1999, the Internet company America On Line was valued at $66bn, compared with a market value of $52bn for General Motors –but it employed 10,000 people, compared with 600,000 for General Motors. Even allowing for stock-market over-valuation, something fundamental has changed. The surge in productivity growth in the USA was twice as high in the second half of the 1990s as in the 1990s, and was in large part the product ,of heavy investment in new information technologies in the first half of the decade. While the USA has led the way, all other OECD countries are following a similar path.

It is not just the national economic life of OECD countries that is being transformed. The knowledge revolution has also left its mark on international trade. The share of high-technology goods in international trade has doubled over the past two decades. It now represents about one-fifth of the total value of international trade – and the trend is unmistakably upwards. Since 1986, the share of value added to exports by high-technology goods has risen by over 50 per cent in the USA, and by over 100 per cent in Britain. Over the same period, the share of non-mineral primary commodities in international trade has fallen by half, to 13 per cent, and terms of trade for labour-intensive manufactured goods are now deteriorating almost as rapidly as those for primary commodities. Meanwhile, payments to holders of patents are increasing by 20 per cent per annum, again reflecting the growing importance –and value –of knowledge in technology transfer.

The clear implication is that countries that they in turn sell access to their lines at controlled prices to other village members. So far, 65,000 villages have been targeted for the next six years. Recent evaluations by the Canadian governments's development ministry point to important benefits for women who are enabled to reduce transport costs, achieve higher prices, and reduce middleman costs.

Education is another area that can benefit. Communications technologies can provide access to resources, and facilitate teacher support and curriculum development. The African Virtual University, based in Nairobi, is aiming to increase university enrolments and improve the quality and relevance of instruction throughout the region. To date it has installed 27 satellite receiver terminals, and it has developed a digital library to compensate for the chronic shortage of scientific journals. In the industrialised countries, governments, schools, and industry have pioneered new approaches to facilitate interactive distance learning. There is scope for adapting these initiatives for use in developing countries. Technology transfer dominates much of the debate on how best to close the 'digital divide '.Some of the Group of Seven industrialised countries are developing major initiatives in this area, including the United States, Japan, and Britain. This is in keeping with the broader received wisdom of the day.

The World Bank in particular has made much of the potential for developing countries to leap over the digital divide by importing new technologies. It points out that while the start-up costs for ICT industries are enormous, import costs for computers and telecommunication equipment are relatively cheap, and getting cheaper. Technological innovation can be imported, so the argument runs, and installed in the local economy. Even at a superficial technical level, this approach understates some of the more complex problems related to technology transfer. The process of technological 'catching-up 'will impose a huge burden on the balance of payments of many countries. Unsustainable debt, deteriorating terms of trade, and, in many of the poorest countries, chronic trade deficits are major barriers to the importation of high-technology goods.

Another problem is rooted in international trade rules. These are designed to raise the cost of technology transfer through intellectual-property protection. Under World Trade Organisation rules, patent protection is provided for twenty years, giving 'owners 'of technology exclusive rights –including the right to extract royalty payments from importing countries. The consequences of rapid technological change are already being felt. Much of the economic analysis of new technology has focused on the hi-tech end of the market. Increasingly, though, success in adding value to exports and capturing a larger share of the final market price of agricultural and mineral exports depends on the processing of market information on prices, storage, and demand. Inability to operate in the information market is already costing desperately poor countries foreign exchange and government revenue. Over the past decade, the share of the 42 Least Developed Countries in world exports has fallen from 1 per cent to 0.5 per cent. Given that exports account on average for 25 per cent of GDP, this has grave implications for poverty reduction. But any attempt to reverse this decline will require a marked increase in the value added to exports through local knowledge, implying a prior improvement in average education performance. Much the same is true for other developing countries. Over the past three decades, only East Asia has significantly increased its share of world trade. Developing countries as a group still account for only about one-fifth of global trade flows. Once again, changing this picture will require a stronger performance in the knowledge-intensive sectors of international trade that are growing most rapidly.

As with any technology, the impact of information technologies on inequality and poverty will depend on how they are deployed and who has access to them. Making access available and affordable to poor countries and poor people should be viewed as a central part of the development process. In Bangladesh, the Grameen Bank, which provides micro-credit to small producers, has built on its experience to extend access to cellular technology. Communications technologies can provide access to resources, and facilitate teacher support and curriculum development. The African Virtual University, based in Nairobi, is aiming to increase university enrolments and improve the quality and relevance of instruction throughout the region.

Education and democracy

There is overwhelming evidence that education generates important benefits for human development. It is associated with more rapid and more equitable growth, it contributes to reductions in child mortality, and it enhances public health. Many of the gains result from the fact that education empowers people, enabling them to exercise greater choice and to exert more control over the events that shape their lives. There is, however, a dark side to education. The broad purpose of national education systems is to prepare children to participate in the economic, political, and social activities of the country, and to accept its values. Education is also used to transmit culture, to reinforce the status quo and, in some cases, to project attitudes that promote ideas of superiority and inferiority. Moreover, for all its liberating qualities, many children experience formal education as a system of learning that restricts initiative and creativity, rather than nurturing them. The relationship between education, democracy and empowerment, is complex. Education is clearly not a sufficient condition for democracy. At the same time, mass exclusion from education is as bad for democracy as it is for poverty reduction. There is also a sense in which education can create an impetus towards democracy, even if this is not what governments have in mind.

Mass education was to be designed primarily to create a supply of not particularly skilled but well-disciplined workers to operate in large-scale industrial units. Repetitive mass instruction was seen as a useful preparation for a system of low-wage employment, and it was inextricably bound up with the maintenance of social order and protection of vested interest. The corollary of the limited aim of mass education was a curriculum designed to promote rote-learning, mastery of basic literacy and numeracy, and respect for authority. William Lovett criticised the pedagogy of his day, condemning it as 'a rote-learning, memory-loading system dignified by the name of education '. Along with other reformers, he argued for education to be geared towards personal development. But rote-learning remained the order of the day until well into the twentieth century. Nowhere was State action in education less oriented towards realising human potential than in the colonies of European powers. It is sometimes forgotten that, in much of the developing world, education systems were developed under colonial authorities whose motivations owed less to considerations of personal development and democracy than to those of cost and self-interest. Their guiding theme was that any education provision should be cheap, financed out of local revenue, and geared to the labour needs of the colonial administration. Where education was provided, it typically involved the export of Western-style education, aimed at preparing a small (predominantly male) population for service in the administrative system. Efforts to establish a causal relationship between education, democracy, and the rule of law have been far from convincing. Many countries that have performed very strongly in education have, by most standards, achieved levels of democracy that compare unfavourably with far weaker performers.

Other countries have combined high levels of educational attainment with highly authoritarian governance –Malaysia and Singapore being two obvious examples. Few governments have prioritised democracy and empowerment in developing their education systems. Economic modernisation and 'nation-building 'have figured far more prominently.

Some have argued that education provided through formal State systems is inherently oppressive, placing an emphasis on the development of 'alternative ' structures. Such approaches are of limited relevance for the vast majority of poor people. The real challenge is to reform attitudes to education and school practices. Evidently, getting girls into schools designed to reinforce their limited role as providers and carers is not a strategy for empowerment. Similarly, the application of rote-learning technologies to equip children with minimal levels of numeracy is not a viable education strategy for the twenty-first century, any more than it was for the nineteenth. Some of the presumed tensions in education reform may be more apparent than real. Social movements in some countries have made education reform an integral part of a broader agenda for political democratisation. In Brazil, education indicators for landless rural communities compare unfavourably with those for much poorer countries in sub-Saharan Africa. Poverty, under-investment by government, and a curriculum widely perceived as being irrelevant to local needs are among the causes. The Movimento Sem Terra (SMT), the landless peoples's movement, has responded by placing education at the centre of its activities. Because the landless are highly mobile, 'moving schools 'have been developed, to follow the communities they serve. Wherever land occupations take place, the MST establishes schools and provides teachers.School curricula have been adjusted to meet local needs –and to assert the importance of claiming basic rights. The environment, agriculture, and the history of social movements in Brazil all figure prominently. Teacher-training programmes emphasise the participation of children and the development of an active learning environment. Adult literacy classes attached to the schools use materials directly relevant to local needs, including literature on health and basic rights.

Constraints on Human Development

The global challenges impose constraints on human development in several ways. First, they create a competition for resources to meet various social needs, all of which appear urgent and legitimate. There is a need to provide the poor and disadvantaged with basic subsistence needs, to remove the sources of social dislocation and disadvantage, to protect the environment, and to control excessive population growth. All these demands on a nation's public and private resources can, and sometimes do, take precedence over the learning needs of the population. In addition, the austerity measures adopted by governments suffering from inadequate financial resources can cause disproportionate cutbacks in societal development efforts.

The education sector, because it produces knowledge and skills, and the health sector, because it protects and extends the value of the population, are critical for development. However, government spending on health and education has declined — in relative and, in some cases, absolute terms—in many of the world's poorest countries.

In twenty-five out of thirty African and Latin American countries for which comparable data are available, the share of the government budget going to health and education has declined in the 1980s. In the world's thirty-seven poorest countries, spending per capita on health has declined 50 percent since 1980, while per pupil expenditure on education has declined by 25 percent.

In this context, the momentum of many societal development efforts has stalled, leaving hundreds of millions of people in conditions of absolute poverty. They are without adequate nutrition to sustain learning or labour, susceptible to diseases that could be controlled, unable to read or write, and so denied access to the very knowledge and skills that could improve the quality of their lives dramatically.

Economic development does not automatically increase the quantity or quality of human development.

A society must decide for itself to devote resources to education and other learning opportunities. The development experiences in the 1980s have demonstrated that social advancement is a fragile process. Without sustained efforts to improve the circumstances of the poorest members of society, overall development gains are undermined.

The enormity of the global challenges and the differences among rates of national and individual development now threaten further deterioration in the quality and equity of life chances. Unless dramatic and effective steps are taken to address these threats, the future may bring even greater poverty and growing polarization within and among societies.

A world in which only an elite few will live in health, safety, and prosperity must be avoided; all people deserve the opportunity to fulfill their human potential and contribute to shaping their society. In times of economic decline, austerity, and competing social and economic demands, basic education must be protected through overt measures. Otherwise, generations will be lost and whole segments of the population excluded from the development process.

The phenomenal expansion of the national education systems since the 1950s has continually increased the number and proportion of children in school and of adults with basic literacy skills. However, the absolute number of outofschool children and youth and of illiterate adults has also increased dramatically in the past thirty years. Today, more than onequarter of all adults still can neither read nor write. The more than 105 million children who are not in school mean adult illiteracy will remain a common problem into the next century.

The difficulty of combating nonschooling and illiteracy is compounded by other problems. Many students drop out before completing their primary schooling; others complete school but fail to acquire the necessary learning. In addition, whatever their previous formal education, significant parts of the adult population have yet to acquire the basic knowledge and life skills that, in addition to literacy, would improve the quality of their lives at home, in their communities, and in support of their nations. The critical problem facing governments and development agencies today is how to specify and meet the basic learning needs of all. These needs cannot be met by a simple quantitative expansion of educational programmes as they now exist although such aggregate expansion may be part of the solution in certain countries.

Despite the efforts and real accomplishments of previous decades, more and more people have needs for basic learning that are not being met. Continuing human development means that future generations of children, youth, and adults will need greater access to and continued participation in primary schooling and equivalent learning opportunities that provide an acceptable level of learning attainment. Given the number of children not currently enrolled in any school at all, it is imperative that each country identify these outofschool populations, determine why they are not participating, and adapt or design appropriate educational programmes to their specific conditions and needs.

In general, those outofschool are likely to be female, to be poor, to be ethnic or linguistic minorities, and to live in urban or periurban slums and remote rural locations. To meet the basic learning needs of such groups, formal education and other educational interventions must deal with the realities of their life circumstances and stress effective measures to attract and maintain their participation and to assure their learning achievement.

The nature and scope of the global challenges, and the effects of economic decline and fiscal constraints on investment in the social sectors, mean that a «business-as-usual" approach to basic education policies and programmes simply will not work. In the long-term, a failure to take decisive action to broaden the range, resources and suppliers of basic education opportunities would only deepen the present shortcomings and disparities, resulting in growing inequities in access to effective learning opportunities, increasing numbers of illiterate adults, and a growing population of youth and adults with inadequate knowledge and skills. Expanded forms of basic education for children, youth, and adults, and innovative modes of delivery and social mobilization to meet the broader scope implied by the term "basic learning" will be required, together with resources sufficient to reverse the declines that are occurring in some countries and to promote real improvements in all countries.

Human development, at the level of individuals involves a process of learning and of applying what is learned to better the quality of life. With more learning, both individuals and groups are better able to derive sustenance from their environment, to participate effectively in society, to meet challenges, to create new solutions, and to transform the world in a positive way. Learning is a catalyst for all development processes, whereas a lack of learning opportunities constrains the individual and societal ability to produce, or to benefit from, development. After four decades of successes and failures in economic development, it has become abundantly clear that economic, sociocultural, and environmental processes are closely linked; development or decay along one dimension profoundly affects the others. Each new development effort, whatever its focus, must recognize the complex interactions among all facets of life on this globe. This interactive nature of change requires a multisectoral, long-term, and international view of development in the design of programmes and policies.

The pivotal determinant of the success of these programmes and policies will be whether a country's population possesses the appropriate basic skills and knowledge.In many nations effective human development can help contain and even reverse the current threat of economic stagnation or decline. There is ample scientific evidence for the contributions of education to social and economic development. For instance, primary education is known to improve the productivity of workers in the factory and in the field and to provide the necessary skills for selfemployment and entrepreneurship. Basic learning of all types can help families earn higher incomes and make better use of their earnings through informed consumption choices and improved household management.

At the macroeconomic level, an analysis of a sample of developing countries indicated that increases in literacy contribute to increases in investment and in output per worker. Literacy, as well as nutrition and income, was also found to correlate with increased life expectancy and reduced infant and maternal mortality. Overall differences in patterns of educational investment, especially at the basic levels, are significant in explaining differences in national rates of economic growth and in other development indicators. Since the majority of workers in developing countries are engaged in subsistence agriculture, the effect of basic education on agricultural productivity has been an important policy issue and the subject of much research.

One study by the World Bank — based on eighteen analyses carried out in thirteen developing nations — concluded that a minimum of four years of primary education increased farmer productivity by an average of 8.7 percent for all countries and 10 percent for those undergoing modernization and growth. The greater the demands on farmers to adapt to changing technologies, credit, and marketing systems, the higher will be the benefits to those possessing basic skills. The effect of primary schooling on wage workers and entrepreneurs is indicated by the higher productivity of primary school graduates, as measured by adjusted earnings differentials.

Both private and social rates of returns to primary schooling have been shown to be high relative to other forms of schooling: in one multinational comparison social rates averaged 27 percent for primary and 1 5-17 percent for secondary education, while private rates averaged 49 and 26 percent respectively. They are also high relative to the common return to capital investments which is about 10 percent. Primary schooling is critical for promoting the productivity of small entrepreneurs because they face additional decisionmaking demands and retain a larger share of the benefits of their own productivity. As in the case of agriculture, primary schooling increases the productivity of both wage earners and entrepreneurs even more in situations of rapid change and development.

Economic disparities are reinforced and reproduced over time by unequal access to basic education and unequal achievement in learning. More equitable access to effective basic learning opportunities will immediately begin to reduce the gap between the least educated and the most educated within a society. Equity in basic learning will also make access to further learning more equitable by assuring that individuals can be selected for these opportunities on the basis of actual achievement, rather than family or community wealth.

The reduction of learning disparities has both immediate and longterm effects. Some of these effects are linked to the importance of education for technological advancement, which has the capacity to affect profoundly the life circumstances of every person today. All countries need citizens capable of working with and through technology. Increasingly, the possession of knowledge and reasoning ability defines individual and national efficacy. In a very real sense, to be deprived of basic education is to be deprived of the essential tools for modern living. Without the skills to participate in a literate, technological world and the knowledge to transform their environment, people will remain on the margins of society, and society itself will lose their vast potential contributions.

Meeting the basic learning needs of all has become of greater importance than ever, not only because of technological and other rapid changes in most societies, but also because of the increased global interdependency of nations in their cultural and economic activities. As a prerequisite for social, cultural, and economic development, education contributes to reducing disparities and building common understanding among people of different countries, socioeconomic origins, and cultural identities. Effective education is a unique means to promote participation of all individuals in their local communities and in this global society.

Marginalized populations depend on their knowledge and problemsolving skills to deal with the hardships created by war, civil strife, and crime, as well as discrimination. Basic education is one means of attacking the root causes of these conditions and, at the same time, of providing immediate knowledge and skills for dealing with their effects. Increasing the level of basic learning helps alleviate conditions of disadvantage and thus contributes to reduction of social disparity. Marginalized populations need basic education to prepare them for effective migration, social and occupational mobility, access to new information and markets, and adaptation to new environments.

Meeting the basic learning needs of these groups will not solve their problems, but it must be a part of the solution. In particular, nonconventional forms of basic education are needed for those whose lives have been disrupted by forces beyond their control. These problems affect all countries: the growing levels of functional illiteracy in the industrialized economies show that they too are not immune to such problems.

To combat environmental degradation, people must not only understand the effect of their actions on the environment but also accept responsibility for them. They must not shift the costs of their actions to people in other geographical areas or to future generations. Increased basic knowledge helps to inform individuals of the real costs of environmental damage and to promote social acceptance of regulations to restrict environmentally damaging acts and measures to promote ecologically sound development.

The replenishment of ecologically imperiled lands can be set in motion by tapping the traditional environmental knowledge of the land's inhabitants. People with local knowledge of food production under harsh conditions, medicinal practices, literary and artistic forms, and local institutions and community processes, are a rich cultural resource. To bring this precious knowledge to bear on contemporary problems of the environment, the people who possess it must be equipped with the basic knowledge and skills that will enable them to function effectively in their societies.

Education, particularly of girls and women, does a great deal to control rapid population growth by promoting collective health and wellbeing. Educated women and men can make informed choices about when to have children and are better able to maintain their own and their children's health. This benefits the society by curbing excessive population growth and improving the overall health of the population. Research has demonstrated that women's educational attainment is strongly related to reduced rates of maternal and infant mortality, and to improved nutrition in the family.

The process by which basic learning affects population growth is complex and varies among countries. Normally it involves several interrelated factors, such as better understanding of family planning options, increased re sources, changes in attitudes, and reduced infant mortality. Where population growth remains a serious barrier to real economic growth, education will offer a significant means of dealing with the problem because of its effects on fertility.

3

Distance Education: Promises and Problems

Although it is thought of as a new term, 'distance learning' has been around for well over 100 years. One of the earlier forms of distance learning was done through correspondence courses started in Europe. This stayed the primary means of distance learning until the middle of this century when instructional radio and television became more popular. As technology has changed, so has the definition of distance learning. Videotaped lectures have been a standard in university and professional courses for the last two decades. Audiotapes and lessons sent through the mail have been used in correspondence courses to teach subjects such as foreign language for quite some time. Today, the Internet and compressed video have taken distance learning in new directions, allowing distance learning to occur in real time.

Distance education and training result from the technological separation of teacher and learner which frees the student from the necessity of traveling to a fixed place, at a fixed time, to meet a fixed person, in order to be trained. From these definitions we can see that the student and teacher are separated by space, but not necessarily by time. This would include compressed video, which is delivered in real time. As stated earlier, this type of live video instruction is the fastest growing means of distance learning today. Because of this, much of the discussion here will be dedicated to the promises and problems of this technology. Many of the promises of distance learning are financial in nature. Universities hope to save money by delivering education to students that are unable to attend classes because of time or distance. The theory is that class size increases while the overhead remains the same. Developing countries are turning to state run distance education programs to take the place of ever increasing enrollments and a lack of physical building space.

Distance-learning techniques to reach those that would by any other means be unreachable. Countries like China are moving from 'elite to mass education,' and that 'traditional universities cannot meet the demand'. China uses a radio and television delivery system to serve 1.5 million students, two-thirds of which are in a degree program. In Australia, Curtain University uses compressed video conferencing to reach remote students in Western Australia, and to enhance classes in Business Studies by connecting with students in Singapore. Other examples can be found in the UK and Norway where several sites have been linked together. Of course there is also wide use in the United States, both in the public and private sectors. It should be obvious by these examples and by the definition of distance learning, that it can meet the promise to deliver classes to a geographically broad and diverse population. Not only that, but the need seems to be strong for such programs. According to the American Council on Education, the number of students in distance learning doubled from 1995 to 1998 totaling 1.6 million. Another market forecast says that by the year 2002 there will be 2.2 million students in distance education program, a full 15 per cent of all U.S. college students. Many Universities are feeling the pressure to control their costs, improve quality of instruction, focus on customer needs, and respond to the competitive pressures. Distance learning technologies have the potential to assist in solving these problems. In 1994, Basom and Sherritt surveyed higher education administrators and state politicians to find out what they thought would be the major problems facing American higher education in the next millennium. The answers they most often received were: meeting increased demands at a time of decreased resources, increasing or maintaining access, using technology more efficiently, and sharing resources across state lines so that colleges won't have to be all things to all people.

Distance learning seems to address all of these issues. Administrators hope that distance learning methods will help make higher education more cost-effective. This type of answer may be seen as a quick fix for many administrators. If not approached seriously however, the distance programs can quickly become second rate. The convenience of time and space is a big promise made by distance learning. Students do not have to physically be with the instructor in space and, depending on the method used, they do not have to be together in time as well. This is a great advantage for non-traditional students who cannot attend at regular times. Satellite campuses such as the ones Arkansas State University have recently opened are drawing out a 'hidden market' of adult students in small towns and recent high school graduates who don't want to go away to a bigger city to get an education. The satellite campuses could conceivably help the school's enrollment to grow tenfold.

Despite the promises and obvious advantages to distance learning, there are problems that need to be resolved. These problems include the quality of instruction, hidden costs, misuse of technology, and the attitudes of instructors, students, and administrators. Each one of these has an effect on the overall quality of distance learning as a product. In many ways, each of these issues relates to the others. We will examine each of these issues separately.

The first issue is the quality of instruction that is given through distance learning programs. Much of the quality of instruction depends on the attitude of the administration and the instructor. Instructors had conflicting attitudes about teaching distance education. After teaching one course, the majority of instructors were willing to teach another, but that they rated the quality of the course as only equal or lower quality than other classes taught on campus. Many times it seems that the administration believes the technology itself will improve the quality of the class.

Technology does not teach students; effective teachers do. They make the point that the issue is not technology itself, but how it is used in the design and delivery of courses. Too often instructors do not design their lessons to take advantage of the technology presented. This affects the quality of the instruction. Research suggests that the effectiveness of distance learning is based on preparation, the instructor's understanding of the needs of the students, and an understanding of the target population. Higher education administrators that many of the decision makers view distance programs as second rate, a "necessary but deficient form of education. In academic departments that have no strong mandates to adjust their curriculum and instruction to fit distance learning beyond cursory cooperation. There are no rewards for doing so and the effort takes away from research time.

The potential cost-effectiveness of using online technologies in distance education is still uncertain. The concepts of costs and effectiveness are not as simple as they first appear. It is possible for a program to be efficient but not cost effective if the outputs which are actually produced do not contribute to the program objectives: that is it may be efficient at doing the wrong things. Human capital and the costs of conversion are expenses that can easily be underestimated. The cost of online courses is affected by how they are implemented: as an enhancement or as the primary teaching medium. If it is implemented as a primary teaching medium, it is considerably more expensive.

The teaching purpose of the different approaches needs to be taken into account. If this is not factored in by administration, there may be costs that are not apparent at first glance. In a study at the University of Northern Colorado that when electronic distance delivery costs were compared with those of instructor travel directly to the site, the least costly alternative was the live instruction with the instructor traveling to the remote site compressing the class into fewer weeks. This alternative was one-third the cost of any other alternative. Starting a compressed video distance-learning program is not cheap. Southern Arkansas University-Magnolia decided to try compressed video as an alternative to other methods.

The startup equipment for the unit was approximately $80,000. Establishment of a permanent T-1 telephone line was another $1,200 per month. These costs are startup only and do not reflect any of the human capital costs as discussed earlier. The California State University System that looked at cost savings in distance learning programs. In really large courses with many sections would cost savings be possible. Courses in excess of 500 students would benefit from this setup, while it was still more cost effective to teach smaller groups in a traditional setting. The startup costs, maintenance costs, and personnel costs should also be factored in to arrive at a true cost for a distance-learning program. The minimum number of staff required for delivery of a compressed video class would be one instructor and two technicians, one at each site. This means a minimum of three people is needed to deliver the same class as one instructor does in a traditional setting. The costs associated with training technicians and instructors should not be overlooked. For effective distance education to take place, the staff delivering the instruction should be well trained.

Besides the cost of the technology, there is the possibility of not utilizing all its potential. Some of these problems arise from a lack of training, some from the instructor's attitudes about using the technology, and still others by hardware problems. It seems to be self evident that instructors need to be trained to use distance learning technology, but too often they are not. Once again, it appears that administration may feel that the technology itself will improve the course. Advancement in technology does not lead to effective distance education. The best distance education practices depend on creative, well-informed instructors. Newer technologies are not inherently better than old ones and many of the lessons learned from the application of older technologies will still apply to any newer technology. Again, the instructor should be trained to take advantage of both their experience and being able to adapt that experience to the new environment of distance learning. The instructors must be trained not only to use technology, but also to shift the way in which they organize and deliver material.

One overlooked factor in the success or failure of distance learning programs is the role that the technicians play in distance learning. Of course they play a large role in the technical delivery, but little is known about the non-technical activities of the technicians that could have an influence on the instructional process. Technicians could indirectly influence the learning environment by orientating participants to the technology, reducing the anxiety of the participants (including the instructor), and by advising the instructor on instructional techniques. This type of role, if viewed negatively by the instructor, can have a huge impact on the quality of the presentation, yet many times the instructor and the technicians do not meet until the initial class meeting. The technicians felt the instructors were given inadequate orientation to the equipment and really could not operate it until they had hands on experience.

The technicians also saw a difference in the instructors who could adapt their styles to the technology, and those who could not. Those who adapted were, in the opinion of the technicians, superior in conducting the classes. So see not only does the instructor need to adapt to the educational environment, they must also adapt to another person in the room that can help or hinder the delivery of the lesson. Much of the outcome depends on the attitude of the instructor.

Equipment and hardware malfunctions can be a great detriment to the effectiveness of distance learning. When a problem occurs in a class everything comes to a standstill and the learning environment is interrupted. If there are too many instances, the entire course can be affected. For instance, if an overhead projector goes out during an instructor's presentation, an alternate way of delivering that information can easily be found. However, if a compressed video presentation has problems, the entire class must be stopped until the problem is resolved. If the instructor goes ahead with the lesson, one site will miss out on that information.

Despite problems with hardware that may or may not get worked out with new advances in technology, we must come back to instructors and their attitudes towards teaching in a distance-learning environment as a major potential roadblock to effective distance education. As in any educational situation, the instructor can set the tone for learning in the educational environment. That instructor must be properly trained and motivated to be effective. An instructor must have technological skills and confidence to use all of the various electronic devices in order to be truly effective in the electronic classroom. Instructors must also change the manner in which information is delivered. While lecture does not work well, multimedia presentations are successful. Of course this means more preparation time for the instructor and the motivation must be there. Adult distance learning that to effectively bridge the gaps between classroom and distance teaching, faculty need to look at the distance teaching from the students' point of view.

The faculty must also be aware of getting instructional materials, handouts, tests, and other class items to both sites simultaneously. It is important for the instructors to develop a sense of community between the sites, achieve maximum participation, and get the participants to buy in to the process. The idea of learning as a collaborative process is very important when students are separated by distance. Collaborative learning processes assists students to achieve deeper levels of knowledge generation through the creation of shared goals, shared exploration, and a shared process of meaning making. It is up to the instructor to be aware of this in the distance learning environment and to encourage collaborative learning and a sense of community among the students. Another important consideration for the instructor is their view regarding the goal of distance education. There are two main thoughts on this. They submit that the goal of distance education in the United States is "to offer the distance student an experience as much like that of traditional, face-to-face instruction as possible". This would mean that distance learning pedagogy would not differ much from that used in an ordinary classroom.

The instructor must decide which attitude they will adopt because it has a profound impact on their approach to instruction. Instructors also have adaptations they need to make to the technology. An instructor used to visual cues may find it difficult to adapt to a situation such as compressed video. The students at the remote site are not always in clear view of the instructor. The lack of visual cues a major adaptation for the instructor. Part of this can be alleviated by good communication with the technician, but as earlier, that communication is not always present. Proximity and eye contact are important factors in education that are limited in the distance learning environment. Inherently recognize the connection these provide, but in the distance learning environment they are "both severely and sometimes permanently compromised".

Instructors have other concerns about distance learning, primarily how it will change their role in education. National survey of attitudes of higher education faculty that there was a moderately positive attitude about distance learning in general, but moderately negative attitudes about their own use of it. Writing about geography educators, Gober worries that if they rely too much on distance-learning techniques, the discipline would "risk losing our collective soul in the rush to convenience, cost-effectiveness, and accountability". Instructors worry about putting their course materials online because once there, the knowledge and course design skill in that material is out of their possession. This puts the administration in a position to hire less skilled, and cheaper, workers to deliver the technologically prepackaged course. Instructors are not always convinced that administration is behind distance learning.

The rewards are not always there for the good distance-learning instructor. "Tenure and promotion usually does not recognize excellent off campus teaching which, in fact, takes valuable time from research agendas". This puts the instructors behind when trying to publish to get their department recognized. The increased amount of time necessary to adequately prepare for distance learning takes away from the activities they will be evaluated on, such as grant writing and publishing. Many of the instructors concerns are valid and should be addressed by administration as distance learning becomes more common, as is predicted to happen. Finally, there are the students and their concerns with distance learning classes. Not all students are suited to this type of learning and not all subjects are best taught via this medium. More mature students are the most likely to find success with distance learning. The successful student needs to have a number of characteristics such as tolerance for ambiguity, a need for autonomy, and an ability to be flexible.

Compared to most face-to-face learning environments, distance learning requires students to be more focused, better time managers, and to be able to work independently and with group members. Many distance learners are different from traditional undergraduates in that they are already in professions. They have well defined goals and are more motivated. Distance education students need to feel a part of a community. This as a virtual learning community. Students in these communities often feel less pressure to perform individually, and more pressure to collaborate and be part of the team. Being involved in a collaborative learning process is an important part of forming the foundation of a learning community. When this is not encouraged, participation is generally low and dialog is absent.

Students also need the attention of the instructors. This may be truer in a distance situation than in a traditional classroom. In a situation where eye contact and proximity are limited, students cannot be disciplined nor affirmed by eye contact and body language. Students may also have a difficult time reading the reactions of the remote location class members. This lack of interaction can cause problems when there is a dissenting opinion that cannot be picked up on with non-verbal cues, and is misperceived as a verbal attack. This type of miscommunication can cause the community problems as the class progresses. It is fair to say that compressed video can magnify the strengths and weaknesses of the instructor. Students are prone to pick up on a lack of organization and direction and respond with apathy and absenteeism.

What may conclude from the promises and problems of distance learning? Are there possibilities for improvement in the future? The technology will undoubtedly keep improving and the price will drop, as technology is prone to do once it comes into general use. Already we see improvement in the delivery systems of compressed video and computer assisted instruction. Despite student problems with distance learning, studies indicate they are relatively satisfied with what they are receiving. A study of students at Indiana University of Pennsylvania found 75% were very satisfied with the instruction they received and 90% rating the technology as satisfactory. Another study was done on a distance learning accounting course at the University of Connecticut. They found that 57.5% would take another such course. Two other findings were generally favorable and included comments on how the course could be improved. The first suggested the instructors needed to be comfortable with the medium, and that the students needed to have more guidance on how to fully take advantage of the presentation. The second showed that students were highly satisfied with the instructors and the course, but that direct interaction with the instructor played no role in the students' satisfaction. It would seem one element that needs immediate improvement is with instructors.

Many excellent ways that instructors can better prepare for the classroom including multimedia use, speaking voice, and even font size considerations. Instructors also need to realize that the technician is an integral part of the experience of distance learning and treat them as such. Many times opinions and communication between the technician and the instructor are not shared either because the technician's role is unclear, or there is a shared perception of a difference in status between the two. Instructors must be motivated to prepare adequately for classes. Part of the responsibility for motivation must lie with the administration and their support of the program. Because teaching a distance learning class involves a new role for instructors, administrators must provide them with the time, the tools, and the training to meet these new responsibilities. Administration needs to train and educate instructors on this role and how to meet the challenges. Higher education administrators that for whatever reasons, higher education administrators and politicians understand the need for technology. But, lacking the heart for distance education, they cannot bring themselves to support it with adequate personnel, simple supplies, and a reasonable operating budge. This sort of attitude from administration can do nothing but trickle down into the instructors and the students. Administrators need to carefully weigh their goals and objectives when taking on a distance education program.

Instructional Technology

With the recent growth of the Internet and other distance technologies, web based course delivery has become an attractive option for expanding the educational opportunities available to students. In this section we are going to discuss a pilot study documents and a comparative evaluation of the three course formats. Many research studies have shown that cognitive factors such as learning, performance, and achievement in distance education classes are comparable to those observed in traditional classes, however, perceptions and satisfaction levels of instructors and students of distance education have not shown the same consistency. Factors such as accessibility to materials, other students, instructors, control of time, and cost can influence individuals' perceptions of distance education. Students were pleased with the performance of their instructor, availability of materials, and performance of technological tools used for conducting the class, while Carr found that undergraduates enrolled in an introductory psychology course performed better in distance education courses, but were generally less happy with them.

Students in the web based course consistently scored an average of five percentage points higher on the final exam than did those in the lecture course, but they consistently reported less satisfaction than the students in the lecture course. Carr surmised that one of the reasons for less satisfaction could be more time required to complete assignments. In a study of adult distance education students, most students did not find that technological equipment used in distance education interfered with the instruction. Distance education students look for many of the same things found in traditional courses including a knowledgeable professor, interaction with the professor, and additional features that create a feeling of community within the class. Student ratings for two courses taught in both a traditional and distance format by the same instructor. No differences in the overall course grade means of the students and in the students' ratings of the course, instructor, teaching, and communication method were found. However, conflicting results were found for the ratings of class organization. For one course, the distance education class was rated as more organized than the traditional class, while for the other course; the distance education class was rated as less organized. The satisfaction, grades, and performance of students in a semester-long graduate social work course taught in a distance format were consistent with previous outcomes in traditional courses of similar content. In addition to web based courses consisting of an instructor created web site, many instructors are now using course delivery platforms such as WebCT or Blackboard. On a study in which courses taught through traditional means were converted into units using WebCT software as the primary means of delivery. Results indicated overall satisfaction with the WebCT software and the organization and content of the units.

The satisfaction levels and perceptions of 39 social work students regarding the use of WebCT in social work education course. All students responded that they found the course materials on the course Web site helpful. Graduate and nontraditional students' responses indicated greater use of the course management tools and nontraditional students responded that they were not disadvantaged by, and preferred access to, Web based courses. Student attitudes toward the Internet and web based courses can influence the future use of the web based instructional materials and how educationally beneficial web based resources are for students. Instructor attitudes toward web based instruction also affect student's experiences with web based courses. The National Education Association administered a survey in which 75% of the instructors surveyed indicated that they were positive about distance education. Most instructors currently teaching a distance education course indicated they would be willing to participate in a distance education course again, however, when asked about the quality of the distance education course, nearly 50% of the instructors indicating they would participate in a distance education course again that the quality of the distance education course, when compared to a traditional course, was lower. Additionally, not one instructor indicated that the distance education course was of higher quality.

The purpose of the pilot study was to compare the efficacy of the three class formats, as well as to learn from the experience. To this end, we compared student performance, student satisfaction, and instructor experiences. In addition the study documented the benefits and limitations of the three delivery alternatives. We believe this was a unique opportunity to compare the three formats. Furthermore, due to the composition of the student population at our school, we believe that our students are more representative of those who might be interested in enrolling in web based classes. Most of the students in our institution work full or part-time and attend classes at night. Intuitively, it would seem that Web delivered classes would be very attractive to this demographic group. The course offered was an undergraduate introductory course in Management Information Systems. It is a survey course, and was selected for this reason. The publisher provided the text, web materials, and an extensive examination test bank. Two instructors taught the three sections, the traditional section covered by one instructor, and the other sections by a second instructor. All sections covered substantially similar material, and completed similar assignments. The course formats were as follows:

— *Traditional section:* The course was offered in a lecture/discussion format with hands-on individual and group assignments in simple web site development. Testing was accomplished via multiple-choice exams using questions selected by the instructor from the publisher's test bank, and administered in class using mark sense forms (Scantron). All class materials were distributed in class and also published on the web for student convenience.

— *Web based section:* This section was offered almost exclusively on the web. Class met briefly once a week to go over hands-on assignments similar to the ones in the traditional format, as well as for testing purposes. Course materials in the form of lectures on streaming media, lecture notes, text based supplementary materials, discussion groups, and testing were offered through the WWW. The course used WebCT as the course delivery platform. Test questions were drawn from the same test bank used for the traditional section. The lectures were videotaped and coordinated with lecture notes in a video-streaming format.

— *Hybrid section:* A third section of this course was offered using a mix of traditional and web based delivery means. Class met for lectures, assignments, and tests, while WebCT was used to deliver course materials as well as conduct discussions and exams. The exams and assignments in this section were duplicates of those used for the web based section.

The sample consisted of students enrolled in the three sections of a junior level Introduction to Information Systems course. The three sections participating in the study comprised all of the sections offered during the academic term studied. This course was required of all students in the School of Business, thus insuring a broad cross-section of our business student population. The number of students enrolled were 41 in the traditional course section, 40 in the hybrid course section, and 53 in the web based course section. Most of the students were juniors.

The instruments used in the study consisted of multiple-choice exams using questions selected by the instructors from the publisher's test bank and a researcher-developed questionnaire. The exams themselves contained a different mix of topics, thus precluding direct exam-to-exam comparison. Nevertheless, since the classes covered the same topics and questions were drawn from the same test bank, a direct comparison of the average of the exam scores was possible. Student satisfaction was considered important for the long-term success of web based course offerings. For this purpose a researcher-developed questionnaire addressing the specifics of the course offerings was administered to the students in the three course sections; the questionnaire included both objective and open-ended questions.

The questionnaire was composed of questions addressing overall student satisfaction and satisfaction with the course format, student motivation for selecting a particular course format, and whether students were willing to enroll in a similar course in the future. The questionnaire used to elicit these responses was simple and did not include provisions for calculation of validity and reliability statistics. In addition to this, students filled out the routine teaching evaluation survey administered to all classes. Instructor experiences were also documented through discussion and anecdotal references. The goal was to document problems experienced, as well as potential solutions to them. Also instructor satisfaction with the course format and supporting materials were of interest.

Student performance was evaluated by comparing exam scores between the two classes using duplicate exams, and as an aggregate using overall exam averages. The goal was to determine if there were significant differences in student performance between classes. Although two different instructors taught the three course sections studied, use of the same text, similar assignments, and test bank questions and format allow for direct comparison. It should be noted that the instructors had also taught the course for a number of years and had a long history of coordinating the content, topic sequence and projects in the different sections. A direct comparison of exam scores for three of the four exams administered in the hybrid and a web based class was undertaken. The first of the four exams was excluded from this comparison due to problems encountered when administering this exam.

Although student performance is an important measure of the success of a web based curriculum, student satisfaction is important for the continued success of such a program. It was therefore important to gauge student feelings about the web based course. This was accomplished by asking the students how they felt about the course, as well as whether they might want to take a course offered in a similar format again. It was also of interest to ascertain the reason the students had selected a particular section and the attendant delivery format. Students were asked these questions as part of the researcher developed questionnaire. First, it was important to establish why students had enrolled in a particular section of this course. The assumption here was that students would select the web based section deliberately. Unfortunately, the course schedule given to students did a poor job of differentiating the web based course from those offered in a regular format. In particular the web based section was listed in the schedule at a specific time and place, with only a cursory note indicating it was to be web based. It is quite probable that many students were unaware that they had enrolled in a web based course.

Students were also asked if they were satisfied with the course. A five point Likert scale with a range from Strongly Disagree to Strongly Agree was used to gauge student satisfaction. Examination of the data show that students enrolled in the web based section were somewhat less satisfied with the course than other students. This was confirmed through the use of a Chi square test of independence, which showed the results as independent at the 0.079 level of significance. The data then, show evidence of different satisfaction levels due to differing course formats. It is quite likely, as will be discussed later, that problems encountered by students in the web class may have had some impact on their satisfaction level. Results from the teaching evaluation survey were also illuminating. Although the survey used is instructionally mandated, three of the questions in the survey seemed particularly relevant to this situation. It is quite evident that the students in the web based class had a different instructional experience than those in the two other sections.

Table 1: Teaching Evaluations

Question	*Traditional Class*	*Hybrid Class*	*Web based Class*
Method of Presentation Easy to Follow	3.632	3.235	2.419
Improved Understanding of Concepts and Principles	3.421	3.059	2.545
Explained Difficult Material Clearly	3.632	3.059	2.484

Finally, students were asked if they would enroll in a similar course in the future. This was intended to draw on the students' experience, and determine future intentions. Presumably, dissatisfied students would not wish to enroll in the same format course again. Most students would be willing to enroll in a similar format course again. There is however, a substantial degree of dissent among those students enrolled in the web based class.

Table 2: Sign-up for Similar Course in the Future (# Students)

Section	*Yes*	*No*
Traditional Class	35	3
Hybrid Class	30	4
Web based Class	33	17

Analyzing the data presented above, it is evident that students were not completely satisfied with the web based course offering. There are a number of factors that may have contributed to this perception. Some of these will be addressed in the next section covering the instructional experience. From a student perspective, though, two factors come to mind. It is quite likely that students having less technological mastery would have a less than satisfactory experience. It is also likely that students who are not self-motivated would find web based courses less satisfactory.

It is important to preface the following observations by stating that this was the first time a web based class was offered in this discipline at this institution. Both instructors had used the web previously to enhance traditional class formats, but a complete web course had not been offered. This was therefore a learning experience, and although efforts were made to follow recommendations, mistakes were made. Several areas that adversely affected the conduct of the web based and hybrid classes were the adoption of a course delivery platform, consistent instructional support, and course material delivery difficulties. The course delivery platform selected for this course was WebCT. This platform was selected to take advantage of the web based materials available from the book publisher.

The web based course section, as well as the hybrid course section used this platform. The hybrid section did not use the publisher produced course materials, relying instead on instructor-supplied materials. WebCT, in the form maintained by the institution's instructional support staff, did not always work consistently. This was a source of frustration for both students and the instructor. For example, it was originally intended that all exams would be administered through WebCT in a proctored lab environment. After a dismal experience with the first exam, this approach was abandoned and the class reverted to traditional mark sense forms (Scantron). There were also problems with the grade delivery facilities and occasionally with the delivery of course materials. These experiences quickly reduced the instructor's and the students' confidence in the course delivery technology. It should be pointed out that these technologies are rapidly evolving and may be less problematic in other instructional environments. Another aspect of adopting course delivery platforms is the extent to which they limit the instructor's ability to control the presentation and format of the class web site. As mentioned above, both instructors had experience with maintaining course web sites, but not with the use of course delivery platforms. In this regard, the WWW/hybrid instructor experienced a steep learning curve with the web delivery platform.

A frustrating aspect of this learning curve was the discovery of the limitations inherent in the use of a course delivery platform. WebCT and other platforms are designed to provide the instructor with the facilities to create a class web site with a number of supporting functions. Unfortunately, in order to deliver this functionality, they require that the instructor strictly adhere to their methods and procedures. This can be particularly frustrating for instructors who are accustomed to directly manipulating the contents of a course web site. In this particular case, certain functions were ultimately provided through a separate web site in order to reduce the amount of effort required in delivering them.

An area that was not well implemented in our situation was that of instructional support. Among the materials provided to the web based class were videotaped lectures available through the web in the form of streaming media. The support to tape and prepare these lectures was lacking, and on occasion lagged behind the class schedule. This lack of support also manifested itself in the sluggish resolution of student problems accessing the materials, and in the lab facilities available to students. Although these problems had some impact on all of the course sections, they were felt most severely in the web based section.The web based class also suffered from problems in consistently accessing web materials through the Internet. These problems fell in several areas. In the case of streaming media, there were problems with student's having the right software to receive it, as well as being able to maintain an Internet connection consistent enough to use it. There were also problems stemming from the students' choice of Internet Service Provider, and their peculiar ways of delivering Internet content. Although data were not collected to verify the extent and nature of these problems, anecdotal reports from frustrated students were abundant. Finally, the students enrolled in the web based section were not uniformly knowledgeable in the use of the web and its technologies. Their knowledge and skills ranged from rudimentary to well advanced. This required the use of some of the limited class time to demonstrate the use of particular features. Unfortunately, this lack of knowledge also meant that some students could not adequately configure their computer systems. Ultimately these experiences probably had a negative impact on students' satisfaction with the web based course.

Student performance was remarkably consistent from one section to another. Whether this can attributed to instructional performance is debatable. From an instructional perspective, this means that other WWW sections can be offered with little concern over how well students will do in comparison with courses taught conventionally. This finding is also in agreement with other distance learning studies. For the WWW delivered course, improvement is necessary from both the students' and instructor's perspective. It is clear that the delivery problems, lack of support, and the student's prior mastery of the Internet contributed to the lower satisfaction levels. Presumably future classes will benefit from some of the lessons learned here, and result in more satisfied students. Some of the things that require improvement are:

— Web based courses should be clearly designated and advertised as such to prevent student confusion at the time of enrollment. Students should be informed regarding course delivery methodology and the requirements for student participation. This is particularly important from the point of view of student satisfaction, as students' expectations must be molded to fit the constraints of web based course delivery.

— Course delivery platforms need to provide more stable and consistent delivery of their content. It would also help if these platforms were more flexible in allowing the instructor to tailor them to meet class requirements.

— Support for web delivered classes needs to be expanded. Both students and instructors require support. Student and instructional needs may differ, but lack of support leads to low satisfaction in both groups.

— Clear and specific specifications for the student's computer hardware, software, and telecommunications must be published prior to course registration so that enrolling students can be ready to participate in the WWW course.

— A final area that may be out of hands of students and instructors is rapid and consistent access to the Internet. Although high speed Internet access is slowly becoming available in urban areas, it will take some time before it becomes widespread. This situation limits the features that instructors can use when delivering web content.

Faculty Role in Teaching at a Distance

The expanding adoption of distance education has led researchers to explore faculty attitudes. Many studies have questioned the educational equivalency of distance courses when compared to the traditional classroom. Distance education is often viewed as second-best to classroom, face-to-face instruction. Faculty philosophically believe that distance courses result in lower levels of cognition.

The level of cognition is equal in both traditional and distance courses. In order to ascertain equivalency a standard of measurement must be agreed upon for effective communication. Communication is essential if innovation is to spread. Changing the philosophical nature of how courses are measured is key to communication. Currently the Carnegie unit (time based) is used to show the equivalency of traditional courses. Unit of measure to be inappropriate for distance courses. Their research indicated that the Capabilities-Based Educational Equivalency model is a more practical instrument for both traditional and distance courses. This model relies on academic achievement rather than time to measure the class equivalency. There is also a current view that distance education courses require a greater effort and time commitment.

Distance education courses can call for up to twice as much time and effort to accomplish the task. However, the findings also support the need for further research in this area to investigate what implications the course content and distance technology used has on the requirements for instructor preparation and delivery of the class. This may also impact philosophical opposition to distance education. Another challenge facing implementation of distance education is faculty skepticism. The transition from elite to mass higher education, with its tremendous growth in the numbers of both faculty and students from more diverse backgrounds, results in a greater variety of notions about what university education should be and whom it should serve. In order for faculty to support distance education, it must be considered congruent with the beliefs and values already held about university education. In turn, for universities to remain competitive they must find ways to employ new models of instructional delivery. To accomplish this task the administration has to first persuade faculty to adopt the model.

Research in the field of distance education has recognized the need for a change and modification of the faculty role in teaching at a distance. It is not the distance education technology that drives the instruction but rather the primary changes in teaching style, technique, and motivation that must take place for instruction of the present and future to function effectively. Many studies cite faculty resistance to instructional technology as a primary barrier to the continued growth of distance education programs. How faculty perceive and react to these technologies is more important than the structural and technical obstacles in affecting the use of technology in distance education. Student success and satisfaction in distance education courses was substantially and positively correlated to their interaction with instructors. College of Agriculture faculty lacked experience in teaching learners at a distance, and that they were much more confident in their technical competence than they were in their methodological ability to use modern technologies in their teaching.

Faculty members who had not participated in distance education perceived the level of support as lower than those who had taught courses at a distance. Faculty generally did not perceive the climate to be supportive of the use of technology. The ability of an organization to adapt to change is influenced by: competence or the knowledge, skills, and abilities of its staff; value or the amount of importance the staff places on the role of these technologies to accomplish teaching and learning; information technology support or the availability of high quality facilities, equipment, technical support, and training. Little is known, however, about how these factors affect faculty adoption of distance education. Tenure status and academic rank have an effect on the adoption of distance education models. Non-tenured, Assistant Professors had the highest distance education competency scores. This led to the conclusion that newer faculty are being hired with the expectation of using distance education technologies and already possess the self-efficacy and skills to integrate technology. It is further noted that faculty who have the comfort and competence are the ones discouraged from participating in distance education due to current policies for promotion and tenure. The study also found that female faculty had the highest distance education value scores and stated a need for further research in this area. As Universities consider and adopt distance education models, more information is needed on teachers philosophical positions towards the distance educational model used to deliver instruction. Such information can be useful in determining strategies, procedures, and processes necessary for delivery at a distance.

As an example, this section examies a pilot study in the College of Agriculture and Life Sciences at a land grant institution by their philosophical position towards distance education competence, value, and information technology support. The research presented identified the connection between value and philosophical position in respect to faculty acceptance and adoption. This provides new information on why faculty members may or may not choose to engage in distance delivery methods and contributes to the growing body of literature on faculty perceptions with respect to distance education. Such information can be useful to faculty and administrators as institutions of higher education strive to make strategic decisions about their distance education mission, vision, strategies, structures, processes, and systems. The objectives of the study were:

— To describe and examine teaching faculty by philosophical position towards distance education.

— To examine differences in distance education competency score by philosophical position to distance education.

— To examine differences in distance education value score by philosophical position towards distance education.

— To examine differences in distance education information technology and support score by philosophical position towards distance education.

The population for the study was all teaching faculty in a College of Agriculture at a land grant institution. A census of the population was surveyed. Department heads were asked to provide a complete listing of faculty members in their department who held teaching appointments. With all departments, Department heads identified a total of 331 faculty members with teaching appointments to be included in the initial sample. There were sixteen of these faculty members who subsequently provided documentation that they did not posses teaching appointments. The population of teaching faculty numbered 315. Of the 315 survey instruments mailed, 196 were returned within two weeks, for an effective initial response rate of 62.2%. After three weeks, a reminder letter was sent to non-respondents along with a second copy of the survey instrument. A follow up e-mail reminder was sent to non-respondents four weeks after the initial mail out. Those non-responding teaching faculty without valid e-mail addresses were contacted via telephone. All non-respondents were contacted via telephone six weeks after the initial mailing, in some cases at home. In each case, they were encouraged to complete the survey and additional instruments were supplied upon request. In all, 252 survey instruments were returned for a final response rate of 80.0%.

The instrument used to collect data was a two-part questionnaire designed by the researchers. The instrument was four pages long and designed to be automatically scanned into a digital file by an optical character recognition (OCR) scanner. Value refers to the nine items used to measure value or the importance of the role respondents believed these technologies have or will have to teaching agriculture. Specific scale items include:

— The Internet/WWW are convenient ways to access information

— Participation in listservs, threaded discussion groups, chats and other electronic communications offers great benefits

— Electronic communications and information will drastically alter how teach in the next five years

— Electronic communications and information will drastically alter what teach in the next five years

— most course materials would be improved by incorporating multimedia

— Animated graphics increase student interest and retention

— Students today prefer a more visual learning experience

— Electronic information technologies provide students with instantly available supplemental course and research materials

— It is important that incorporate electronic information technologies in the course(s).

Information technology and support refers to the eight items used to measure the perceived availability of equipment, facilities, and training to determine the extent to which the campus environment supported the use of technologically mediated instruction on- and off-campus.

Distance education competency, value, and information technology and support scores were used in the conduct of the study. Overall scale and subscale scores were calculated by summing the appropriate items and their scores used in the analysis. The Competency scores were computed by summing responses to the 11 competencies items. Value scores were calculated by summing the responses to the 9 value items explained above. Information technology and support scores were contrived by summing the 8 items. The total distance education score was determined by summing responses to all of the 28 items.

Table 3. Total Distance Education Score

Distance Education Scores	*M*	*SD*
Distance Education Competency Score	32.0	8.3
Distance Education Value Score	33.2	5.7
Distance Education Information Technology and Support Score	23.4	5.7
Total Distance Education Scores	88.6	

Most teachers (85%) were not philosophically opposed to distance education. Fifteen percent of teachers were philosophically opposed to distance education. The total distance education score was not significantly related to the participants' philosophical position towards distance education. Faculty members' overall perceived level of competence in the use of distance education electronic technologies, their perceptions with respect to the role these technologies have or will have in teaching agriculture, and their perceptions regarding availability of equipment, facilities, and support were similar regardless of a faculty members philosophical position towards distance education.

The distance education competency scor was not related to the participants' philosophical position towards distance education. Therefore Faculty members' perceived level of competence in the use of distance education technologies were the same regardless of their philosophical position towards distance education. Faculty members overall indicated a neutral attitude toward their competence with distance education technology.

Teachers not philosophically opposed to distance education had higher distance education value scores. This finding may be key to understanding a faculty member's philosophy towards distance education. Faculty members' who had a positive philosophical position toward distance education tended to "agree" with the statements defining distance education value. Faculty members' who had a negative philosophical position towards distance education tended to "disagree" with the statements defining distance education value.

Faculty members' perception of distance education information technology and support were the same regardless of their philosophical position towards distance education. In general there was a neutral attitude in their perception of distance education information technology and support.

The majority of educators are not philosophically opposed to distance education. Total distance education score, distance education competency score and distance education information rechnology and support score were not significantly related to the philosophical positions towards distance education of the participants. However, the Distance Education Value Score was directly related to the philosophical position of the respondents. The faculty who had higher distance education value scores had low philosophical opposition scores. This leads to the belief that the increasing value of distance education must be communicated more effectively in order to impact the philosophical positioning of those opposed to distance education. In order for faculty to support the distance education model it must be congruent to their current beliefs and values held about university education. Those faculty members who did not believe distance education was the educational equivalent to traditional courses had lower distance education value scores and therefore are philosophically opposed to distance education.

The ability of an organisation to adapt to these changes is influenced by: competence (knowledge, skills, and abilities of its staff) and value (amount of importance the staff places on the role of these technologies to accomplish teaching and learning). With more research it may be possible to tie adverse philosophical position to tenure status and academic ranking which could contention that newer faculty already possess the skills and self efficacy to integrate the technology. Which, in turn, that further training and assistance in the use of instructional technologies is needed for the faculty members not as experienced with the distant education model. Female faculty scored higher on the distant education value scale, additional research on a sample population with more diverse gender representation needs to be done to find if there is in fact a correlation between philosophical position and gender. As higher education attempts to meet the growing demand for courses delivered at a distance identification of potential barriers to faculty acceptance and adoption are needed.

Distance Education Policies

Different policies impact the growth of distance education, or put more simply, does policy make a difference in the distance education effort? By all evidence, the growth in distance education courses and enrollments has been phenomenal. For instance, the US National Center for Education Statistics found that from Fall 1995 to academic year 1997-98, the number of courses and degree or certificate programs doubled, from 25,730 to 52,270 courses and from 860 to 1,520 programs. Student enrollments also doubled in the same timeframe, from 753,640 to 1.6 million enrollments. However, teasing out the role policy may play in this growth is very difficult, since it is clear there are strong market forces at work in this phenomenon. For example, students are encouraged for a number of economic reasons to pursue additional education through distance technologies and institutions are influenced to provide distance education in order to serve the students in their perceived market and to reap the increased state funding that results from serving greater numbers of FTE students. To be honest, the motivation behind much policy-making is to avoid lawsuits resulting from not having policy or to lay the groundwork for a successful defense based on having, and following, an adopted policy. And yet it is very common to hear from a number of policy bodies—from legislatures to state boards of higher education—that policy on a particular matter is needed. The belief seems to be that policy will help clarify the situation, provide a guide for future behavior, or change the behavior of individuals in a manner deemed more appropriate or beneficial.

Certainly, the evidence is very mixed that policy affects human behavior. There are three practices deemed good for undergraduate education, found that despite several much-publicized policies on the importance of and ways to improve the education of undergraduates, the three practices did not markedly increase in frequency. What is more typical in studies of faculty behavior, who reviewed the attitudes of administrators and faculty toward distance education and, having found them to be similar, still concluded that revised policies on rewards for faculty were needed. Even though the literature on policies affecting behavior is limited, there are an ample number of studies on current practices for faculty compensation and workload in distance education. The colleges of education and found that 42% provided monetary or other consideration (e.g., release time) for faculty teaching distance education courses (deans also indicated that only 40% had a formal intellectual property policy on ownership of distance education courses).

The National Education Association survey of members found 63% of respondents did not receive additional compensation and 84% received no reduction in courseload. There are 44% of faculty surveyed teaching an interactive video course taught the course in load (without additional compensation) and 51 of 64 respondents felt there was no recognition for their distance education efforts. As for policies on intellectual property, or ownership of distance education courses, 45% indicated the institution owned the rights, 11% indicated the faculty had the rights, and 24% indicated those rights were shared (20% indicated "other," which was not explained).

What is perhaps most intriguing about policy and faculty behavior is how counterintuitive it sometimes appears. In studies of faculty involvement with distance education, many institutions did not reward faculty for their online teaching, nor were promotion and tenure decisions influenced positively by a faculty person's developing web-based courses. And yet distance education continues to grow, largely through the efforts of faculty. In a subsequent study, investigated faculty beliefs on compensation and workload issues and uncovered three factors: return on and equity of investment, intrinsic motives, and commitment. In other words, faculty appear to be motivated by intrinsic factors to the greatest extent, the commitment of the department or college to a lesser extent, and least of all by recognition or credit in performance evaluations. This latter finding may be due to the continuing lack of recognition for these activities at many institutions.

In a study of faculty compensation, institutions were more likely to pay faculty for delivering a course than developing one, although considerable variability in policies were found. There are 30 institutions found that only 12 had workload and/or compensation policies; seven additional institutions were in the process of discussing policy in these areas. Most frequently, institutions apply existing policies to distance education and do not pay instructors for updating courses but support faculty training by paying conference fees or granting release time to do so. These studies indicate that the world of policy regarding faculty compensation and workload is in considerable flux, although most institutions seem to have decided to handle these issues no differently than other efforts on campus. In a factor analysis of motivators and inhibitors for teaching online, faculty and administrators and found four scales (in order of loading): intrinsic motives (e.g., challenge, improve teaching), personal needs (e.g., release time, monetary reward), inhibitors (e.g., lack of release time, lack of support), and extrinsic motives (e.g., requirement of department, support of administrators). For faculty, responses were also split between those who had participated in distance education and those who had not; those who had taught online were more likely to name intrinsic motives while those who had not named more extrinsic motives. Administrators were more likely to name personal needs and extrinsic motivators as influencing whether faculty participate in distance learning.

Faculty motivated to try online teaching were interested in the Internet or online teaching and rated the experience more satisfying than faculty whose motivation was a fear of being left behind. The motivation for involvement with distance education and found that faculty were (again) motivated by intrinsic factors (e.g., intellectual challenge), inhibited by lack of release time and technical support. Extrinsic factors (e.g., credit toward promotion, merit pay) did not affect their involvement. The top motivating factors for faculty were money, credit toward tenure, and release time. In another study of incentives, that faculty were motivated by such incentives as providing innovative instruction and using new teaching techniques; monetary awards were neither an incentive nor an obstacle.

The biggest obstacles were time and training. These studies present a consistent picture of the intrinsic motivators that push faculty into getting involved in online learning, and that administrators overestimate the importance of extrinsic motivations. On the other hand, these studies also seem to imply that to involve the faculty who are not motivated by the same factors, it may well take money, time, and rewards. While the emphasis on intrinsic rewards is interesting, what is more interesting is how impervious faculty have been to negative rewards (or the lack of extrinsic rewards). This is an interesting quandary, where policy discourages a behavior that some faculty pursue anyway while other faculty avoid the activity due to the lack of extrinsic rewards.

Although there are probably multiple answers to this issue, reward and tenure policies aligned to support online learning may encourage some of the more reluctant faculty to pursue online teaching. On the other hand, a favorable policy may not be sufficient to change faculty behavior; it is not necessary, but it does enable faculty involvement for those so motivated. Clearly, one should recognise that faculty are not only very different in their personal characteristics, but they are differently motivated in different situations. They are imbedded in multi-layered environments, influenced to a greater or lesser extent by their personal views and values, departmental and college goals, university ambitions, system or state values, and even regional or national trends. So it is not a simple notion to ascribe faculty motivations to one thing or another, let alone to the existence of a specific policy adopted by one layer of this complex environment. And yet it is an intriguing task to ask the question about the impact of policy, and to attempt to tease out its role in what is happening to higher education.

What follows is an example of policy analysis, partakes, at different times, of rational and intuitive methods, drawing upon both traditional data collection as well as an understanding of the interconnectedness of complex systems. Crucial to this process is explicating the variables and relationships proposed to exist in the system as well as the human factors that affect decisions and actions within the system. Analysis is strongly grounded in the analyst's judgment and intuition of the problem, for solution of nonquantifiable problems demands a role for subjective human judgment. That should not mean that the judgments can not be explained, rationalised, and supported and made understandable so that others can judge for themselves the quality of the analysis. Policy analysis is, by its very nature, a messy process, but it is not chaotic. An attachment to an email to the membership of the Western Cooperative for Educational Telecommunications (WCET). The membership includes over 150 institutions that pay dues to participate in WCET and are thus a group that is largely aligned with the pro-distance education values of the organization.

Seven institutions submitted data to the investigator, and only five of these were deemed usable for the analysis (two institutions had only begun delivering distance education so had a short track record to evaluate in terms of the impact of various policies). The outcome measure of interest was distance education enrollments, and two types of policies were investigated: faculty-related policies and institutional/state policies. The institutional survey included questions on the number of distance education enrollments (by headcount or FTE) per academic year and the number of fully distance courses offered by academic year. The three policy areas of interest to faculty were:

1) faculty compensation (whether faculty were paid for course development),
2) faculty workload (whether faculty taught distance education courses in load or as overload), and
3) intellectual property (whether the policy allocated ownership of distance education courses to the institution, the faculty, or both).

In addition, institutions indicated whether specific funding for distance education was available from the state, whether a state plan for distance education was in place, whether distance education appeared in the institution's mission statement, and whether geographic service areas delineating where institutions could offer distance education were in place. The additional data on funding, strategic plans for distance education, mission statements, and service areas were specifically asked to determine whether these policies would influence distance education growth as much or more than the policies that more directly impact faculty.

The five institutions are located in the west, the midwest, and the south. They include one community college, two regional four-year institutions, and two research institutions, and thus institutional enrollments are varied, but range from over 2,000 to 20,500 total headcount students in the most recent year. Distance education headcount enrollments ranged from over 1,000 to over 7,000 students in the most recent year. Because not all institutions are experiencing the same conditions (be they economic state-level politics), it is difficult to compare experiences or overly generalize from these cases, but only to comment on the unique experiences of the five institutions. There are five cases based on institutional data and discuss various policy conditions that may inform our understanding of each case.

Case A: received state funding in its early years of offering distance education courses and programs, but its largest enrollment increases were in later years, when there was no state funding. Faculty policies (compensation, workload, intellectual property) were supportive of faculty, including compensation for developing courses, distance education taught in or out of load as the faculty person chose, and an intellectual property policy that shared with faculty the rights to and benefits from of a distance education course. In terms of state policies, service areas had been eliminated, and a state plan for distance education was in place. Distance education was not specifically mentioned in the institution's mission statement.

Case B: had not received state funding for its distance education program in its first year, but in each year thereafter. Growth in enrollments was higher in the first and last years. Faculty policies were supportive of faculty, including compensation for developing and delivering online courses and distance education courses taught in load. Despite its long history with distance education, the institution had just begun to develop an intellectual property policy for online courses. State policies were also supportive, including the elimination of service areas, a state plan for distance education, but no mention of distance education in the institution's mission statement.

Case C: had never received directed state funding for its distance education effort, although it also saw high enrollment growth tied to high growth in the number of new courses added to its offerings. Faculty policies were supportive of faculty, including compensation for developing and delivering online courses, distance education courses taught in load, and an intellectual property policy that shared with faculty the rights to and benefits from of a distance education course. Other policies were not so supportive, including the existence of service areas, no state plan for distance education, and no mention of distance education in the institution's mission statement.

Case D: had received state funding every year of its distance education program, but had not added new courses in year 3 and had increased its new courses by 80% in year 4. Largest increases in enrollment were in the first and fourth years of distance education offerings. Faculty policies were supportive of faculty, including compensation for developing online courses, distance education courses taught in load, and an intellectual property policy that shared with faculty the rights to and benefits from of a distance education course. State policies were also supportive, including the elimination of service areas, a distance education plan, and a specific mention of distance education in the institution's mission statement.

Case E: had received state funding in only its last year of operation. Faculty policies were supportive of faculty, including compensation for developing online courses, distance education courses taught in load, and an intellectual property policy that gave faculty the right to own and benefit from their distance education courses. State policies were mixed; service areas had been eliminated but no state plan for distance education had been developed. Distance education was not mentioned in the institution's mission statement.

The question is how can we make sense of these situations? And there may be answers in understanding some basic qualities of the policy environment as well as faculty faced with novel or innovative situations such as involvement in distance education.

— The policy environment as existing on a continuum from policy-free to policy-restricted, with several points in between. For this analysis, let us focus on the two extremes. The policy-free environment is characterized by having no policy in place and decisions likely made on a case-by-case basis. The policy-restricted environment would be characterized by having policies for all eventualities and decision-making that is based on those policies.

For the entrepreneurs, a policy-free environment is probably ideal, offering them maximum freedom to operate as they will. However, the entrepreneur in the policy-restricted environment may operate in the same manner, ignoring discouraging policy and suffering more difficulties as a result. Whether policy could stop the entrepreneur is an interesting question; for now, let us assume that the strength of motivation for the entrepreneur is stronger than policy. For this analysis, let us group together the risk-averse and reward-seeking faculty, due to their common characteristic of being affected by external factors, either positive (rewards) or negatives (risks). For these faculty, the condition of having no policy might be especially troublesome, as it provides them with few indications of where risks are located and what activities might produce a reward. Living in a policy-restricted environment may be more comfortable for these individuals, offering them clear clues as to what to avoid and what to pursue. And given the strength of their need to avoid risk and gain rewards, one would expect them to respond differently to different policies. For example, to these individuals, a positive policy—one setting policy on rewards for teaching online courses—would encourage them to try out this new activity (other things being equal, such as demands on time, etc.).

On the other hand, a lack of policy (or a policy that did not reward this behavior) would be a barrier, largely preventing these individuals from pursuing teaching online. For the reluctants, it is likely that having no policy is frightening or a confirmation that the activity is a dangerous endeavor, which would be reason enough not to pursue it. The policy-restricted environment may feel more reassuring to these individuals, although one suspects that for truly reluctant individuals, there may be no policy good enough to encourage a change in behavior. This construct explains a number of behaviors already captured in the review of literature and the five cases. First, the faculty who have, so far, taught distance education courses may be heavily drawn from the entrepreneurs, who revel in policy-less environments and ignore policies that might discourage their involvement in distance education. If there is no extra compensation or no adjustment to their workload, they teach online anyway. The lack of explicit rewards or clear intellectual property policy may be troublesome, but it does not stop them doing what they want to do.

However, for the risk-averse and reward-seeking faculty, the lack of policy on rewards and compensation keep them away from teaching online courses. For these individuals, the creation of positive, supportive policy may be important to encourage them to consider online teaching. If these faculty types are the early majority and late majority of Rogers' terminology, they are the largest number of faculty and therefore, the most predominant type in institutions of higher education. It is probably because of these faculty that we hear the constant urging to revise policy to make distance education more attractive.

Each institution should initiate a policy initiative immediately? Not without considering four alternatives. However, before considering these alternatives, an institution needs to understand at least three issues.

— It must have a grasp of how its faculty are distributed across the entrepreneurial and other categories and how a policy discussion will be interpreted.

— It must have a clear vision of what involvement in distance education or online learning will do for them, or not, as the case may be.

— It must have an understanding of the severity of its other challenges and whether this is an appropriate or necessary time to undertake change.

The first policy alternative is to do nothing. Although often pursued by default, it is a legitimate and honorable policy alternative, if chosen based on understanding the institution and its faculty, its direction and challenges. For example, if distance education is not deemed to be a useful direction for the institution, or the faculty too risk-averse or suspicious of others' motives to discuss new policy, then an institution may be well-advised to stay its course and/or spend its valuable time and energy meeting its other challenges. The second alternative is to revise current policies to be more supportive of distance education. If this alternative is chosen, one assumes that the institution believes this is a good time to initiate a policy discussion, that the majority faculty may not undertake this effort without appropriate policy being in place, and that this is a good direction for the institution. The third alternative, and another popular policy alternative, is to study the issue. This might be an appropriate alternative for institutions where timing may currently not be propitious for change, where the study process may be designed to help educate more individuals on campus, or that the direction of the institution require some thoughtful preparation.

The last alternative may be to deliberately avoid policy development for now, but use incentives available to the institution to encourage involvement in distance education, such as targeted funding. This may be an appropriate response for an institution with ample resources and greater faith in incentives than in having supportive policies in place or one with more faculty who are reward seekers than risk aversives. There is no one right answer to these policy choices, only answers that will be better or more appropriate for one institution at a point in time. These alternatives can be combined consecutively or pursued concurrently. However, these policy choices will help, or not, based on the institution's knowledge of its strengths and weaknesses, its environment and the market in which it must compete for resources, be they students, faculty, funding, or public regard. In any case, undertaking a change in policy is not for the faint of heart. It is one of the most difficult and time-consuming activities any administrator can pursue and it generates all types of suspicions and responses from faculty and others who may have something to lose or gain by the change, or only think they do.

4

Challenges of Learning

The world's human population has remained relatively stable for thousands of years prior to our era, growing only slightly, but not dramatically, for most of the time thereafter. An estimated 250 million people inhabited our planet around the year zero. The number had roughly doubled around 1650 and it had doubled again around 1850. By that time, advances in medical science, notably the work of the likes of Pasteur, started to ensure that the doubling period would become shorter and shorter. Only slightly more than 30 years were needed for the most recent doubling of the world population from 3,000,000,000 in the mid-sixties to 6,000,000,000 now. As a consequence, we are rapidly reaching the limits of the resources that our planet possesses to sustain its ecology. Naturally, the latter prospect leads to ever increased levels of activity among the six billion of us and the exponential curve that represents the growth of the human population sparks off other exponential growth curves representing the technological and economic development we generate.

Learning is a crucial dimension of the human existence. The latter notions are based on the assumption that hange is a given, the former one envisions human beings as part of the changing environment, i.e. as actors who engage in intelligent behaviour as they see things change around them, aware that by doing so they, too, produce change themselves. Such conscious, intelligent behaviour, based on what is sometimes called 'deep understanding', is the result of true learning.

Knowledge now becoming obsolete various times in a lifetime, questioning one's own assumptions has become crucial. Against that backdrop, Penzias noted the frightening situation that children, as soon as they go to school, cease to ask questions.

Both the schooling tradition and many of the alternative pathways to learning that complement it, such as much of the distance education tradition, still treat knowledge as a commodity, as something that can be passed around, that represents value in monetary terms, and that has an existence independent of the relationship between the beholder and her or his world. Currently emerging notions of the knowledge society tend to reinforce such perceptions.

One of the greatest challenges therefore is to move beyond the paradigm that defines learning simply as the acquisition and accumulation of knowledge. We must come to grips with, and be constantly cognizant of, the dimension of development, growth or process of knowledge - of science - in which uncertainty prevails, while moving towards attaining deeper understanding.

A second major challenge relates to the dialogical nature of learning and therefore its essentially social nature. This aspect finds clear expression in the notion of learning to live together, one of the four pillars - perhaps the most important one - on which, according to the 1996 report to UNESCO of the International Commission on Education for the Twenty-first Century, learning throughout life should build. This important and overriding dimension of any successful learning experience has long gone unnoticed. Due to the dominance of the traditional schooling paradigm, learning was usually seen as something that is done alone, a view that is perhaps most strongly expressed in how learning gains are being assessed.

Even now that this important aspect of learning is getting increased recognition, educators and evaluation specialists are often at a ioss as to how to reflect this in assessment practices. As a consequence, moving away from the old paradigm is hard. Whence the enormity of this challenge. A third major challenge has to do with the nature of knowledge itself. Societal processes of dealing with a vastly growing body of knowledge - growing both in extent and complexity -have, over the centuries, led to increased specialization.

A tendency has thus emerged to deal with the complexity of the world by breaking it down into parts that, when dealt with in isolation, could be comprehended. This process has greatly contributed to the advancement of science. However, it has also led to a view of the world, and thus to ways of dealing with it, that are no longer able to account for its complexity. This is becoming problematic as many of the issues the world has to deal with now have, in a very fundamental way, to do with the phenomena of exploding change and rapidly increasing complexity referred to earlier. Whence the need to overcome the shortcomings of the disciplinary structure of knowledge, moving beyond also multidisciplinarity and interdisciplinarity, to start seeing things in a transdisciplinary perspective. In short, we need to rediscover the unity of knowledge.

Fundamental changes are required in the ways in which, both at individual and societal levels, learning and the conditions that promote and facilitate it are being conceived. The major societal institution consciously set up to deal with learning needs, the school system, is in for a fundamental overhaul in terms of content, procedures, internal organization, and the ways in which it interacts with the outside world. At the basis of that overhaul should be the recognition that learning is much wider than the school itself. That being the case, the school has an important, if not crucial, role to play in helping people to prepare themselves for a life of lifelong learning. Equally fundamental in this process of change must be the notion that learning is a social process. The school should thus be envisioned as a learning community.

That community is made up of actors - students, teachers, parents, etc. - whose roles flexibly oscillate between learning and facilitation of learning. It should allow those different actors to appreciate the excitement of learning as they experience it individually, but also allow them, as a group, to experience how the group as a whole gains in knowledge and grows in significance as an organic part of the larger society in which it is integrated. School-community linkages are thus essential. Exposure to the idea of organizational learning at the preparatory level is of major importance to recognize opportunities for such learning beyond the school context. Thirdly, the problems with which the school interacts should be real ones. If once again the school is seen as part of the larger world surrounding it, there is no shortage of real problems to deal with.

Problem-based learning is essential to stay focused on the unity of knowledge, even if for practical purposes very specific detail may be pursued and a fair effort may be invested in exploring the tremendous wealth of disciplinary knowledge. After all, one must attain disciplinary insights before they can be transcended and transdisciplinary visions ensue. Such a focus on problem-based learning will have profound implications in terms of curricular reform as well as for the way in which the school is organized and the pedagogical principles it applies.

The recognition that the learning environment is larger than the school is an important one. The school, in fact, should in the first place be seen as one of its components, and a very essential one at that, provided it be adequately conceived. Another important recognition is that the learning environment at large be seen in an ecological perspective.

Learning communities of different kinds and at different levels of organizational complexity function within it. They use its resources, interact with each other and with the environment at large, each of them being a potential resource for all other learning entities - whether learning individuals or collectives of individuals - that constitute the environment. To clarify this notion, let us look at the following example. One component of the larger learning environment could be a community of individuals, such as often from among originally marginalized youths, who, while attempting to become a more meaningful part of their society, engage in, say, the mastery of basic skills and formation of attitudes and motivations to that effect. Those same youths, however, may also be part of a family environment that constitutes another level of learning community in which processes of learning take place particularly at an intergenerational level. Alternatively, or sometimes simultaneously, they may be part of a youth culture such as found in the inner city environment of many an urban context. They may furthermore be found in chat rooms on the Internet, virtual spaces of learning in which they interact with others whose identity may become less explicitly known to them.

On a more continuous basis, they are being exposed to media such as TV, radio, the press, and the cinema. This is yet another set of learning contexts of which, unfortunately, the importance gets attention mostly when it leads to negative consequences. The extent to which such consequences can be negative should meanwhile have opened our eyes to how those same media can be made to benefit humankind.

At yet another level of organizational complexity, those same youths may live in towns that have defined themselves as learning cities, thus offering to their various constituent learning communities a wealth of opportunities of mutually beneficial interaction. It is not at all difficult to extend the above description much more lengthily, contemplating the learning effects of people's pertaining to spiritual communities; economic communities; their political affiliations; their wonder at what world, what universe they live in, and thus their scientific interest; their longing for beauty and fulfilment, i.e. their appreciation for and capacity at art. One could also go on and consider that the youths of our example grow older, becoming mature adults who acquire and take on continually changing roles as circumstances and opportunities lead them to do so. Whatever their stage in life, there will always be reason to learn. The structures that have historically evolved in response to the need for human beings to learn are largely no longer adequate. They reflect societal assumptions, particularly those pertaining to the industrial society, that have ceased to hold. Yet, it is understandable that until only a few decades ago learning was still mainly perceived as what one would do to prepare oneself for the rest of one's life.

Until then, change was relatively slow and futures could be foreseen with a relative degree of certainty. The adult generation of a particular time could reasonably predict what would be necessary for the generation that followed to prepare itself for its role in society via schooling. That generation, once schooled, would do the same for the next one. Hence, interaction with change followed a generational pattern. Not so any longer. No one graduating from school can any longer have the illusion to have completed her or his learning career. Quite to the contrary, learning will be the major business of the professional future of anyone who now leaves school.

For learning to play such a more prominent role in life we can no longer be satisfied with the rather narrow and rigid institutional contexts to which it is often confined. Learning spaces should not be restricted by the boundaries of the school. A reconceptualization of the learning environment must recognize the multiplicity of learning spaces. Such spaces can be defined in physical terms, but they are equally expressed in terms of the interactions among people via such media as the Internet and they also have an important time dimension, a-synchronicity becoming an increasingly important feature of many learning experiences and the communities that generate them.

Some of the elements of the learning environment that one can envision in the perspective of Horizon 2020 are already there. They are present in the school systems, particularly those that struggle to redefine themselves in terms of the requirements of the post-industrial era. They are equally present in the growing practice of distance learning to the extent that such practice generates and sustains dynamic learning communities, rather than creating replicas of the traditional school model.

They can be found in the - often inspiring - instances in which increasingly available and accessible interactive technologies are being used in imaginative ways to create learning communities whose members are spread around the globe, sometimes gearing their learning towards issues of global importance and relevance. They are found in the example of teachers who become aware of their role as learners and learners who realize their potential to facilitate the learning of others.

They are present when members of different generations develop the capability to mutually learn from each other; when learning becomes a shared experience among people who speak different languages and who are able to appreciate and explore the diversity of cultures among them; when centuries old local knowledge systems and modern science start interacting with each other in a constructive fashion, etc. In such an environment, traditional distinctions such as those between formal, non-formal, and informal learning, as well as those between distance education and face-to-face instruction, will become increasingly irrelevant. One is that care for the learning environment must be the shared responsibility of a broad partnership of stakeholders, particularly including the learning communities themselves. The other one is that any predetermined choices, such as those that emphasize particular technologies or approaches as the basis for its development, are unproductive.

Educational Inequalities

As economic activity becomes increasingly knowledge-based, disparities in educational opportunity will play a more important role in determining the distribution of income and poverty.Global inequalities of educational opportunity are not just a matter of crude differences between North and South. Disparities between developing countries are also marked, with important implications for the distribution of income between developing regions. Comparisons between regions and countries provide an insight into average performance. But in education, as in other areas, averages conceal differences based on wealth, gender, region, ethnicity, and other factors. National inequalities in education are often greater than North –South inequalities. Just as the latter reinforce highly unequal patterns of income distribution in the global economy, inequality in the distribution of national opportunities for education enables the wealthy to capture a disproportionately large share of national wealth. These national inequalities cast the global education crisis in a new light.

The crisis is fundamentally a crisis for the poor, since there are only a few countries in which the rich have not achieved universal basic education. The final section uses a disaggregated version of the EPI to capture the extent of inequality across a wide range of dimensions by ranking different regions of the same country. Contrasts between a typical primary school in

Europe or the United States and a similar facility in rural sub-Saharan Africa or South Asia capture some of the dimensions of global inequality in education. In much of the developing world, 'school 'is often a dilapidated mud building with crumbling walls. More than 80 children, many of them undernourished, might be crammed into a classroom, sitting on the floor with scarcely a book, pencil, or notepad to share. Their teachers, most of them untrained, may have second jobs to make ends meet.

Rote-learning will be the order of the day. Water and sanitation facilities are likely to be grossly inadequate. Primary schools in industrialised countries face problems of their own –but they are problems of a different order. Teachers are well trained, class sizes are smaller, paper and pencils will be in plentiful supply. The school will have a library, and probably computers. The walls will be decorated with the work of the children, maps, and other visual aids. Each child will have access to a set of core textbooks. While the national media and parents 'associations may take the view that schools are in a state of perpetual crisis, it is a crisis of a different order than that which prevails in the developing world.

The material contrasts between the education systems of rich and poor countries reflect huge disparities in financing capacity. The problem is not that poor countries spend a smaller share of their national wealth on education than rich countries. In fact, sub-Saharan Africa spends a larger share of its GDP –around 5.6 er cent – on education than the OECD countries spend, though many countries in the region spend far less than the average. Measured in terms of public effort, Africa has been investing more in primary education than other regions, and also increasing that effort over time. The problem is that disparities in wealth translate into huge disparities in spending, which in turn produce highly unequal outcomes in terms of public provision for basic education. This is especially true when, as in Africa's case, economic decline reduces the absolute value of any given proportion of GDP invested in education.

Some indication of the financial divide separating education systems in the developed and developing worlds can be provided by a simple profile of expenditure. With one-fifth of the world 's population, the industrialised countries account for more than four-fifths of total public spending on education. At the other extreme, South Asia accounts for almost 25 per cent of the world 's population, but for only Economists typically think about poverty and inequality in terms of income.On average, the OECD countries spend $4636 per student through public finance for primary and secondary education, compared with $165 per student in developing countries and $49 in sub-Saharan Africa.

To take relative spending in 1980 as the point of comparison, per capita public spending on education in sub-Saharan Africa and South Asia is now 60 per cent lower than average spending in the industrialised world. In Latin America, it is one-third lower. Only East Asia has closed the financing gap in education, although this picture has almost certainly changed in the wake of the financial crisis. While inefficiencies in public spending contribute to the education gap separating rich and poor countries, differences in national wealth, related in turn to the distribution of global income, are the main determinant of the financing gap.

Demographic factors are reinforcing the effects of differential growth rates and initial income inequalities.

In the industrialised countries, the size of the population aged under 15 has contracted by about 6 er cent since 1995, while per capita incomes have grown at more than 2 er cent a year. Spending per pupil has risen significantly as a result, even though the share of GDP allocated to education has been static.

In developing countries, the population aged under 15 has grown by one-third over the same period, while problems of economic stagnation and debt have, in many cases, reduced financing capacity. The importance of demographic trends can hardly be overstated. At any given level of average income and unit cost of schooling, countries with higher rates of population growth will face relatively higher per capita costs in progressing towards education for all. In the developed countries, children aged 6 –11 typically comprise 5 –8 per cent of total population, and population growth is now zero. In sub-Saharan Africa, the 6 –11 age group typically represents more than 15 per cent of the population, rising to 20 per cent for countries such as Tanzania, Zambia, and Uganda. It is not just that the education budgets of these countries are infinitesimally smaller than those of developed countries, but that these smaller budgets must cover a primary-school population that is three times larger in relative terms. Financing differences are marked at all levels of education, but the biggest gap is to be found at the primary level. Taking into account only recurrent budgets, per capita spending on primary-school pupils in Nepal and India is about $12, compared with $5130 in the United States. Annual spending per primary-school pupil in Britain is equivalent to $3553 –around 130 times more than in Zambia. At one level, these simple spending comparisons give an exaggerated picture of the problem. The costs of materials, buildings, and teachers 'salaries are obviously higher in the developed countries, so that the same provision costs more.

At another level, financial comparisons understate the problem. They do not, for instance, capture the high levels of private spending on education in the industrialised countries. In the developing world, millions of households do not own a single book; the consequent restrictions on children 's academic development are obvious. By contrast, recent research in Britain, the USA, and Australia found that more than 80 per cent of children of primary-school age had 25 or more books at home. This illustrates how private spending capacity widens the already extreme differences in opportunity associated with differences in public spending. Comparisons of public spending fail to capture another dimension of financial inequality. Pressure on recurrent expenditure in many of the poorest countries means that teachers 'salaries often account for more than 95 per cent of spending –leaving almost nothing for the purchase of teaching materials, or the maintenance of schools. Non-salary recurrent expenditure at the primary level in much of sub-Saharan Africa is less than $2 per pupil, which explains the generalised lack of textbooks and other teaching materials.

While inequalities in education provision and quality are greatest between developed and developing countries, countries in transition are also facing acute problems. They too are falling further behind the high-income industrialised countries, with a major crisis on the horizon in parts of Eastern Europe and the former Soviet Union. Highly developed education systems are collapsing in the face of declining public investment and falling living standards. Compulsory and free basic education up to the mid-secondary level, high levels of gender equity, and, especially in the sciences, good standards of learning were among their achievements. Today, however, the education systems of the region are crumbling in a context of economic stagnation, rising inequality, and declining State provision. In education as in other areas, there is a growing danger that the positive inheritance from the past will be lost in the process of transition to market economies. Oxfam has witnessed at first hand the collapse of education systems through its work with marginal communities in Armenia, Azerbaijan, and Georgia, the former Soviet republics in the southern Caucasus region. For these communities, the rising direct costs of schooling, such as expenditure on textbooks, meals, transport, and other services that were previously provided free, combined with wider economic pressures, notably declining wages and unemployment, put education out of people's reach.

At the same time, the reduced provision of schooling, especially in areas affected by conflict, and its deteriorating quality are widely perceived as problems. The precise mix of demand and supply factors varies from place to place. But the crisis is real, and it has profound implications for economic recovery and social equity. The following are among the problems which must be addressed to prevent further decline of the education systems in these transition economies:

— *The erosion of compulsory and free basic education*: Most Central and Eastern European countries have restored enrolment to pre-transition levels. This is not the case in the former Soviet republics, which have witnessed dramatic declines in enrolment both at the primary level and in general secondary education. UNICEF has estimated that as many as one in seven children may now be out of school in Central Asia and the Caucasus. Half a million Russian children aged between 6 and 10 are now missing from each grade in the school system.

— *Rising costs*: The cost to families of educating children has risen dramatically. Budgetary constraints mean that schools are now encouraged to raise their own funds. Parents are meeting a growing share of school budgets and teachers' salaries out of their own pockets. Textbooks, once free, are now being charged for, along with notebooks and pencils. These rising costs come during a period when family incomes have been eroded by declining wages, rising unemployment, and inflation. At the beginning of 1996, the price of a package of basic materials for school in Azerbaijan was about $50. The average monthly wage was only $13.

— *Declining public provision*: For many countries, 'transition' has become a euphemism for a shrinking national economy. In 1997, real GDP in the Caucasus countries was less than 40 per cent of the 1989 level, less than 60 per cent in Russia's case. Economic decline on this scale inevitably diminishes the government's capacity to finance basic services through public revenues. Unfortunately, the problem has been exacerbated by political decisions to reduce the proportion of revenues allocated to basic services, including education.

— *Deteriorating quality of schools and schooling*: Precipitous declines in public spending have taken their toll on school infrastructure and service provision. Buildings and equipment have suffered disproportionately, with many schools in a state of chronic disrepair. One in five of Georgia's schools has been classified unsafe and unfit for occupation. In most of the former Soviet republics, teachers' salaries are now below the poverty line, forcing many to take second jobs. Low teacher morale, like deteriorating school buildings and declining public investment, is a sign of diminishing educational opportunity.

The quality of education often left much to be desired, with a great emphasis on learning facts by rote, rather than on child-centred development. School-management and teaching practices were generally rigid and authoritarian, with little parental involvement. There were also limits to equity, with rural areas often disadvantaged, and ethnic groups suffering discrimination. But, while reforms to central planning were urgently needed, responsibility for developing a coherent education policy and for funding equitable access seems to have been abandoned. The transition to a situation in which household income determines access to educational opportunities is inherently inefficient in economic terms. The fact that this transition is occurring at a time of rapidly rising poverty and social inequality carries grave implications for social equity and cohesion today, and for future prospects of social and economic recovery.

Good-quality primary education provides the foundation on which individuals and countries can progress to develop higher levels of skills and learning. As production becomes increasingly knowledge-intensive, the development of secure livelihoods will require not only universal primary education, but high levels of transition into secondary and higher education. Many developing countries are ill equipped to make the transition. The combination of low enrolment and low completion rates in much of the developing world means that children spend far less time in education than children in developed countries. On average, a child entering primary school in the developing world can expect to receive eight to nine years of education, compared with the 15 –17 years that can be expected in developed countries. As always, however, the average conceals as much as it reveals:

— 'School-life expectancy 'in sub-Saharan Africa is five to six years. It is less than three years in Burkina Faso, Mali, Niger, and Mozambique.

— In Bangladesh, 'school-life expectancy 'is less than four and a half years for girls and six years for boys.

Even these cases obscure the full extent of the problem. This is because averages capture the aggregate picture for the entire population, but conceal differences between average outcomes and those for the poorest sections of society. In poor households, school-life expectancy is invariably far lower, and the proportion of children not attending school is far higher. But in many developing countries the wider consequence of poor-quality education and limited progression through the primary-school system is an exceptionally low rate of transition into the secondary-school system.

The 2015 target of universal primary education has focused international concern on the primary-school system, often to the exclusion of secondary-school education. But the quality of secondary provision is of profound importance, for at least three reasons. First, basic education alone is not enough to ensure the adoption of new production methods and diffusion of new technologies, especially those associated with information and communications. The expansion of secondary schooling is vital for the development of the higher levels of education upon which national prosperity increasingly depends. Effective secondary schooling fosters the development of more flexible and abstract reasoning skills of the type associated with high-growth sectors of manufacturing and service industries, and there is evidence that secondary schooling is positively associated with the development of export production in higher-value-added areas of production.

Second, limited opportunities for progression to secondary education have the effect of reducing demand for primary education. This is because many parents see primary education as a stepping stone to the secondary education that their children need in order to maximise their income-generation and employment opportunities – a perspective supported by research that indicates high rates of return in secondary education.

Third, success in accelerating progress towards universal primary education will inevitably increase demand for secondary education. At present, many secondary-education systems are unable to absorb even the trickle of students who progress through the primary-education system.

The current state of secondary education poses acute problems. At least 700 million people live in countries with gross enrolment rates of less than 40 per cent, and another one billion in countries with rates in the range of 30 –70 per cent. Enrolment rates in the former group of countries have not increased significantly over the last decade, and only modest advances have been recorded in the latter group. As in primary education, sub-Saharan Africa poses the greatest challenge. The region accounts for fully two-thirds of the countries with gross enrolment rates at the secondary level of less than 40 per cent, with fewer than one-third of primary-school children progressing to the secondary level. There are 19 countries in the region with gross enrolment rates of less than 20 per cent, with a large group falling far short of this level. This group includes Malawi, Mozambique, Burkina Faso, Chad, and Mali, all of which have enrolment rates of less than 10 per cent, and Tanzania, where the secondary-school enrolment rate of 5 per cent is the lowest in the world. East Asia, South Asia, and Latin America have closed the gap, but they still remain far behind the industrialised countries. Moreover, there are large gender gaps in secondary education, with girls accounting for a far smaller share of enrolment in South Asia in particular. This is the inverse of the situation in industrialised countries, where boys are under-represented.

The transition point between primary and secondary schools is at the midpoint in a cumulative cycle of inequality. Limited progression through the secondary system produces a limited transfer into the tertiary system. Only 3 per cent of African children, 8 per cent of South Asian children, and 17 per cent of children in East Asia progress beyond secondary school. With the exception of Latin America, significant gender gaps remain at higher levels of education. The contrast between developing and industrialised countries is striking. Several OECD countries have a higher rate of enrolment of young women at the tertiary level than sub-Saharan Africa has achieved for girls at the primary level. More than half of the children entering the education systems of the industrialised countries today will progress through secondary school to the tertiary system. As an OECD report puts it, 'once learning is realised on this scale in upper-secondary education, it is hard to resist the demand for tertiary studies'.

At the other extreme, insufficient learning at the primary level in sub-Saharan Africa means that there cannot be a sustained increase in enrolment at the lower-secondary level. Some of the differences are especially stark. While millions of girls in South Asia and Africa never step inside a school, women now account for the majority of tertiary enrolments in most OECD countries.

As the process of globalisation integrates developing countries ever more deeply into a knowledge-based global economy, differences in educational opportunity at the secondary and tertiary levels will increasingly distort the benefits of economic growth in favour of rich countries. Without a sustained expansion of coverage and an improvement in education quality at the primary and secondary levels, developing countries will fall further behind at the tertiary level. In turn, as tertiary education becomes more important to innovation, economic growth, and employment, the wealth gap and the education gap will create a vicious circle of economic decline and rising global inequality.

The communications revolution arrives in the schools of the industrialised world, there is a grave danger that developing countries will be excluded from new areas of learning. And as information technology is integrated more extensively into production systems, the risk of future marginalisation will intensify. In the industrialised countries, telecommunications technology has already revolutionised education. Technological trends in hardware and software have increased the availability and usefulness of computers for education. Digitalisation has led to the development of computers with multimedia capacity, presenting text, image, and sound to the user. On the software side,' graphical user interfaces 'have made it possible to control computer functions by pointing at pictures rather than by typing text, and to develop interactive programmes for users. Compact discs have made available a vast range of audio and visual learning devices, considerably reducing the costs of accessing information in the process.

Educationalists increasingly recognise the potential benefits of computers for improving the quality of teaching and learning, and expanding the range of information available to children. Learning opportunities are being revolutionised in particular by the Internet, a worldwide information highway, with easy access via the World Wide Web. Searching among different websites has been facilitated through simple interface 'navigation 'tools, which enable schools to download documents from other computers. Increased access to user-friendly equipment that enables computers to communicate with each other has created what amounts to a 'virtual 'worldwide library. Access to computers at school is becoming increasingly widespread in the industrialised countries, starting at the primary and the lower-secondary levels. Growing numbers of children also have access to home computers –although the 'digital divide' between rich and poor households is growing. In the Netherlands, more than half of all households have personal computers, 15 per cent of which are connected to the Internet. Estimates for the USA place the ratio of computers to children at the primary and secondary levels at 1:6. In the SA, Britain, and Denmark, one-third of 14-year-old science students report using computers.

For those with access to information technologies, there are obvious advantages. Students who are familiar with basic computing will adapt more easily to the profound changes that are happening in labour markets with the spread of information technology. They will benefit from higher incomes and wider employment opportunities, and their countries will benefit from associated gains in productivity and competitiveness. Failure to close the information-technology gap now opening up between school systems in the rich and poor worlds will inevitably result in increasing income inequalities. But the gap cannot be closed by technology and finance alone. The problem is that the extension of computer technologies to schools requires substantial financial expenditure for the purchase of equipment and the training of staff.

Governments in the industrialised world have turned to the private sector for assistance. But education authorities in the developing world face enormous financial and technical obstacles in obtaining basic computer equipment, with the result that inequalities in access to information technology will start to increase at a far earlier age. Much has been written about the scope for extending computerised learning systems to the poorest countries. Unfortunately, much of it is divorced from reality. The emphasis has been on the creation of international funds to transfer education technologies through partnerships between development-assistance programmes and private companies. However, many of the poorest countries lack even the most basic infra-structural requirements. Most schools in sub-Saharan Africa and South Asia do not have the electricity and the telephone lines needed to use computers and access international web sites, let alone the financial resources to purchase them.

In countries such as Mali and Mozambique, where there are fewer than four telephone lines for every 1000 people, and where per capita student spending at the primary level is less than $1, the prospects for effective use of new education technologies are limited. As the effects of inequalities in access to information technology at the primary and junior-secondary levels feed through into the higher and vocational levels of education, the knowledge gap will inevitably widen.

North –South inequalities in access to the knowledge and skills imparted by education will shape future patterns of income distribution in the global economy. However, developing countries themselves are not a homogeneous group. There are marked inequalities in educational attainment across and within regions. These inequalities will also have a bearing, not just on income distribution and future shares of international trade, but also on prospects for human development. Attempting to capture the extent of educational inequality poses serious methodological problems. Most reporting systems refer to data on enrolment rates, completion rates, literacy standards, and gender-based inequality. But measurements in each of these areas are treated in isolation, which can create a misleading picture of overall performance. Countries that achieve a high level of success in enrolment may perform poorly in terms of completion rates.

Conversely, education systems may achieve high rates of completion for those who enter school, while large sections of the population never actually attend school. The Education Performance Index (EPI) provides a more integrated measure of performance across a wider range of dimensions. We use the EPI to rank more than 100 developing countries on a composite indicator for education. The same countries are then ranked on the basis of income. Some of the results are predictable. The EPI confirms that deprivation in education is closely associated with overall levels of poverty. Those countries that are most desperately in need of education to escape the poverty trap have the weakest human-resource base. Of more interest are the marked discrepancies between educational attainment and average income. Income differences are an important factor in explaining human-resource differences between countries, but they are not the sole consideration. While low-income countries have lower levels of access to education, many score far higher on the EPI than would be redicted on the basis of national wealth. Conversely, many middle-income countries score far lower. These findings suggest that good public policy in education can overcome the disadvantages associated with low income; and bad public policy will reinforce these disadvantages.

The measurement of educational performance has become a highly politicised activity, especially in the industrialised countries. League tables have been developed to differentiate 'successful 'from 'failing ' schools, but a vigorous debate has ensued over what should be measured, and what weight should be attached to various aspects of performance. The EPI provides a different type of league table. It brings together in a composite index a range of features of deprivation in educational attainment, to arrive at an aggregate judgement on how countries are performing in relation to each other. There are serious problems in developing a composite index. Education data are scandalously poor in many countries. For the mid-decade review of the World Declaration on Education for All, UNESCO produced detailed data on net enrolment rates, completion, and gender equity for most developing countries. However, many of the enrolment rates are little more than 'guestimates', some of which are out of line with evidence derived from household surveys.

According to the World Bank, reliable net enrolment data exist for only about 70 countries. For all their flaws, and despite problems with the data, composite indicators are useful tools. They help to simplify a complex reality on the basis of something more meaningful than a single indicator. When combined with league tables of income, they can also help to compare the performance of countries at very different levels of average income, highlighting important issues of public policy. The EPI provides a simple composite indicator by concentrating on three aspects of educational performance: namely, coverage, completion, and gender equity. Each of these indicators has a critical bearing on the 2015 target of universal primary education. The specific measurement criteria used are as follows:

— The net enrolment rate, which captures the proportion of children aged between 6 and 11 who enrol in school. This serves as a proxy for the coverage achieved by the school system.

— The completion rate, or the proportion of students who progress beyond Grade 4.

— Gender equity, expressed in terms of the ratio of female to male enrolment.

The EPI measures the average shortfall from a perfect score across the three elements. The higher the score, the larger the shortfall. Data were compiled for 104 countries, which were then ranked on the basis of their performance in each area. An extreme deprivation line was established, representing a threshold where on average more than one-third of children were out of school, fewer than one-third were completing school, and the gender gap in enrolment exceeded 33 per cent. Finally, the EPI ranking was set alongside an income ranking, using World Bank data for purchasing-power parity in order to provide some insight into the relationship between education performance and average income levels. Two preliminary observations must be made about what the EPI is –and what it is not. First, the EPI does not capture a number of important aspects of education performance. Gender equity in enrolment is an important but limited indicator of gender discrimination in education at school and beyond. It does not capture the consequences of gender-biased teaching material, the low self-esteem associated with low expectations on the part of teachers and parents, or the excessive work burdens imposed on young girls.

The EPI is of similarly limited value in measuring education quality. Completion ratés are a proxy, but a weak one. In terms of coverage, gross primary-enrolment rates are more widely available than net enrolment data, but they are much less useful. All enrolment data suffer from the problem that they are only a proxy for school attendance. But the difficulty with the gross enrolment rate is that it automatically increases if grade repetitions rise, giving a misleading indicator of performance.

The achievement of gender equity at very low levels of enrolment, or relatively high rates of enrolment with wide gender gaps, should not be obscured by a simple average figure for ranking purposes. For this reason the EPI uses a weighting system that penalises countries for poor performance in each area, thereby limiting the extent of substitution. Deprivation in basic education as measured by the EPI is closely associated with income poverty and wider human-development indicators. Of course, correlation is not causation. Income poverty does not simply reflect educational attainment. Even so, with education increasing in importance as a determinant of income and wider life-chances, the interaction of deprivation in education with other aspects of deprivation will intensify. The danger is that failure to overcome educational inequalities will in turn lead to more intensive patterns of marginalisation, especially in sub-Saharan Africa.

There are some obvious reasons why poor countries experience particular problems in providing basic education opportunities. Low average incomes limit the capacity of governments to finance and deliver schooling –the supply of education. Household demand for education is also linked to average income levels and the incidence of poverty. Poor households are less likely to be able to afford school fees, and more likely to depend on child labour. The overall relationship between income and educational performance is therefore entirely predictable. But the average relationship obscures a more complex picture. Large numbers of countries are under-performing in relation to their income levels; and others are achieving far more than might be expected. There is, in fact, a vast potential for educational opportunity that is being missed because of bad policy choices.

That potential is illustrated by the contrasting performances of good performers, who have achieved a higher EPI rank than their income rank, and bad performers, who have failed to achieve an EPI ranking commensurate with their average income levels. Comparing EPI and income rankings confirms that, in education as in other areas of human development, some countries have performed better than others in converting economic potential into benefits for people. The benefits of economic growth and rising income in reducing income poverty and child mortality and raising the average level of educational attainment are well established. However, there are striking deviations from this relationship. These are graphically illustrated by the EPI, which shows that many countries have failed to create educational opportunities commensurate with their national wealth.

Latin America has failed in a spectacular fashion to develop a basic education system with a level of coverage and performance consistent with average income levels. Several countries occupy an EPI ranking far below their income rank, among them Colombia, Guatemala, Venezuela, Argentina, the Dominican Republic, Brazil, and Chile. The Latin American case demonstrates the benefits of a composite indicator. In contrast to poor performers in sub-Saharan Africa, most countries in Latin America have achieved a high level of enrolment, and gender gaps are generally small. However, dropout rates are so high that the average number of years spent in school by the poor in countries such as Brazil is less than that of the poor in countries at much lower income levels, such as Kenya and Zimbabwe. In the cases of Colombia and Guatemala, high dropout rates are aggravated by substantial gender gaps.

The EPI –income comparison confirms the assessment of the Inter-American Development Bank that, taking regional wealth levels into account, Latin Americans –or, more accurately, poor Latin Americans – suffer the world 's worst public education systems. On average, the region 's workforce has had 5.2 years of schooling. If Latin America 's primary-education system had been as effective as the international average for its income levels, the figure would be more than seven years. Moreover, the percentage of children who drop out of primary school is twice the level that would be predicted on the basis of average-income comparisons.

Under-performance in education is both a cause and a consequence of the extreme levels of income inequality in Latin America. Failure to improve performance at the base of the education system will reinforce these inequalities over time. In some cases, the gap between EPI ranking and income ranking is of extraordinary dimensions. Among the worst cases are Kuwait, Saudi Arabia, Qatar, and Oman. Kuwait and Saudi Arabia respectively account for the largest and second-largest differentials between EPI ranking and income ranking. The underlying reasons for the discrepancy vary. In the cases of Kuwait and Saudi Arabia, the central problem is a relatively low net enrolment rate. Completion rates for both countries are high, and the gender gap in enrolment is small. In Qatar, the gender gap in enrolment is the primary problem. For Latin America and the Middle East, the discrepancy between educational performance and potential raises some important policy questions, notably about public-spending priorities. Both regions show that relatively high levels of public spending and average income do not provide an automatic passport to reasonable levels of educational attainment. However, it is not only middle-income countries and regions that have failed to convert economic wealth into more widely shared opportunities for basic education. There is a large group of low-income countries that are underachieving in relation to their average income levels.

The countries in sub-Saharan Africa clustered beneath the EPI 'extreme deprivation 'threshold illustrate the point. Thirteen of these countries have an EPI rank lower than their income rank, including the following:

— Angola, which has an EPI rank 31 places below its income rank, demonstrating the devastating consequences of the country 's civil war.

— Senegal and Benin, each of which has an EPI ranking 16 places below its income ranking.
— Côte d 'Ivoire, Mozambique, and Niger, with in each case an EPI ranking 8 –9 places lower than the income ranking.

The UNDP's Human Development Report has consistently shown that poor countries can 'over-achieve 'in human development in relation to their income levels. The EPI confirms this fact in relation to education. But it also shows that poor countries can massively underachieve, highlighting the damaging consequences of factors such as bad policies, conflict, and an unfavourable external economic environment. One of the worst underachievers revealed by the EPI is Pakistan. The country occupies 99th position in the EPI league table, or 38 places below its income ranking. Pakistan has an average income equivalent to three times that in Burkina Faso and four times that in Mali, yet it ranks below both countries. This reflects the combination of exceptionally low enrolment rates, a large –and widening –gender gap, and low completion rates. In each of these cases, failed government policies have aggravated problems associated with low income, contributing to a significant shortfall in performance. Inadequate financial commitment, poor planning, weak administration, and, above all, failures of political leadership have contributed to missed opportunities for education. These missed opportunities imply high costs for human development. China has a slightly higher average income than Pakistan, but its citizens are three times as likely to enrol in school and almost twice as likely to complete school. The gender gap in enrolment is six times narrower than in Pakistan. Zimbabwe has a lower average income than Guatemala, but enrolment and completion rates are far higher. Guatemala has a 30 per cent gender gap in primary-school enrolment, while Zimbabwe has no gender gap at that level.

The EPI captures average educational attainment levels for countries. However, national averages obscure deep structural inequalities in education related to enrolment. Household wealth is the single most important factor associated with these inequalities. The poor systematically underachieve in relation to the non-poor, although wealth gaps take different forms in different countries. They also interact with other sources of inequality, including rural –urban differences, gender disparities, regional factors, and ethnicity. These inequalities do not exist in isolation, but are overlapping and mutually reinforcing. Transmitted across generations,they shape the distribution of opportunity and perpetuate the wider structures which consign people to poverty and marginalisation.

Most governments in developing countries recognise the principle that education is a fundamental human right. Many enshrine that right in constitutional provisions.In practice, however, the right to education is universally enjoyed by the rich, but not by the poor. In education, as in other areas of social development, wealth matters. Differences in income shape opportunities for education, which in turn shape future patterns of wealth distribution. There are three broad regional patterns emerge for poor households:

— low enrolment and high dropout rates in much of sub-Saharan Africa;

— low enrolment and a less marked dropout rate as far as Grade 5, followed by a sharp increase thereafter in South Asia;

— high enrolment and high dropout rates in Latin America.

The case of sub-Saharan Africa demonstrates how high levels of poverty produce particularly intensive forms of deprivation, starting at enrolment. In Senegal, the enrolment rate for children from the richest 20 per cent of households is more than double that for the 20 per cent. Once in school, children from the wealthy households are four times more likely to complete Grade 1 and five times more likely to reach Grade 5. In Mali, four out of five children from poor households do not progress beyond the first grade of primary school. Only 2 per cent complete primary school –less than ten per cent of the national primary-school completion rate. Although wealth gaps are widest in West Africa, they are significant across a wide range of countries. In Zambia, for instance, enrolment rates for the richest households are more than one-third higher than for the poorest households. In South Asia, as in Africa, the proportion of 15 –19 year-olds from poor households who have not completed Grade 1 is very high. Almost half fail to progress beyond this stage. Thereafter, retention in school is much higher than in Africa until Grade 5, when dropout rates increase. In India and Pakistan, children from the wealthiest 20 per cent of households have almost achieved universal primary enrolment, while less than half of those from the poorest households enrol. Thereafter the wealth gap widens slowly until Grade 5, when it becomes a chasm. Only 2 per cent of children from the poorest households in Pakistan complete Grade 9, compared with 60 per cent of children from wealthy households. The Indian wealth gap is narrower, but still exceptionally large. Children from wealthy households are around six times more likely to complete Grade 9.

One of the advantages of disaggregated data is that they provide a clearer insight into where the main shortfalls exist in relation to the target of universal primary education. In India, there is a 38 per cent shortfall from universal completion of Grade 5. But only 4 per cent is attributable to children from the richest 20 per cent of households. Almost two-thirds of the primary-school education deficit is attributable to children from the poorest households, which underlines the need for education policy to be integrated into broader anti-poverty strategies.

The Latin American case differs from those of sub-Saharan Africa and South Asia. The pattern here is one of high initial enrolment, followed by a widening wealth gap to Grade 5 and beyond. The education gap is both created by the enormous wealth differences in Latin America and helps to sustain them. In Brazil, the initial enrolment rate for the poor is similar to that for the wealthy. But whereas four out of every five children from the richest households complete primary school, only 15 per cent of poor households do so. In some countries, wealth gaps in education reach remarkable dimensions. Completion rates for Grade 9 are some thirty times higher for children from wealthy households in Guatemala than for children from poor households. One of the most striking findings to emerge from household survey data in Latin America is that the level of attainment among children from poor households is not only lower than in East Asia, which politicians in the region typically use as a point of comparison: by Grade 5 it is lower than in sub-Saharan Africa countries such as Zambia and Zimbabwe. Once again, data disaggregation helps to identify the main deficits in relation to the achievement of universal primary education. In Brazil,

Peru, and Bolivia, poor children dropping out account for more than 90 per cent of the shortfall in primary-school completion. Striking as they are, average differences between rich and poor households understate the full extent of the wealth gap in education. Differences in the median grade completed by children in differing wealth rankings reveal even wider disparities. The median represents the middle point in the survey data, and thus avoids some of the problems associated with compiling simple averages. It can be used to compare attainment levels in terms of average years of education across a range of wealth groups.

There are significant differences across all regions. In India, Pakistan, Senegal, Burkina Faso, Côte d 'Ivoire, and Mali, the median grade completed by children from poor households is zero, because fewer than half finished at least one year of schooling. In Africa and Latin America, the median wealth gap typically translates into a situation where children from poor households spend 4 – 7 years less in education than children from wealthier households. The wealth gap in India and Pakistan amounts to 9 –10 years. It is not only highly unequal countries that suffer from wide wealth gaps in education. Vietnam has one of the world 's most equal patterns of income distribution, but the net enrolment rate for children from the poorest quintile is 10 per cent lower than for the top quintile at the increase the coverage of education provision, while at the same time reducing dropout rates among poor children.

In Latin America, improving the physical availability of schools and the accessibility to all social classes is less of a problem than retaining the children from poor households after they have enrolled. But in all regions, the closure of wealth gaps in education and an increased emphasis on equity are the starting point for accelerated progress towards the goal of education for all.

In developing countries, men living in rural areas are twice as likely to be illiterate as those living in urban areas. Differences between rural and urban women are only slightly less extreme. Such disparities reflect differences in access to basic education. Limited educational opportunities in rural areas are caused by a combination of factors, ranging from the administrative cost and difficulty of providing services to more remote areas with scattered populations, to the unwillingness of teachers to live in isolated regions, and to demands for child labour. Public-spending priorities that concentrate resources on urban areas add to the problems of rural people. Overcoming wealth gaps in education is of profound importance to the achievement of the 2015 human-development targets. Bringing the average number of years spent in school by poor children up to the level of their wealthier counterparts would raise the average incomes of poor households, and produce more equitable patterns of income distribution.

Both outcomes would contribute to the halving of extreme income poverty. Similarly, increasing the average number of years spent in school by girls from poor households would help to reduce child-death rates. Different regions face different challenges if the wealth gap is to be closed. In sub-Saharan Africa and South Asia, the pressing need is to it across generations. Schools in poor rural areas are less accessible, less well equipped, and less able to provide an education of reasonable quality. For instance, 50 per cent of the rural poor live more than 10km from a school, compared with 10 per cent of urban poor households.

Rural schools have fewer qualified teachers and lower completion rates. As a result, the rural poor, who might be expected to reap some of the most significant human-development benefits of education, have the most restricted opportunities. Inequalities in educational opportunity restrict the ability of rural Zambians to work their way out of poverty. Education can act as a great leveller, but all too often it serves to reinforce disadvantage. Even in countries marked by poor levels of overall attainment, rural populations are frequently left far behind. Only 3 per cent of pupils attending rural primary school in Tanzania proceed to secondary school, compared with 10 per cent of their urban counterparts. One reason for the discrepancy is that only 17 per cent of rural school pupils pass their primary-school leaving exam, compared with 29 per cent in urban areas.In South Asia, rural –urban disparities are particularly marked, interacting with gender differences. The province of Sindh in Pakistan demonstrates the interaction in a particularly powerful fashion. For a young girl living in rural Sindh, her chance of going to school is half that of a young girl in urban Sindh; and she is twice as likely to leave before completing school.

Inequalities in education between men and women extend across a wide range of dimensions, including enrolment, completion, and the quality of teaching. Cultural, social, and economic factors combine to place young girls and women at a serious disadvantage that starts at school and extends into adulthood. The facts of gender discrimination speak for themselves:

— Women are 60 per cent more likely than men to be illiterate.

— There are 42 million fewer girls in primary school than boys.

— Gender gaps in enrolment have not narrowed significantly, even at the primary level. In South Asia, the net enrolment rate for girls is 20 per cent lower than for boys; in sub-Saharan Africa and the Middle East, it is 10 per cent lower.

— There are 12 countries in sub-Saharan Africa where the gender gap in enrolment exceeds 20 per cent.

— An average six-year-old girl in South Asia can expect to spend about six years in school –three years less than an average six-year-old boy. Even where progress has been made towards improving equity in enrolment, disadvantages in other areas often remain intact.

For instance, India has closed the gender gap in primary-school enrolment by 10 per cent since 1980, albeit to 22 per cent, which is still exceptionally high. Less success has been achieved in reducing the dropout rate for girls.Gender disparities cannot be considered in isolation. They interact strongly with inequalities linked to household wealth and rural –urban differences. In almost all cases, poverty reinforces gender inequity, so that girls born into poor households face far more restricted opportunities for education than girls born into wealthy households. In India, nine out of every ten girls from the richest quintile of households are in school, compared with fewer than half for the poorest two quintiles. This wealth-related gender gap widens over the duration of the school career. More than 80 per cent of girls from the wealthiest households complete Grade 8 –almost the same percentage as for boys from the same household. In the poorest households, only one in ten girls completes Grade 8 –and boys are three times more likely to reach this level than girls.

In many countries, wealth gaps aggravate already extreme inequalities between girls and boys. For instance, Nepal has one of lowest ratios of girls 'to boys 'enrolment in the world, and rich and poor families alike are less likely to send girls to school. But in poor families, the enrolment rate for girls is one-third of that for boys. Raising the average incomes of poor households would, in this case, almost certainly reduce gender-based inequity. Rural –urban differences magnify gender differences almost as much as household wealth does. In Pakistan, completion rates for primary school are twice as high in urban areas as in rural areas. But in rural areas the completion rate for boys is three times higher than for girls, while in urban areas it is only 50 per cent higher. Clearly, cultural, social, and economic factors associated with life in rural areas and with rural poverty exercise a powerful influence.

Important as wealth is, it cannot be taken as axiomatic that any increase in household income will improve gender equity. The relationship between income disparity and the gender gap is complex. Where the education of girls is regarded by parents as being of less value than the education of boys, economic pressures associated with low income will have adverse consequences for gender equity.

Girls are likely to be the last into school and the first out when times are hard. However, this tendency is not universal. Evidence from sub-Saharan Africa suggests that, while boys are often enrolled first in school, they are often the first to be withdrawn in situations of economic adversity where local employment practices preclude the use of girl-child labour to generate cash incomes away from the home. Whatever the national variations, it is clear that income growth and poverty reduction per se do not provide an automatic route to improved gender equity. The initial response within poor households to any increase in income may be to increase male enrolments, thus causing the gender gap to widen.The case of Yemen graphically demonstrates the complex interaction between the gender gap and other disparities. Gender gaps in enrolment are exceptionally wide, with girls accounting for only one-third of children in Grade 1. However, the national average conceals large urban – rural differences, with girls far better represented in major urban areas. In Sana 'a City, they account for more than 40 per cent of enrolments, compared with less than 20 per cent in rural Sana 'a. This is consistent with the broader pattern in many countries. In contrast to many countries, however, the correlation between wealth and the education status of women appears to be weaker in Yemen.

Illiteracy rates for poor and non-poor women are almost equivalent, at slightly above 80 per cent. Simply raising household incomes under these circumstances will have a limited effect, a fact that indicates the importance of more deeply rooted cultural factors.Uneven progress in providing access to education has resulted in deep regional disparities within countries –disparities which, in some cases, rival those between rich and poor countries.

Educational disadvantage tends to be concentrated in regions with the highest levels of poverty, as the following examples demonstrate.While Brazil is a middle-income country, the nine States of the northeast are among the poorest regions in the world. The poorest 50 per cent of the population in these States have per capita incomes broadly in line with the average for South Asia.This is the highest concentration of poverty in Latin

America, with human-welfare indicators which are far worse than in the rest of the country.

Inequalities in education perpetuate the human-welfare gap between the northeast and more prosperous regions. Over half the children in the rural northeast receive less than four years of schooling, and one quarter of the population has had no schooling. The Philippines.The Philippines has achieved relatively high rates of net enrolment. Regional differences related to poverty and service-provision account for much of this deficit. Four out of five pupils in Central Luzon complete primary school, compared with an average of one in three children in Northern Mindanao. Poverty incidence in Northern Mindanao is twice as high as in Central Luzon. Over the past two decades, Indonesia 's progress in education has been impressive. Gender differentials have narrowed at all levels, and near-universal primary-school enrolment has been achieved. But issues of quality and progression through the secondary-school system have come to the fore, especially in the Outer Islands. Net enrolment rates vary between 100 per cent in Jakarta and 58 per cent in Irian Jaya; dropout rates are less than 5 per cent in Central Java, but 23 per cent in East Timor. The incidence of poverty on the Outer Islands is about 33 per cent, compared with 20 per cent in Java. Similar differences are observed in human-development indicators.

Some of the developing world 's widest educational disparities exist between Indian States. In Kerala, almost all children in the 10 –14 age group are literate. By contrast, one-third of boys and two-thirds of girls in Uttar Pradesh are illiterate. The difference can be traced back to the primary-school system. Around one-quarter of all boys and half of girls in Uttar Pradesh have never enrolled. In the States of Bihar, Rajasthan, and Uttar Pradesh, the gender gap in enrolment is 25 per cent or more; in Kerala and Tamil Nadu it is less than 7 per cent. Inter-State differences have a profound bearing on the wealth gap in education, as noted above, there is a large national gap in enrolment between rich and poor households in India. But the wealth gap varies widely across States. In Kerala the enrolment gap between the richest 20 per cent and poorest 40 per cent of households amounts to 9 per cent; in Uttar Pradesh it rises to 56 per cent. This gap extends into children 's school careers. Attendance rates at school for children from the wealthiest 20 per cent of households are broadly similar for Kerala and Uttar Pradesh. However, the attendance rate of children from the poorest 40 per cent of households in Uttar Pradesh is 48 per cent – around half of the rate achieved in Kerala. Such differences starkly illustrate the fact that poverty is not an automatic barrier to higher levels of educational attainment.

Public-policy choices, made in this case by State government, are capable of overcoming the disadvantages associated with low incomes. For instance, average incomes in Kerala are lower than in either Tamil Nadu or Punjab, yet nine out of ten children in Kerala complete Grade 5, compared with fewer than five out of ten in the two wealthier States. Inter-State differences also have an important bearing on gender-related wealth gaps. The gender gap in enrolment for children from the poorest 40 per cent of households is close to zero in Kerala, but reaches as high as 32 per cent for Uttar Pradesh and 44 per cent for Rajasthan. As with other disparities, regional inequalities interact with gender disparities and urban –rural differences.

In Pakistan, the proportion of the overall adult population who have completed school to primary level or beyond varies from 26 per cent in Baluchistan to 41 per cent in Sindh. However, for rural women in these two provinces, the figures fall to 6 per cent and 8 per cent respectively. Regional inequality on this scale draws attention to the need for public action to close the gap in opportunities for households in different parts of the same country. Inequalities relating to ethnic minorities and indigenous people are strongly linked to regional disparities, and to the distribution of poverty. Deprivation in this area is among the most intensive of all forms of educational deprivation. But here too averages can have the effect of obscuring crosscutting patterns of deprivation. Within indigenous communities, inequalities based on household wealth and gender are often as pronounced as the inequalities in opportunity that separate indigenous and non-indigenous people.

East Asia has achieved some of the most impressive gains in education, increasing coverage and completion, and narrowing gender gaps. Pockets of intense deprivation associated with ethnicity remain intact, however. The case of the Philippines, which has achieved near-universal enrolment in primary school, illustrates the problem. During 1997, Oxfam conducted an education research programme in the Arakan Valley, in the eastern part of Mindanao island.The valley 's highland regions have been recognised by the government as the ancestral lands of the Manobos people. While the Manobos value education for their children, not least because they learn skills that are useful in negotiating with traders, schools are usually inaccessible. In one settlement covered by the Oxfam research project in 1997, the nearest school was a four-hour walk away over rough and steep trails. As a result, more than two-thirds of children were not in school. The Philippines case is not untypical. Countries such as China and Vietnam are often held up as model performers, because of their success in achieving levels of educational attainment that compare favourably with those for countries at far higher levels of average income.In one sense, this is justified. But despite the rapid progress achieved in extending educational opportunity, ethnic minorities have often been left behind. Enrolment and completion rates in the 25 provinces with the largest ethnic-minority population are far below the national average.

In Vietnam, ethnic-minority groups living in remote, mountainous, and poorer areas –such as the Northern Uplands and Central Highlands –have far lower rates of enrolment and completion than wealthier regions such as the southeast. Although ethnic-minority groups account for only 13 per cent of the population, they represent half of the children who are not in school; and children of ethnic minorities make up less than 4 per cent of the school population. School-completion rates are also far lower for ethnic minorities. Nationally, just over two out of every three students complete primary education. In Vietnam 's Central Highlands, the completion rate is 56 per cent. Research by Oxfam among Hmung communities in Lao Cai province in the Northern Upland region found enrolment rates as low as 40 per cent, and completion rates of only 38 per cent. Differences in educational opportunities partly account for the high concentration of poverty in the Northern Upland and Central Highland regions.

India 's caste system provides another stark example of education discrimination. Members of the 1091 scheduled castes and 573 scheduled tribes have historically suffered intense educational disadvantage. Often isolated both physically and geographically, these groups have lower enrolment rates, higher dropout rates, and wider gender gaps. Past discrimination is reflected in the fact that the literacy rate for scheduled castes and tribes is more than 30 per cent lower than the national average. Although there is evidence of disparities narrowing, this is happening at a slow pace. Research carried out by Oxfam in the Indian State of Gujarat shows the persistence of inequalities related to scheduled tribes. More significantly, four out of every five children had dropped out of school by Grade 5, even though the overall completion rate for Gujarat is 50 per cent. In Latin America, indigenous people living in remote highland areas have simultaneously suffered simultaneously from exclusion and inclusion. They have more limited access to public education systems, and these systems often represent a hostile environment in which children are taught in an alien language in an institution that does not respect their culture.

In Peru, educational opportunities are concentrated in the coastal areas, with chronic under-provision in regions such as the southern highlands. By the age of ten, a child in Ayacucho, a predominantly indigenous area, will have received three years of education –one year less than a child in the capital Lima. Thereafter the disadvantages become cumulative, as the low quality of education takes its toll. Only one-quarter of children in Ayacucho complete primary school. On average, taking into account repetition and dropout rates, it takes 15 school years per child to finish primary education in Ayacucho, compared with seven years in Lima. As in other regions, and with other dimensions of inequality, educational deprivation serves to reinforce poverty, with the most deprived communities experiencing the most severe exclusion. In Mexico, the 'poverty belt 'states of the Pacific South account for more than 80 per cent of the incidence of subsistence poverty. Some 5 million people are affected, more than the number of extreme poor in all of urban Mexico. An estimated two-thirds of those who live in the municipalities with the highest degree of poverty are indigenous people. Most of these municipalities lack access to basic amenities such as safe water and electricity –and they have the most limited access to education. Illiteracy rates for indigenous peoples are five times the national average, and net enrolment rates 20 per cent lower. In municipalities with a proportion of indigenous people greater than 30 per cent, each adult has on average four years 'less education than the national average. The strong association between education deprivation and poverty among indigenous people intersects with gender disparities. Indigenous people suffer extreme disadvar.tages, but indigenous women are particularly affected. Indigenous people in Guatemala receive on average 1.3 years of schooling, compared with a national average of 4.2 years. Indigenous females receive on average half as many years of schooling as indigenous males. In Bolivia, more than half of indigenous males and two-thirds of indigenous females do not complete primary education.

5

Impact of Learning Devices

Over the course of the industrial revolution, motors shrank in size and cost, disappearing inside household appliances and workplace tools to create new kinds of machines. Through a similar process are now embedding computers and telecommunications into everyday context, making possible three innovative types of learning devices. Smart objects, with embedded microprocessors and wireless networking, explain their own functioning and help us create articulate educational environments that communicate with their inhabitants. Information infrastructures provide remote access to experts, interlinked archival resources, virtual communities, and distributed investigations involving many participants in different locations. Shared synthetic environments, by immersing us in illusion, help us develop a better understanding and appreciation of reality. The new messages emerging from these new media can dramatically improve instructional outcomes, but such an evolution of educational practice depends on careful design of the interface among the devices, learners, and teachers.

High-performance computing and telecommunications are driving the rapid evolution of devices that facilitate learning. Imagine information technologies as forming something akin to a biological ecosystem, with each type of device a different species. First came the telegraph, then the telephone, then radio, television, videotape players, videodisc players . . . . Now this ecosystem is incredibly crowded; every few months a new species appears, such as the personal digital assistant. From their individual niches, a bewildering variety of species cooperate, compete, and become extinct, just as in nature's ecological systems. The coming generation of computers and telecommunications is different from prior evolutions of information technology because it is dramatically reversing the century-old trend toward a crowded ecology of devices.

Different species are fusing together; the radio, television, telephone, copier, fax, scanner, printer, and computer will eventually coexist in a single box. Soon, the ecology of information technologies will have only a few superspecies remaining that synthesize and extend the capabilities of all current devices. One way of understanding this evolution is to classify these synthesis devices into three typesùsmart objects, information infrastructures, and shared synthetic environmentsùbased on their relationship to our surroundings. Smart objects are artifacts in our immediate context that can explain themselves and, acting in concert, help us understand our surroundings.

Information infrastructures are ways of extending our nervous systems so that we can communicate and learn across barriers of distance and time, exploring and contributing to remote archives and virtual think tanks. Shared synthetic environments are entire virtual contexts into which we immerse ourselves, much as Alice walked through the looking glass to become part of an artificial reality. Thinking about new educational media from this perspective highlights the crucial issue of how our relationship to these various devices shapes and makes possible different types of learning. As microprocessors and wireless networking grow cheaper and more powerful, it is rapidly becoming more feasible to design embedded capabilities (including speech, imagery, and intelligence) into common objects, thereby enhancing their educational value. Smart objects used for learning might include, for example, intelligent manipulatives for young children. Imagine a child stacking blocks by size, from biggest to smallest, to form a tower.

The global marketplace and the communications and entertainment industries are driving the rapid evolution of regional, national, and global information infrastructures that enhance our abilities to access and interlink materials in remote archives. These powerful channels for transmitting data are ways of extending our nervous systems so that we can communicate and learn across barriers of distance and time, exploring and contributing to virtual think tanks. As a result, the means for creating, delivering, and using information in business, government, and society are swiftly changing. To successfully prepare students as workers and citizens, educators must incorporate experiences into the curriculum that enable students to create and utilize new forms of expression and that can be activated just in time, at any place, and on demand. The information superhighway metaphor, now widely used to convey the implications of high-performance computing and communications, is an inadequate analogy. It is the equivalent of someone in 1896 declaring that the airplane will be the canal system of the 20th century. Backward-looking metaphors focus on what can automateùhow can use new channels to send conventional forms of content more efficientlyùbut miss the true innovation: redefining how communicate and educate by using new types of messages and experiences to be more effective.

Since emerging forms of representation, such as hypermedia and virtual reality, are in their early stages of development, we are just beginning to understand how they shape not only their messages, but also their users. Many people are still reeling from the first impact of high-performance computing and communications: shifting from the challenge of not getting enough information to the challenge of surviving amid too much information. The core skill needed in today's workplace is not foraging for data, but filtering a plethora of incoming information. The emerging literacy we all must master requires immersing ourselves in a sea of information and harvesting patterns of knowledge, just as fish extract oxygen from water via their gills. In this environment, educators must understand how to structure learning experiences that make this kind of immersion possible.

Preparing students for full participation in 21st century society will require expanding the traditional definitions of literacy and rhetoric to encompass 'immersionlike' experiences of interacting with information. Two new forms of expression that take advantage of the unique power of information infrastructures are knowledge webs and virtual communities. Both illustrate how information infrastructures can have a major impact on conventional instruction by expanding learning resources beyond the individual teacher and classroom materials, to encompass rich, widely distributed sources of information, expertise, and fellowship.

'Knowledge webs' give people distributed access to experts, archival resources, authentic environments, and shared investigations. A well-informed person in immediate vicinity for guidance, to consulting printed information or watching a news program, to visiting exhibits like zoos to learn about different types of environments, and to conducting informal experiments to understand how reality works. Often, these information gathering and creation activities are constrained by barriers of distance, restricted access, scheduling difficulties, and limited personal expertise in investigation methods. Via information infrastructures, educators and students can join distributed conferences that provide an instant network of contacts with useful skillsùa personal brain trust scattered geographically, but offering just-in-time answers to immediate questions. Eventually, these informal sources of expertise will utilize embedded 'groupware' tools to enhance collaboration.

On the Internet, online archival resources are linked increasingly into the World Wide Web, accessible through 'webcrawler' programmes such as Netscape. In time, guides based on artificial intelligence will help users navigate through huge amounts of stored information. Another type of emerging electronic environment is the virtual exhibit that duplicates museums and other real-world settings. Virtual exhibits make possible a wide variety of experiences without the necessity of travel or scheduling. Distributed science projects enable students to conduct shared experiments dispersed across time and space; often each team member learns more than would be possible in isolation about the phenomenon being studied and about scientific investigation. Combined, all these capabilities to enhance information gathering and creation form knowledge webs.

Access to data does not automatically expand students' knowledge; the availability of information does not intrinsically create an internal framework of ideas that learners can use to interpret reality. While presentational approaches transmit material rapidly from source to student, often this content evaporates quickly from learners' minds. To be motivated to master concepts and skills, students need to see the connection of what they are learning to the rest of their lives and to the mental models they already use. Even when learners are drilled in a topic until facts are indefinitely retainedùwe all know that the sum of a triangle's internal angles is 180 degrees this knowledge is often 'inert'; most people don't know how to apply the abstract principles they memorised in school to solve real-world problems. To move students beyond assimilating inert facts and toward generating better mental models, teachers must structure learning experiences that highlight how new ideas can provide insights in intriguing, challenging situations. The curriculum is already overcrowded with low-level information; teachers frantically race through required material, helping students memorize factual data to be regurgitated on mandated, standardized tests. Using information infrastructures as a fire hose to spray yet more information into educational settings would make this situation even worse. Without skilled facilitation, many learners who access current knowledge webs will flounder in a morass of unstructured data. A vital, emerging form of literacy that educators ought to be communicating is how to transform archival information into personal knowledge.

Moving students from access through assimilation to appropriation is no simple process, however. Teachers must provide unsophisticated learners with educational experiences that enable them to construct their own knowledge and make sense of massive, incomplete, and inconsistent information sources. In order to create a learner-centered environment in which students can take full advantage of information infrastructures, it is vital that educators augment the traditional curriculum with collaborative, learning-through-doing activities based on linked, online materials and orchestrated across classrooms, workplaces, homes, and community settings.

Virtual Communities

Virtual communities that provide support from people who share common joys and trials are a second means for enhancing student learning through information infrastructures. We are accustomed to face-to-face interaction as a way of getting to know people, sharing ideas and experiences, enjoying others' humor and fellowship, and finding solace. In a different manner, distributed learning via information infrastructures can satisfy these needs at any time, in any place. Some people or reflective or seeking a little emotional distance may even find asynchronous, low-bandwidth communication more 'authentic' than face-to-face verbal exchange. They can take time before replying to compose a more elegant message or refine the emotional nuances they wish to convey. This alternative conception of authenticity may reflect a different kind of learning style than the visual, auditory, symbolic, and kinesthetic distinctions now used. Virtual communities are an important component of new pedagogical strategies based on information infrastructures, one that can dramatically improve learning outcomes.

Learning is social as well as intellectual. Individual, isolated attempts to make sense of complex data can easily fail unless the learner is encouraged by some larger group that is constructing shared knowledge. In addition, institutional evolution is a communal enterprise; educational innovators also need emotional and intellectual support from others who have similar challenges in their lives. Moreover, formal education comprises only a small fraction of how students spend their time. No matter how effective the schooling, students are unlikely to make major gains in learning if the other parts of their lives are not educationally fulfilling.

Virtual communities can help bring about close cooperation and shared responsibility for learning among all the educational agents of societyùfamilies, social service agencies, workplaces, mass media, schools, and higher education. For example, involving families more deeply in their children's education may be the single most powerful lever for improved learning outcomes. Virtual parent-teacher conferences and less formal social interchanges provide new opportunities for involving parents who will never come to a PTA meeting or a school-based event. In many regions across the United States, community networks are emerging that, among other missions, enhance education by enabling distributed discourse among all the stakeholders in quality schooling. Peer tutoring is another educational use of virtual communities. This instructional approach aids all students involved, on both an intellectual and an emotional level, but is difficult to implement in traditional classroom settings. Outside of school, virtual interactions, enhanced by groupware tools, make it easy for students to relate to each other and also prepare them to use distributed problem-solving techniques in adult workplaces. Telementoring and teleapprenticeships between students and workplace experts are other ways of applying the capabilities of virtual communities to distributed learning.

Creating a sense of communion among a distributed group linked by low-to-moderate bandwidth networking is a complex challenge. Some people favor technology-mediated communication as their most authentic way of sharing ideas and enjoying fellowship. Most people prefer face-to-face interaction, but find that the convenience of just-in-time, any-place access to others often outweighs the disadvantages of distributed sharing of ideas, experiences, and support. Groupware tools, a capable moderator, and shared interactivity and control are important for sustaining the vitality of virtual communities, as is occasional direct contact among participants. To succeed in sustaining communion among people, distributed learning must balance virtual and direct interaction.

A relationship based only on telephone conversation lacks the vibrancy that face-to-face interchange provides. Similarly, while digital video will broaden the bandwidth of virtual interactions via information infrastructures, teleconferencing will never completely substitute for direct personal contact. A variety of social inventions to emerge that provide the best of both worlds. Just beginning to understand how knowledge webs and virtual communities can reshape the content, process, and delivery of conventional distance education. Information infrastructures are the new type of learning device that is spurring this evolution, just as the steam engine was the driver for the industrial revolution.

- Shared synthetic environments, the third type of emerging learning device, are entire virtual contexts into which we immerse ourselves, just as Alice walked through the looking glass and became part of an artificial reality. Communal virtual worlds that students can enter and explore have many educational uses. For example, single-user simulations allow an individual to interact with a model of reality, such as flying a virtual airplane. Distributed simulations extend this capability by enabling many people at different locations to inhabit and shape a common synthetic environment. As an illustration, the U.S. Department of Defense uses distributed simulation to create virtual battlefields on which trainees at remote sites develop collective military skills. The appearance and capabilities of graphically represented military equipment alter second by second as the virtual battle evolves. Shared synthetic environments are a representational container that can accommodate a broad range of educational uses, such as virtual factories, hospitals, or cities. Moreover, this type of distributed learning strategy uses 'edutainment' to build on the curiosity, fantasy, and motivation that the entertainment industry stimulates in youngsters. While home video game consoles are not now particularly powerful, in 8 to 10 years they will be quite sophisticated in graphics and distributed simulation capabilities, but still relatively inexpensive because so many are sold.

Since video game consoles are widely found even in poor and rural households, they offer a promising installed base of learning technologies if we develop educationally rich material that takes advantage of these systems. Even without the added enhancement of visual imagery, the rise on the Internet of text-based shared synthetic environments (i.e., MUDs, MUSEs, MOOs) illustrates the fascination that people have with participatory virtual worlds. The continual evolution of distributed simulations based on participants' collaborative interactions keeps these shared virtual environments from becoming boring and stale. In contrast to standard adventure games, in which you wander through someone else's fantasy, the ability to personalise an environment and receive recognition from others for adding to the shared context is attractive to many people. Part of why we read fiction or watch dramatic productions is to escape the ordinary in a manner that increases our insights or refreshes us to plunge back into real-world challenges. Shared virtual experiences on the national information infrastructure can complement books, plays, television, movies, and concerts by taking us beyond the daily grind; the challenge, however, is to move past escapism into metaphorical comprehension and catharsis.

Advances in high-performance computing and communications also provide the means for sensory immersion, whereby learners are involved in 'artificial realities.' Wearing computerised clothing and a head-mounted display, the participant feels as if he is 'inside' an artificial reality, rather than just viewing a synthetic environment through a computer monitor's screen; virtual reality is analogous to diving rather than to looking through an aquarium window. Using sensory immersion to present abstract, symbolic data in tangible form is a powerful method of attaining insights into real world phenomena. 'Visualization,' for example, is an emerging type of rhetoric that enhances learning by using the human visual system to find patterns in large amounts of information. People have very powerful capabilities to recognize patterns among images; much of our brain is 'wetware' dedicated to this purpose. As a result, when tabular data of numerical variables such as temperature, pressure, and velocity are transfigured into graphical objects that shift their shape, texture, size, color, and motion to convey the changing values of each variable, learners also gain increased insights. For example, graphical data visualizations that model thunderstorm-related phenomena (downbursts, air flows, cloud movements) can help meteorologists and students understand the dynamics of these weather systems. As information infrastructures increasingly enable people to access large databases across distances, visualisation tools can expand human perceptions so that we recognize underlying relationships that would otherwise be swamped in a sea of numbers.

One good way to enhance creativity is to make the familiar strange and the strange, familiar; adding sound and even tactile sensations to visual imagery can make abstract things tangible, and vice versa. Expanding human perceptionsùfor example, allowing a medical student to see the human body through X-ray vision like Superman's is a powerful method for deepening learners' motivation and their intuitions about physical phenomena. Current research centers on assessing the potential value of sensory immersion and synthetic environments for learning material as disparate as electromagnetic fields and intercultural sensitivities.

During today's much larger war in the information services industry, educators that have innovative alternatives to "talking heads" instruction can find vendors happy to share the costs in exchange for help with the regulators, legislators, and judges who are determining which coalitions will manage the nation's information infrastructures. As with business, however, the evolution of technology creates new markets and expanded competitors for schools and colleges. As one illustration, prestigious universities may develop nationwide offerings of standard courses, such as Psych 101, taught by telegenic, internationally recognized authorities. Under this strategy, presentations with high production values would be coupled with frequent, interactive teleconferences, mentoring via electronic mail, and occasional face-to-face meetings of locally enrolled students led by a practitioner. This approach would not intrigue learners interested in a residential college experience, but could be very attractive to students at commuter campuses. With sufficient economies of scale, this delivery method would have lower costs than our present system of similar standard courses duplicated at every institution. While many faculty would disparage this type of instruction, state legislatures could easily see it as an attractive way to cut their expenditures for higher educationùa method applicable to every course for which a substantial textbook market exists. In this particular evolution of distance education, colleges and universities would be reshaped as profoundly as American business has been altered by the technologies that helped create the global marketplace.

Given their responsibilities for socialization and custodial protection, public schools would be less affected by the erosion of geographic monopolies through distributed learning technologies. But the home schooling and educational voucher movements see emerging learning devices as an attractive alternative means of delivering instruction. If smart objects, information infrastructures, and shared synthetic environments are not incorporated into public school classrooms, teachers may find a decade from now that they have a smaller fraction of students enrolled and fewer taxpayers willing to provide funding. Educators must help all students become adept at distanced interaction, for skills of gathering information from remote sources and of collaboration with dispersed team members are as central to the future American workplace as learning to perform structured tasks quickly was to the industrial revolution. Also, by increasing the diversity of human resources available to students, distributed learning can enhance equity and pluralism, while preparing young people to compete in the world marketplace.

Virtual classrooms have a wider spectrum of peers with whom learners can collaborate than any local region can offer and a broader range of teachers and mentors than any single educational institution can afford. In a few years, high-performance computing and communications will make knowledge utilities, virtual communities, shared synthetic environments, and sensory immersion as routine a part of everyday existence as the telephone, television, radio, and newspaper are today. This evolution of learning devices won't be a 'silver bullet' that magically solves all problems of education, however. Thoughtful and caring participation is vital for making these new capabilities truly valuable. How a medium shapes its users, as well as its message, is a central issue in understanding the personal impact of emerging learning devices.

The telephone creates conversationalists. The book develops imaginers, who can conjure a rich mental image from sparse symbols on a printed page. Much of television programming induces passive observers; other shows, such as Sesame Street and public affairs programs, can spark viewers' enthusiasm and enrich their perspectives. Through the evolution of smart objects, information infrastructures, and shared synthetic environments, our society is encountering powerful new interactive media capable of great good or ill. Today's 'couch potatoes', vicariously living in the fantasy world of television, could become tomorrow's 'couch funguses', immersed as protagonists in 3-D soap operas while the real world deteriorates.

Impact of Technology on Teaching

Some schools of education are in the vanguard of introducing technology into teacher preparation. Yet most schools of education have not yet fully integrated technology into their programs for preparing teachers. There is a long road ahead. Two million new teachers will be hired over the next decade. Will these new teachers be comfortable and skilled in using technology? What will it take to transform schools of education so that faculty feel comfortable e-mailing students, using listserves for projects and instruction, and introducing candidates to software that enhances instruction? As technology moves from the periphery to the center in P-12 schools, so must it move from the periphery to the center in teacher preparation. This is the culmination of a year of deliberations by US's National Council for the Accreditation of Teacher Education (NCATEs) Task Force on Technology and Teacher Education. NCATE commissioned the task force to help guide the development and implementation of technology expectations for teacher candidates and for accredited schools of education, and to guide the organization's use of technology in the accreditation process.

NCATE is in a unique position to provide leadership. In 1995, NCATE introduced technology expectations for schools of education. In 1997, NCATE , which recommends that NCATE emphasize technology as central to the teacher preparation process. In the year 2000, NCATE will introduce its latest set of accreditation standards which will undoubtedly raise the bar for the use of technology in teaching and learning in schools of education. Just as NCATE expects accredited institutions to use technology in teaching and learning, its institutions should look to NCATE to use technology in the accreditation process. NCATE intends to streamline the accreditation process so that schools of education can send and receive information to each other and NCATE electronically, reducing paperwork and saving time, money and effort. We look forward to working with you as technology transforms education through this century and beyond.

It is impossible to deny the tremendous effect rapid technological growth has had on our society. This explosion of new technologies has changed the way we live—from the way do business to the way communicate with each other. Technological advancements are also affecting the way teach and learn. The business world demands that schools prepare educated workers who can use technology effectively in the global marketplace. The president and vice president of the United States, governors, state legislatures, and other policy-making groups are increasingly convinced that technology is a central element of educational reform and improved student learning. New skills needed in the workplace are catalysts that spur technology use in the classroom.

Computer to student ratios have declined steadily from 50:1 in 1985 to 20:1 in 1990 to an estimated 9:1 in 1997, affecting traditional classroom practice and even the culture of the schools. Student enrollment is growing at the same time that the nation's experienced teaching staff is declining, due to regular retirement. An estimated two million new teachers will be hired during the next decade. Classroom teachers hold the key to the effective use of technology to improve learning. But if teachers don't understand how to employ technology effectively to promote student learning, the billions of dollars being invested in educational technology initiatives will be wasted. The nation's teacher education institutions must close the teaching and learning technology gap between where we are now and where we need to be. Although progress has been made and exemplary practices exist, recent research indicates that most teacher education programs have a long way to go. Teacher education institutions must prepare their students to teach in tomorrow's classrooms. Rather than wait to see what tomorrow's classrooms will be like, they must experiment with the effective application of computer technology for teaching and learning in their own campus practice.

Today's teacher candidates will teach tomorrow as they are taught today. The NCATE Task Force on Technology and Teacher Education, a group of educators from diverse institutions and backgrounds, was assembled to consider ways that NCATE can provide leadership and support initiatives to meet the technology challenge facing teacher education institutions. The group met three times during 1996-1997 to identify and discuss the issues. The first section presents the task force's vision of what teachers must be able to do in order to take advantage of technology for instruction and student learning, identifies current teacher education program deficiencies, and suggests what teacher education programs need to do to correct the deficiencies and bring vision into reality. The second section advances three broad recommendations regarding what NCATE can do to:

1) stimulate more effective uses of technology in teacher education programs,
2) use technology to improve the existing accreditation process and to reconceptualize accreditation for the 21st century, and
3) improve and expand its own operations through greater uses of technology.

The task force finds that a watershed for education and training has been created by rising costs for P-12 and higher education, by educational reform efforts at the state and federal levels, and by developments in modern information technology that have already affected the U.S. economy and society. Marginal efforts to improve teacher education will not satisfy the spirit of the times or the practical demands placed on education by the nation. Vigorous action by NCATE and its member institutions is necessary to effect substantial reform. From time to time, someone invents a product or develops a practice which has an unforeseen and massive impact on society. The printing press, created by Johann Gutenberg approximately five and a half centuries ago, was such an invention. The results of the printing press, and all of its modern successors, are so much a part of our lives it is difficult to imagine an existence without the ability to read, and the books, journals, and newspapers that support a reading public. It is also difficult to imagine how one could organize instruction without textbooks and various associated readings.

For teachers and students alike, learning at all levels of education has been primarily a process of reading what experts have written, discussing what has been read, and listening to teachers explain or expand upon textbooks. In most cases, schooling has become a process for understanding, retaining, andwhat is found on the printed page. Inventions of the twentieth century have the potential to influence society as much as did the printing press. The computer, video, and telecommunications of various kinds are having an impact on every aspect of our society: work, leisure, entertainment, household tasks. These inventions are also transforming the way we approach knowledge and sources of expertise.

Today, people are no longer required to read about an event; they can see media versions of it unfold before their own eyes and make their own interpretation. Consequently, the ability to obtain and interpret information quickly and accurately is even more important than in the past. There is no longer a question about whether the new technology will be used in schools. Nearly everyone agrees that students must have access to computers, video, and other technology in the classroom. Many believe these technologies are necessary because competency in their use is an important feature of career preparation; others see equally important outcomes for civic participation.

Most importantly, a growing research base confirms technology's potential for enhancing student achievement. What is less certain is how and when these technologies will change the nature of schooling itself.

For example, the technologies are already providing an alternative curriculum for students that is scarcely acknowledged by the formal school curriculum. Nevertheless, they have been mainly employed as additions to the existing curriculum. Teachers are employed who know how to use them, but knowledge of and skill in the use of technology has not been necessary for all teachers. These attitudes are surely short-sighted if technology infusion is to take root. The introduction of computers and other technologies into schools is occurring at the same time that three decades of research in the cognitive sciences, which has deepened our understanding of how people learn, is prompting a reappraisal of teaching practices.

As new technologies become more readily available and less expensive, they will likely serve as a catalyst for ensuring that new approaches to teaching gain a firm foothold in schools. Despite the technology changes in society, being a teacher in American schools too often consists of helping children and youth acquire information from textbooks and acting as an additional source of expertise. Teachers are provided role models of this approach to teaching from kindergarten through graduate school; their teacher education courses provide hints for making textbook-oriented instruction interesting and productive, and as teaching interns, they both observe and practice instruction based upon mastering information found in books. Teachers may be forgiven if they cling to old models of teaching that have served them well in the past.

All of their formal instruction and role models were driven by traditional teaching practices. Breaking away from traditional approaches to instruction means taking risks and venturing into the unknown. But this is precisely what is needed at the present time. Teachers need to understand the deep impact technology is having on society as a whole: how technology has changed the nature of work, of communications, and our understanding of the development of knowledge.

Today, teachers must recognize that information is available from sources that go well beyond textbooks and teachers—mass media, communities, etc. and help students understand and make use of the many ways in which they can gain access to information. Teachers must employ a wide range of technological tools and software as part of their own instructional repertoire. Teachers should help students pursue their own inquiries, making use of technologies to find, organize, and interpret information, and to become reflective and critical about information quality and sources. Teachers must participate in formal courses, some of which may be delivered in nontraditional ways, e.g., via telecommunications; they must also become part of ongoing, informal learning communities with other professionals who share their interests and concerns.

Finally, teachers need an 'attitude' that is fearless in the use of technology, encourages them to take risks, and inspires them to become lifelong learners. Once, a teacher who was well prepared in the subject she taught, experienced in the design of interesting classroom activities, and on top of information conveyed by the textbook, could contemplate a long career in teaching without having to change her style or practice very much. Those days are over. Future teachers take their cues from the practices they observe in classrooms during teaching practica and internships. If students are taught the latest technology uses as part of their teacher education programs, but don't see effective technology practices in the schools, they are unlikely to incorporate technology use in their own teaching.

Schools are powerful socializing agencies that greatly affect new teachers' perceptions about what does and what doesn't work in practice. The new technology will transform the role of the teacher as thoroughly as did the introduction of printed textbooks. More than in the past, teachers must become advisors to student inquirers, helping them to frame questions for productive investigation, directing them toward information and interpretive sources, helping them to judge the quality of the information they obtain, and coaching them in ways to present their findings effectively to others. This will require teachers to become even better prepared in the content of the subjects they teach, and the means by which the content can be taught and learned.

Re-educating the existing teaching force will not be easy and will require extensive professional development over many years. The problem will be greatly compounded if those teachers entering the profession now and in the future have not been adequately prepared to use new technology. Public attention has been focused on the reform of elementary and secondary schools without attending to the preservice preparation of teachers who will work in these schools. However, with an estimated need for 2 million new teachers over the next decade to replace retiring teachers and to meet increased student enrollment, well-designed preservice teacher education is a critical factor in reforming our schools. Responsibility for preservice teacher education is not limited to a college or department of education within a university. In general, teachers take more courses in general education and in their academic majors and minors than they do in professional studies.

Any effort to remake teacher education must consider all of the undergraduate and graduate experience of teachers, as case illustrations 4 and 5 demonstrate.

Not using technology much in their own research and teaching, teacher education faculty have insufficient understanding of the demands on classroom teachers to incorporate technology into their teaching. Many do not fully appreciate the impact technology is having on the way work is accomplished. They undervalue the significance of technology and treat it as merely another topic about which teachers should be informed. As a result, colleges and universities are making the same mistake that was made by P-12 schools; they treat 'technology' as a special addition to the teacher education curriculum—requiring specially prepared faculty and specially equipped classrooms—but not a topic that needs to be incorporated across the entire teacher education program. Consequently, teachers-in-training are provided instruction in 'computer literacy' and are shown examples of computer software, but they rarely are required to apply technology in their courses and are denied role models of faculty employing technology in their own work. The reasons for these deficiencies in teacher education programs are relatively easy to explain, if difficult to excuse.

— Many teacher education programs lack the hardware and software essential to strong programs. Teacher education programs often are given low priority for special technology funding on their campuses and therefore are denied essential technology.

— Many teacher education faculty lack the knowledge and skill to incorporate technology into their own teaching. Similar to P-12 teachers, they have not been provided the training they need to use technology successfully.

— A majority of teacher education departments and colleges have not been able to invest in the technical support required to maintain a high quality technology program.

— Some higher education faculty are out of touch with what is happening in schools. They have little understanding of the vast changes that are occurring in P-12 classrooms as a result of the introduction of technology and how they must change their own instruction to stay abreast of changes in the schools.

— Teacher education programs are driven by an academic culture that rewards and recognizes individuality among faculty.

There are few incentives for bringing faculty together around a common vision about what the teacher education program should be. There may be individual faculty who believe that more emphasis should be given to the role of technology, but in any program it is likely that faculty who either oppose technology altogether or who at least do not wish it to be a priority are present as well. Furthermore, development of technological applications of software, while extremely time-consuming, is often not as highly valued for tenure as is more traditional publication and research. Too, because college faculty also are expected to be experts in their own fields, there is little or no tradition of identifying absences of knowledge and skill among college faculty and providing faculty development to overcome these deficiencies.

Bringing about the needed changes in teacher education programs will not be easy. Change will not occur by simply adding a course or recruiting a new faculty member who understands technology. What is required is a transformation of the culture of teacher education, one in which technology is seen as changing relationships between students and teachers and between learners and knowledge.

Teacher education programs should be guided by a vision of what their programs might become if they took full advantage of information technology. For example, teacher education programs devote substantial time and expense to providing 'early experiences' for their students. These typically involve sending students individually or in groups to spend time in school classrooms observing teachers. Sometimes these experiences are tightly linked to the instruction taking place in the university classroom, but illustrative examples of theory in practice can rarely be planned and cannot be analyzed as they occur. Two-way interactive video allows teacher education students to observe a P-12 class from their university classroom. Their professor can point to events that deserve special consideration, without interfering with the P-12 class. Technology can also serve as the catalyst for reconsidering the entire architecture of teacher education: e.g., how, when, and where candidates will acquire the knowledge and skills they need; and the linkage between preservice and in-service professional development.

The integration of technology should be accomplished in relation to other efforts to reform teacher preparation, not as a separate reform initiative. No vision about the future of teacher education is likely to prove useful if it is not closely tied to a set of assumptions about the future of schooling and the impact of technology on school instruction. This visionary process is one that must remain fluid and subject to amendment as conditions and opportunities change. The job is not to create a vision statement that remains fixed for years; the task is to begin a process in which the faculty begin to dream about the kinds of schools and teacher education programs society requires and how to obtain them. Above all, the process demands a faculty prepared to experiment and to try new ideas.

With a vision in hand, the teacher education faculty need to plan how their vision can be realized. The "plan" must be more than a technology acquisition plan that focuses on how to acquire, allocate, and amortize hardware and software. The plan must be tightly linked to other planning processes in the college and include suggestions for integrating technology across the curriculum, for providing faculty development, and for building the support structure the program will require. Steps for reallocations within the existing budget as well as ideas for seeking external funds are also a part of a good plan. The budget planning process must also include the recurrent costs associated with technologies—which include maintenance as well as upgrading. Perhaps the most important part of a sound plan is the specified outcomes for the students who are enrolled in the teacher education program

Teacher candidates can progress along a continuum, starting as consumers of technology (reliance on faculty-developed applications) to become producers of technology-based applications for use in their teaching. In addition, teacher education programs should pay careful attention to the National Standards for Technology in Teacher Preparation, developed by the International

Society for Technology in Education (ISTE). ISTE recommends that all teachers acquire competencies in basic computer/technology operations, in personal and professional uses of technology, and in the application of technology for instruction. Few, if any, teacher education programs are currently meeting all of these standards. Few schools or departments of education will be able to achieve their plans and to reach their visions in a brief period. Therefore, plans must remain flexible in order to take advantage of new and unforeseen circumstances: new technology, new faculty, new funding opportunities. What is important is to have a plan that is directed toward the vision with the flexibility to alter the plan appropriately as efforts take place. Continuous and systematic planning is more important than achieving a final plan.

Perhaps the best way the faculty can inspire teachers-in-training to use technology is to cast themselves as learners and to experiment fearlessly in the applications of technology. The teacher education faculty can make themselves role models of lifelong learning if they create for themselves situations in which they must learn from each other and from their students. Except at the level of graduate seminars, faculty are not accustomed to place themselves in situations where they are members of a learning group. College faculty can lean upon more skilled faculty colleagues who can coach them while they improve their own abilities. Such efforts demonstrate a model of teaching behavior that should be encouraged among P-12 teachers. It is not necessary for all faculty members to exploit every technology in their classes. Nor is it necessary for faculty to reach consensus on how technology should best be employed.

The fact is that, in the early stages of understanding how technology can be used most effectively to support teaching and learning. Given the circumstances, it is best if many pedagogical approaches are tested, several theories of learning applied, and a variety of technologies are used. The results of each experiment should be assessed carefully. Encouraging faculty to be reflective about their work and evaluate results of instruction can also advance an important domain of knowledge, while building faculty competence. This is not a time when teacher education programmes can confidently predict how technology will change the profession. This is a time of transition, which calls for experimentation. If teacher education programs adopt a vision of what they wish to accomplish and become, and specify technology's role in support of this vision, and if they encourage an attitude of experimentation in which the teacher education faculty and the teachers-in-training learn to use the technology effectively together, then the other factors that must change will logically follow. These include:

— An appropriate infrastructure that allows powerful applications of technology to occur. For example, the technical infrastructure must not only accommodate uses on campus but also allow distance learning connections with P-12 schools and teacher education programs in other colleges and universities.

— Incentives for faculty in terms of release time for professional development, new course development, and recognition for experimental teaching at times of tenure and merit review;

— Technical support that provides reliable maintenance of existing equipment and assistance for new software applications;

— Sufficient access to technology for faculty and students;

— Better linkage to P-12 schools and to other sectors of the university or community where students receive portions of their training;

— Continuing relationships with corporations and foundations for funds to support innovations in teacher education.

Colleges and universities must use a multifaceted approach for implementing technology, developing technology use by faculty and staff, continually upgrading facilities and equipment, and maintaining ongoing involvement with elementary and secondary schools and businesses.

6

Web-based Learning: Challenges and Opportunities

As more courses in higher education move to an online format, a major concern is a potential loss of personal interaction between the professor and student. There is evidence that a growing number of courses delivered in an online format tend to be configured and delivered in an asynchronous manner more often associated with traditional independent study and correspondence work, i.e., students working independently to complete posted assignments at their own pace. While this format serves the purpose of meeting the needs of the non-traditional learner in regard to delimiting issues of time and distance, and in many instances is a viable option, it leaves a "missing link" in the learning curve for students because they lack the opportunity to benefit from the experience of structured dialogue, interaction with faculty and peers, and the sense of community that can be created in a traditional on-site classroom environment. Learning involves two types of interaction: interaction with content and interpersonal interaction. Online courses must adopt a pedagogical framework more closely aligned with social learning theory for students to maximize the benefits of online instruction. Although many professors create their own courses, publishing companies are responding to the growing online course market by creating a wide variety of pre-packaged courses.

The resulting phenomenon has been termed unbundling and refers to courses that are developed by 'content experts' and then are facilitated by a faculty member. The role of the professor shifts from that of authority to the role of course manager. The increasing availability of these fabricated online courses is likely to further the trend of lowered personal interaction between the professor and student. An essential component of any course is the culture or environment that exists within that course, i.e., the expectations, understanding of members' roles, process of how the course will evolve, and establishment of rituals, celebrations, traditions, etc. Whether the course is taught online or on-site, the culture established within the course serves either as an enhancement or barrier to the quality of student learning. Where interaction, collegiality, and collaboration are a valuable part of the culture, there is a better exchange of ideas and development of problem-solving skills. Course cultures with a high degree of interaction benefit from the concept of team learning.

Interactivity and a positive culture create a sense of synergy where group learning and productivity become greater than the total sum of individual students learning and productivity. These qualities are lost in the asynchronous online course format. The importance of creating within the culture a learning community that is synergized. Most online course delivery systems include a synchronous communication tool, such as the chat room, as well as interactive asynchronous tools such as e-mail, listserv, threaded discussion, and bulletin board. When used effectively, each of these can be used to maintain high levels of communication between and among class members and the professor and to promote desired levels of interactivity. The following is an overview of some of the strategies used by the authors to maintain quality interactivity in the online environment.

Chat is a real-time, electronic form of communication. It affords both the instructor and students the opportunity to engage in real time discourse and dialogue. The quality of interaction is determined by the established culture of reflection, preparation, and risk-free participation. Instructional delivery via chat requires the instructor to extract himself from the traditional didactic teaching format and instead embrace a more fluid attempt to lead students to the acquisition of desired learning outcomes. Such expectations can be achieved via Socratic teaching methods whereby the instructor poses leading questions/ statements to which students engage each other in inductive reasoning to arrive at the desired level of understanding. In this setting the instructor is a facilitator of specific content rather than a 'deliverer' of content.

The instructor must be prepared to adjust, adapt, and modify the questions and/or issues to be raised based on the flow of student responses. Experientially, strictly maintaining a highly structured, sequentially planned format reduces the free-flow of ideas by both parties, thus ostensibly diminishing the potential quality of the chat experience. An instructor who wishes to maintain 'tight control' of a course may not be suited for online course delivery. Therefore, it is vital to the success of the overall chat experience that the instructor maintains an understanding for the need of flexibility and modification during the chat session. A successful approach to accomplishing this task while ensuring student learning is to begin with the identification of desired student learning outcomes and then select possible questions and/or thought-provoking statements that will lead students to these outcomes, while maintaining the understanding that these questions/statements will be selected, modified, and/or omitted based upon student responses throughout the chat discussion. The overall success of chat sessions, student satisfaction, and ultimately the degree to which students benefit from the learning experience, will be determined by the degree that the instructor is able to adjust and monitor the process. The capability of using separate chat rooms further extends the opportunity for the instructor to engage students in the learning process by placing students in either random or predetermined groupings for the purpose of extending the application of acquired knowledge.

Students may be placed in small groups to solve problems, draft group responses to questions/issues, work on extended projects, and develop reactions/constructive criticism to another group's work effort. After sufficient time for small group work, students can return to the general chat room to share/debate responses. This movement from whole group to small group and back to whole group makes learning more meaningful and further cements the concept of team learning and a shared vision. When these interactions are relevant to real-world application, there is a greater potential for students to value the experience and gain the desired knowledge, a byproduct of this being increased student motivation. Another benefit to using real-time chat is the immediate feedback students and instructors receive. Research shows that tudents participating in online courses where chat is used effectively on a consistent basis often identify frequency and quality of feedback as a major benefit. Constructive, interactive feedback helps shape student progress through the course in the synchronized learning environment.

Course delivery packages such as Black Board and WebCt include the capability for private e-mail within the course for communication among students and between students and instructor. The frequency of e-mail, quick responses to e-mail, and quality of messages are important functions sometimes overlooked by online instructors. While the tasks of remaining current with e-mail readings and responses are time-consuming, the rewards far exceed the inconveniences. An online instructor may also wish to set up an electronic mailing list either through a university server or other means, to which all class members subscribe. Commonly referred to as a Listserv, the electronic mailing list is similar to e-mail except when a message is sent, all subscribed members simultaneously receive the same message.

This application is another valuable resource in the toolbox of online course delivery. Its major advantage is that it affords students the opportunity to communicate with the entire group via a single message. This group messaging and ease of communication enhances the sense of community that can be created in online courses. This ability to communicate with all students via one message can also be used by the instructor as an instructional tool. One example might be to structure a case-study simulation where students utilize the communication tool to collectively solve a problem. Because the instructor is also a subscriber s/he receives copies of all messages sent via the Listserv, therefore, it is easy to monitor student progress, raise questions, help students refocus, and/or throw 'rocks in the road', i.e., add problems to be solved along the way. The Listserv, when used in this fashion, further allows students to transfer knowledge to real-life situations, hence increasing knowledge retention.

An electronic bulletin board serves the same function as the cork or felt wall-mount versions common in many offices. It is the place within the online course where students and the instructor can post announcements and messages. The bulletin board can be a place for students to find updates, changes, important messages, assignments, and group correspondences. Because files such as lecture notes, power point presentations, etc., can be attached to messages posted on the bulletin board, groups can post projects for others to view and provide feedback. Also, logs from the live chat sessions can be recorded and posted for students to download and review. This is a great way for students to process information presented in the fast-paced chat or for a student who was absent from chat to acquire missed information. Because the bulletin board is an asynchronous communication tool, the quality of student work is often enhanced by the increased degree of freedom the student has to select optimal times for posting and responding to bulletin board messages.

Additionally, students have more time to reflect, research; and compose their thoughts; therefore, the expectation of student products should be elevated above the fast-paced exchange of ideas in the chat environment. The bulletin board can be used for students to post individual and group assignments/projects for review and evaluation by peers and their professor. This application of the bulletin board further allows students to learn from their own work and the work of others and to benefit from an opportunity to receive interactive feedback on both from their peers and the instructor of the course. This provides a unique opportunity for achieving a level of interaction and feedback that even the traditional on-site classroom has difficulty achieving in a face-to-face environment.

One powerful application of the bulletin board is the use of a threaded discussion. This application allows the instructor to organize a thematic threaded discussion by posting a topical statement, question, problem, case study, etc., and then directing students to respond based on their knowledge, experience, readings, and interactions with other students. Using threaded discussions equalizes student participation, something difficult to achieve in a traditional classroom setting. Unlike conditions present in a chat room situation, which is constricted by time, the threaded discussion affords students a longer period of time to frame ideas and respond to the original posting and to subsequent student postings. Students are able to develop their thinking and writing skills, which is extremely important considering the fact that proficiency in writing seldom demonstrated during chat sessions where speed takes precedence over grammar, spelling, and syntax. Like the chat room application, the threaded discussion can be free-flowing and the role of the instructor is to supervise flow and direction of student thinking. The instructor can monitor and if necessary refocus the avenue students may be taking a threaded discussion by posting intermittent feedback. Students also have the ability to read and download the threaded discussions for further review and processing of information.

Students in online courses develop a high degree of camaraderie and reported developing personal relationships outside that of the course. The degree of community created in these courses was evidenced by the students' desire to participate in a social gathering after the course ended.

Personal interaction between the professor and student, and students to student, is an extremely important component of the educational process and must be considered when online courses are developed. In a rush to provide convenient access to more courses, professors must maintain a commitment to maintaining close human relations and effective practices in the delivery of information via distance education. Course adoption policies should ensure that both content and level of interaction are evaluated regardless if the course is developed by faculty members or adopted from a publisher. Although all courses should not be held to the same standard, efforts should be to at least consider the degree of interactivity that is appropriate for the content of the course.

WWW Interface

Information overflow can be tackled through adapting the information to a particular user or a group of users. The information overflow problem in one particular domain, the documentation of an object-oriented software development method, and designed an interactive, adaptive hyper-media system which utilizes WWW as its interface. Until now, the WWW potential for interactivity has been very limited: the user can choose to follow or not follow links to other pages of information. It is important that the adaptive system is integrated with a highly interactive interface for two reasons. With an interactive system it will be easier for the user to correct any mistakes made by the adaptive system based on erroneous assumptions about the user. The second reason is that any modeling of the user can only be based on the users interaction with the system. If those interactions are limited to 'clicking' on links in the hyper-media system, very little can be known about the user. The target domain requires that the interactive interface should be multi-modal, including both static text, generated text and generated graphics as output, and accepting both direct-manipulation and free form query input. These demands have forced us to design new ways of interacting with a WWW page that stretch the original hypertext metaphor. When realising the system, goal has been to create a modular solution.

Separate the user model from the information in the database andalso separate the actual generation of the html-code from database. The separation of user model and information in the database is necessary since the information in the database is changed over time. The target domain, a number of authors work with recurrent releases of the information database. It would be impossible to require that they would mingle the target domain information with user modeling control sequences. The second separation is necessary to ensure that can update interface as the page viewers and html-standards are changed and enhanced. For example, recently re-implemented presentation of the information to fit with the new Netscape viewer which includes Java virtual machine interface. This could be done without changing anything in database of the software method. The system is named PUSH (Plan- and User Sensitive Help).

The information in database is concerned with a Software Development Method (SDP). It is an object-oriented method. The method consists of processes that are activities done during the project phases, and objects that are e.g. specifications, pieces of code and similar, produced as a result of the method. Objects are the input and output of processes. In addition, objects are related to one-another with defined relationships as is a or part-of. Finally, processes are related to one-another so that one process comes before another, is part of another, or should be run in parallel. As can be understood from all this, the user is confronted with a difficult and complex information space. The already available on-line manual consists of more than 500 documents of 5 to 20 pages of text and pictures. The task in the PUSH, was to reorganise that manual into an adaptive and highly interactive multi-modal hypertext system. Several studies on how the users understand the method and how they search for information about it, and the design of the adaptive hyper-media system presented here is based on those studies.

The issue of trust is crucial when design adaptive systems that alter their behavior in response to the users' actions. No matter how clever inferences make about the user characteristica, and will never be anything but a guess. One way of increasing the trust in the system, is to place some of the control over the system in the hands of the user. That is why believe that system should be interactive and allow the user to alter the output from the system. System is interactive on several levels. It is interactive at the interface level, allowing the user to manipulate the output from the system. It is also interactive in terms of allowing the user to control the adaptivity. In order to realise the interactivity at these both levels, have a dynamic interaction between the users' actions and the information system behind the scene. There are no ready-made html-pages that the user can down-load, instead create the pages on the fly in response to the users' actions and history of actions. Apart from the goal to make the output from the system interactive, second design goal is to utilize the hypertext metaphor and de facto standard interaction with the WWW. It will be easier to learn interface if it does not divert too much from the prevailing web style of interaction. This goal conflicts with the interactivity goal since WWW offers few possibilities for interaction. Still, want to rely on the basic metaphor of pages and links as a means for moving between pages.

The basic structure of prototype is therefore that each object and process in the target domain will be presented in one answer page each. This page contains all the relevant information about the object or process, even if some of the information is hidden from the users immediate view. The limitation of the potential nodes in the hyper-space to only one node per process or object also serves another purpose, namely to help users with the 'lost-in-hyper-space' problem. By limiting the nodes to be the whole description of a process or object, make the hyper-space substantially smaller. An alternative would have been to divide the information into small, stand-alone units presented in one page each. This would have meant thousands of potential pages in this domain, so clearly that is infeasible given the goal that users will be trying to learn the structure of the whole method, not only tiny pieces of information about certain aspects. The problem with approach is that each page on a process or object might, if fully expanded, contain a lot of information. It is therefore crucial to structure the information within the page, and have means for navigation within a page.

The page is divided into different parts. The graphics frame serves two purposes. Firstly, it provides a comprehensive view of the information space at the current position; the graphs display all objects related to the current query as well as their relative positions. This gives the user an overview of the domain and also a means for navigation. Secondly, the graphs allow the user to navigate in the information space by clicking on objects in the graph. As the user clicks on an object the view changes to portray the new object and it's neighbors, and at the same time the appropriate textual information is retrieved and presented. The presentation in the graphs meets the needs of users who are not so knowledgeable in SDP. They need to see how the objects are related to one another. The graphs in interface are not static pictures which are ready-made in database.

The graphs from the object-oriented database the lies in the background. This means that whenever database is updated, e.g. an object might be added or a relation changed, the graphs will immediately reflect the change.

When the user has clicked on a certain process or object, they can also get a textual description of that process or object. There are many aspects that may be described: how to produce the object, how to work in the process, examples of objects, the purpose behind the process or object, etc. The user can either ask for a general summary, or just one specific aspect. In the figure above, the user has asked for a general summary of the process 'iom'. A set of 'information entities' are made available to the user. The summary and the underlying purpose of the process. The text frame is scrollable, and so there is more text available further down in that frame. An information entity is a stand-alone piece of information about one particular aspect of an object or a process. It is not necessary to read one information entity before another—there are no references between the entities. The domain, and studies of similar domains, show that this is not an impossible requirement on technical documentation: it is often written as a set of small stand-alone pieces of information. In the underlying knowledge representation, the information is organized as objects (one for each process or object in SDP) with attributes.

The attributes are the objects relation to other objects and also the information entities which describe the objects. So, each information entity constitute an attribute of the object. When construct the textual presentation, some information entities will be ready-made texts in the database, other texts generate from the information about the object. An object-oriented terminology to describe database, in other adaptive hyper-media systems, objects are named frames and their attributes are slots. In the interface, an information entity can be viewed as either a piece of text, or a part of the graphs. Sometimes an information entity is doubled so that display, for example, input objects of a process in the graphs, and also as a piece of text. The user can be dissatisfied with the provided information in the answer page, and is therefore allowed to manipulate the textual parts of the page. They can close or open the information entities through clicking in the guide frame next to the textual frame. By clicking on the name of the information entity displayed in the guide frame, the text will be inserted into the page. Another click on the information entity name in the guide frame will close that part of the text. This is what is named stretch-text. By opening and closing parts of the text, the user can create an answer page that is better fitted to their needs.

The user to pose follow-up questions on concepts that are crucial to the understanding of SDP. In order not to disturb the users reading of the text, the alternative questions are only visible after clicking on the button next to the hotword. If the user chooses to follow one of these links, an explanation of the concept is inserted into the text frame below the current information entity. So, if had clicked on 'Describe object-oriented analysis', an explanatory text would have been inserted between the 'summary' text and the 'purpose' text. At the same time, insert the concept into the guide frame. The hotwords and their associated follow-up questions allows the user to increase their knowledge of SDP. If they are already knowledgeable in SDP, they do not have to read irrelevant information about these basic concepts.

Finally, the user can also navigate by composing questions via menus, which is an important alternative to navigation in the graphs. A more specific question could be 'provide an example of iom', which would result in an answer page with only one information entity open: the example text. Allowing the user to pose questions is crucial if want to meet the needs of experienced users. They do not want to spend time navigating to a particular piece of information, but instead just 'jump' to it.

Even if the interactive WWW interface outlined above will be a powerful tool for information retrieval in this domain, still have the problem of information overload. One answer page might turn out to be several pages long, and know both form own studies and from studies of WWW usage, that users tend not to read more than the first page of information. This has caused us to try to find aspects of the users that can be used as a basis for information filtering. The user's information seeking task was a good tool for determining which information entities would be most relevant to the user in a specific situation.

A hierarchy of information seeking tasks as a result of a task analysis on user's behavior in their daily work situation. Examples of tasks are: 'project planning', 'learning the structure of SDP', 'working in an activity within a process', etc. So how can know which information seeking task the user is performing in any particular situation? Knowing about the task is by combining a user-controlled and a self-adaptive approach. (Self-adaptive are such that the whole adaptive process is done by the system alone: the system initiates, proposes, decides, and executes the adaptive behavior. The adaptive hyper-media tool should optimally be a tool to aid the users in their daily work, not an obstacle that they have to actively adapt in order to make it work smoothly. The users to set which task they are working with initially, and then use plan inference to update their assumed current task continuously.

The user can at any time change the inferred task to some other task, although limit the set of potential tasks to those which will actually change the explanation in the current situation. Given that know of the information seeking task, utilize a set of simple rules that connect a question plus a task with the most relevant information entities. The whole solution with the multi-modal, interactive WWW interface, and the adaptivity, will provide the user with explanations which meet their needs. Since users differ in many respects, approach has been to find a mix of non-adaptive and adaptive techniques that together meet the individual user. Adaptive to the information seeking task, but not to the knowledge of the user, or to their cognitive characteristics and preferences. In studies, did find that both the users knowledge and their spatial ability influenced their understanding of the domain and the documentation of it. By allowing the manipulation of the answer page, and in particular by the follow-up questions on concepts crucial to the understanding of SDP, cater for the difference in knowledge held by the users. With the two ways of navigation in the information space, menus and graphs, and by presenting some information both in graph and textual form attempt to cater for differences in spatial cognition.

System architecture

To make the more or less non-interactive WWW environment as interactive as possible several methods have be used: a Java program for client side graphics handling, a CGI program for dynamic generation of web pages, as well as an underlying adaptive database, implemented in SICStus Prolog objects. They have all played a part when brought together in the Netscape browser. The result is a platform independent, highly interactive, adaptive system for filtered information retrieval on the World Wide Web. This whole architecture is transparent to the user, who only sees Netscape. There are several reason why the dynamic generation of web pages is preferable to keeping static pages on disk. For one there is the aspect of presenting information that is tailored to a specific user. Furthermore, if the information can be put together in a multitude of ways, the sheer number of possible variants can make static pages impractical. In the PUSH system, pages are created in two distinct ways. One is for presenting the results of a new query to POP (the database part of the PUSH system) and the other is for filtering or modifying the currently displayed page. As a query is made to POP, certain data that is tailored to the current user is retrieved. This data is in the form of plain text containing tags signifying hot-words that lead to further queries. The data is channeled to the Page Generator, a CGI program, via a socket. The Page Generator parses the information and builds the finished page by incorporating HTML code into the textual data to construct interface tools such as clickable buttons and menus. When finished, the complete page is piped to the Netscape browser and displayed. The page is also cached to disk. It contains hidden formatting instructions that make it possible to alter the appearance of the page without accessing the database.

A graphics engine implemented as a Java applet takes care of the graphics functionality. At the onset of a query session when the initial page is served to the Netscape browser, the Java code is loaded. (Code written in the Java language runs on a virtual machine inside the web-browser. The same applet code can therefore be loaded into Netscape regardless of platform.) Throughout the query session, the Java program then receives and displays the graph data in it's frame in the Netscape browser. The graph data is read each time it is updated. This happens when the view of the information space changes, i.e. when a new object is viewed. Since there are follow-up questions in the text that do not result in a change of the object that is being viewed, but rather in an insertion of the answer into the existing text, the graphs serve to reinforce the sense of a current object.

The PUSH system is accessed remotely using the Netscape Navigator. A typical session starts with a user retrieving the initial PUSH page, which is the only page that is stored on disk. This is a template page that contains the interactive controls for choosing a query, as well as the Java applet displaying an initial overview of the information space. At this point the user is issued a session id that distinguishes the session from other potential simultaneous sessions, and an individual Prolog process is started. Each user communicates with their own Prolog process via a dedicated socket and both socket and prolog process exist as long as the session lasts. At the end of a session the user's prolog process is terminated so as not to hog the server system. Each query starts the Page Generator CGI which sends the query parameters to the POP Prolog program. Since each query changes the state of the POP program to allow different follow up questions depending on the current context, and since the Page Generator is a CGI program that lives until the current query answer has been presented to the user, a scheme for saving the current state is needed. For example, the Page Generator must have a way of knowing to which of perhaps several different POP prolog processes to talk to, so the socket name is saved in each presented HTML page as a hidden input field. An example of such hidden instructions is the insertion of the menu of potential follow-up queries associated with a hotword when the user clicks on the hot-word button. This will not invoke a call to the Prolog process, but can be handled the Page Generator.

Remote access to a system such as PUSH, using the WWW, has a number of advantages:

— The Netscape Navigator and the Java language enables users on a number of different platforms to access common data using a common interface.

— The application software only needs to be implemented in one place, thus sparing users from the sometimes difficult task of down-loading and installing the software locally.

— All software and data updates are done at the server site. This means that the remote users can be assured that they have access to the latest information as soon as it is available. It also means that all users have access to the same information which is important when users are collaborating remotely.

— Adapting to new and improved protocols and standards such as HTML 3 or new versions of Java, is easier.

— Approach here may be compared with Kay and Kummerfeld's, that mingle the html-format and user modeling instructions with the information in the target domain (1994). In [Rice et al. 1995] much the same argument about WWW and its availability across platforms is made.

At the present time the PUSH system uses beta versions of the Netscape Navigator (2bj) and the Java programming language. This puts certain restraints on the system. Apart from what is to be expected in terms of bugs or missing documentation, the Netscape Navigator has no support for socket communication in the Java implementation. This means that the graphical data for example, must instead be saved to disk by the POP program and read by the Java applet. Several enhancements will be feasible within short. One of the advantages of using a widely spread web browser such as the Netscape Navigator as well as the up and coming Java language, is that as soon as advances are made to these products they can be taken advantage of in the

PUSH system. The graph data is transferred from the POP program to the Java applet by means of a file. Improvements to look forward to are the Java socket capabilities in Netscape, enhancements to the HTML standard, and for example HTML parsing and presenting capabilities in a Java text-area.

This will allow us to completely remove the Page Generator component and instead have one, more complex, Java applet communicate with and present the information of the POP prolog server. For example, we hope to replace the current somewhat awkward way of posing follow-up queries to hot-words by pop-up venues. Another great improvement to the system will be to allow authorized users to update the information database in POP by viewing and editing and finally uploading the content from a remote location.

The prototype is not completely stable due to the problems with Java and Netscape. Even so, were able to conduct a first evaluation of the interface parts of system. The purpose was to collect information that would help us to bootstrap the adaptive parts of the system. At the same time as collected that information also logged the users actions and posed a number of queries to them on how the perceived the interface. Since the study was fairly small, only thirteen subjects, and done on a buggy prototype, the results should be viewed as tentative. At the time of the study of the interface, only had the graph and text frames. The guide frame had not yet been implemented. The design with the guide frame as a picture to the subjects after their session with system, and they all expressed a feeling that this would improve the interface. The subjects first got familiarised with the tool by just 'clicking around'. The four different actions possible: clicking in the graphs, posing queries via menus, opening and closing stretch-text and posing follow-up queries on hotwords. They filled in a form about their background knowledge. They were then presented with different 'tasks' and asked to pick one which fitted with what they knew about a particular part of the process, usually did, their background knowledge and work-style, etc. (as 'reverse engineering', 'project planning', 'learning structure', etc.). They were then asked to tell us which information about a process and an object would be most relevant given the task. In addition, some subjects performed two search tasks for specific pieces of information. Finally, the subjects were asked to answer a set of follow-up questions on their impressions of the interface.

So, in summary, it seems as though subjects made use of the possible actions at the interface and they did not have too big problems with getting lost or understanding how to interact with the system. As this was used to bootstrap the adaptivity, asked the subjects whether "tasks" were realistic and whether they kind of adaptivity envisioned would be feasible. All seemed to find the scenarios realistic. Many added that what determined which information would be most relevant was also the project status. If they were just about to start a process, they would require information related to the learning task, while towards the end of a process, they would require very specific information on how to document the results of the process in the objects and the relations between the objects, etc. Adding the project status to system and using it as an additional source of information for the adaptive behavior, is considered and will be included in future work. By stretching the limits for what can be seen as a standard WWW-interaction, have been able to implement a multi-modal interface to adaptive information filtering system in a closed domain. It should be noted that regard the combination of the interactive interface and navigation in the information space as part of the solution of how to meet the individual users needs.

Analysis of Web-based Education

This section presents an international analysis of courses on the Internet, and it provides strategic recommendations about issues of importance to online education. The results and discussions are based on literature reviews, catalogue entries submitted by 130 institutions in 26 countries, and 72 interviews with key persons at these institutions. The catalogue data were collected from March 98 to February 99 and the interviews were conducted in the spring of 1999. The CISAER catalogue includes entries from institutions in all continents. In addition to four transnational institutions, the catalogue includes entries from institutions in 26 countries. It is likely that there is an overrepresentation of institution from countries that have English as an official language since the primary research language was English. Still, it would be quite easy to include many more entries from North America, since the listing from this area is intentionally partial. Among the 130 catalogue entries, 45.4% were from the English language countries: USA, UK, Australia, Canada, and Ireland. Institutions in Europe (60.8%), North America (21.5%), and Australia with New Zealand (7.7%) overwhelmingly outnumbers institutions in South America (3.1%), Asia (3.1%), and Africa (0.8%). Even though the researchers have a better knowledge of Europe, North America, and Australia than they have of the rest of the world, the survey testifies that these continents overwhelmingly dominate web-based education. There is a steady growth of institutions that offer online courses to students in other countries, and the analysis presents many examples of international collaboration and thinking. However, most of the global initiatives seem to be experiments and ambitions rather than main priorities.

A large number of the institutions offer quite few web courses. As many as 23.1% of the institutions have only one web-course, and 46.2% of them to offer less than 5 courses. Only four institutions have 100 courses or more. From this, one can infer that much of the activities are experimental and not pivotal for the institutions. The survey also showed that 29.3% of the institutions they have 100 or fewer students. Only four institutions have more than 5000 students. The relatively low enrolment numbers also indicate that web-based instruction is not pivotal to these institutions. One may conclude that there is a dominance of web-courses in the fields of computer and information sciences and by courses in education. Except from these two fields, web courses cover a very broad range of subjects. The number of subject areas that was offered varied considerably between the institutions. Nearly half of the institutions offer courses in only one category and only five offered courses in five or more categories. None of the surveyed institutions seem to provide enough online courses and support services that this analysis would characterize them as virtual or online universities. The survey shows that 60.0% of the 130 institutions belong to the university and college sector, 10.0% to the traditional open university and distance education sector, and 9.2% were classified as companies or corporations.

An administrative system should be able to handle students, teachers, courses, and course material. An online college may have to handle thousands of students, hundreds of teachers, and a large number of courses with password restricted web pages, discussion forums, distribution lists, class rosters, and student presentations. It may also have to provide administrative systems for the dispatch of textbooks, handling of tuition and examination fees, and organization of local examinations. These services constitute a major challenge for many traditional institutions. Institutions that plan to offer large scale and professional online education need an administrative system, which is integrated with the web. To accomplish this, institutions may follow several strategies.

The simplest strategy is probably to collaborate with an institution that already has a functional administrative system. Another solution, which requires more technical competence, is to develop an in-house system based on common Internet services. The third option is to purchase a standard system for online education. These standard systems are continuously being improved, but they may still need much local adaptation. They may only meet some of the administrative needs, and they could place some pedagogical limitations on the courses. A discouraging, but important observation is that a number of institutions do not use the web for administrative purposes. Outsourcing is an option that does not seem to be much used, only one instance was identified. Many of the institutions have developed in-house administrative solutions in combinations with standard Internet software. The standard administrative systems that were mentioned in the interviews were FirstClass, WebCT, and Lotus Notes.

It is implicit in many of the interviews that advertising of programs and courses is an important function of the web-services. The tuition fees for web-courses seem to vary considerably among institutions and courses. Some courses are free and open to everyone, and others seem to have full or partial external funding. The institutions that operate with tuition fees seem to have fees that are the same or not very different from fees in traditional courses. The analysis has revealed few, if any, examples of institutions with substantial income from student fees. Likewise, there seem to be few institutions that can claim that provision of web-based courses has been an economic success, if they disregard external research and development grants.

The tutors seem to be both part-time teachers that are engaged just for the online courses and full-time teachers that also teach some online courses. It is also interesting to observe that distributed experts and students take part in the tutoring. An analysis of the interviews indicates that the tutors at least conduct the following functions:

— Organizational functions: structure discussions, pacing, put forward initiatives

— Social functions: monitor groups

— Intellectual functions: answer questions, guiding students on the Internet

— Assessment functions: give feedback to assignments, correct submissions

Human tutoring seems to be much more common than machine tutoring, but some institutions include machine tutoring in addition to human tutoring. Most institutions seem to combine individual tutoring with group tutoring. The focus between the two could however vary. Online teaching is in many courses supplemented with face-to-face meetings, video- or audio-conferences, or telephone contact. Some institutions have course development teams; others use the tutor as the sole designer of a course. The different models probably have implications for both quality control and development time.

The interview analysis implies that accreditation of online courses and programs is very similar to the institutions' traditional accreditation schemes. Degrees, diplomas, certificates, and statements of completions are all widely used. The accreditation seems to be the same independent on whether the course or program is offered online or not. Many institutions basically state that the accreditation is the same as for campus courses. Accreditation could be an important competitive advantage and several strategies could be followed to achieve the necessary accreditation. Collaboration with institutions in other countries could result in bilateral accreditation.

While summative assessment of online courses seems to be very traditional and often has a face-to-face component, formative assessment is more experimental and based on online activities. Most of the institutions apply several assessment methods in a course or program. Tutor assessment is the most common form of assessment found in the interviews. The interviews reveal many examples of self-assessment, but they imply that computer assessment is relatively scarce. However there are several examples of online quizzes, multiple choice tests, and some examples of interactive exercises. The interview analysis implies that peer assessment is relatively scarce. The interviews indicate that some courses have no assessment simply because they are self-study courses with no tutors.

Both enrollment and progress can be more or less flexible. However, the two main models found in the interviews are group enrollment and progress and individual enrollment and progress. These models represent two different strategies that have important consequences for marketing, administrative systems, and pedagogical approaches. The interviews testify that group based enrollment and progression is far more used than individual enrollment and progression. The analysis identified 46 institutions that used the group model and 12 that followed the individual model. In addition, 11 institutions offered both models. The preponderance of the group model could come from conventional thinking that sustains the semester and term system in traditional educational systems. Another possible reason is that the institutions have a well-considered perception that teamwork and collaborative learning is hard to achieve with individual enrollment and progress.

One can however argue that many students will prefer individual flexibility and that many institutions lack systems, structures, and competence on individual enrollment and progression. If so, one may hypothesize that open universities and distance teaching institutions should be more disposed of individual flexibility than traditional universities and colleges. However, the analysis has not found evidence to support this hypothesis.

The interest in online education is high, and it seems to proliferate rapidly and globally. A Canadian competitive analysis that the primary expansion strategies are more and diverse programs, international students, and new and nice markets such as corporate training. The CISAER interviewees foresaw a future with more web-courses, additional online services, better quality of the courses, enhanced focus on teacher training, further collaborations with other institutions, and additional organizational consequences.

There are a number of barriers that must be overcome before online education can become a large-scale success. Among them are financial barriers, resistance to change, bandwidth limitations, access limitations, insufficient search facilities, copyright issues, and barriers to online assessment. The financial barriers are important. The analysis showed that few institutions had substantial income from student fees. At the same time, the cost of development and maintenance could be high. In addition, national regulations in some countries deny institutions the opportunity to charge tuition fees. The interviews testify that there are a number of barriers to effective use of online assessment. Among them are public and institutional regulations, traditions for physical attendance, technical limitations, student identification, and detection of plagiarized digital material.

Bibliography

Attig , G., Promchan, S., Rojroongwasinkul, N. *Ten Steps to Children's Integrated Learning and Development*. Paper prepared for UNICEF Education Officers Meeting. Bangkok, September 1998.

Bamber, C., Berla, N., Henderson, A. *Learning from Others: Good Programmes and Successful Campaigns*. Washington, D.C., Centre for Law and Education, 1996.

Connell, H. *Reforming Schooling: What Have we Learned*? Paris, United Nations Educational, Scientific and Cultural Organization, 1998.

Kuper, W, . 1999. In: *Disadvantage, Dialogue and Development Co-operation in Education*. Report of the IWGE Meeting, June 1998, Munich. Paris, UNSECO Institute of Educational Planning.

Lindquist, E. Public Managers and Policy Communities: Learning to Meet New Challenges. *Canadian Public Administration*, Vol. 35, No. 2, Summer.

Shaeffer, S.; Govinda, R., *Towards a New Framework for School Management: Creating Stronger Partnerships for Better Education*. New York, UNESCO-UNICEF Project on Innovations in Basic Education.

UNESCO, *Learning: The Treasure Within*. Report to UNESCO of the International Commission on Education for the Twenty-first Century, Delors Commission, 1996.

UNESCO, *Assessing Learning Achievement.* Paris, United Nations Educational, Scientific and Cultural Organization, 1999.

______________, *Education for All: Achieving the Goal.* Mid-Decade Meeting of the International Consultative Forum on Education for All, June 1996, Amman, Jordan.

UNICEF, Progress, Challenges and Future Strategies in Basic Education, June 1999.

UNO, *Learning for Life: Innovations for Youth* No. 2. Paris, United Nations Educational, Scientific and Cultural Organization, 1999.

Wright, S.; Morely, D., Learning Works: *Searching for Organizational Futures.* York University, Toronto, ABL Group, Faculty of Educational Studies, 1989.

World Declaration on Education for All and Framework for Action. 1990. World Conference on Education for All - Meeting Basic Learning Needs. Jomtien, Thailand, March 1990.

Index